'This volume brings ... Morris in answering modern challenges to a Biblical doctrine of the atonement of Christ. Wells' work is characterised by John Calvin's "brevity and clarity", and is very powerful as it penetrates the heart of Christ's work for us sinners on the cross. Paul Wells faces head-on the modern (and not-so-modern) challenges to a Biblical viewpoint on the atonement. He evaluates knowledgeably and fairly some of the most significant denials which - with considerable popularity amongst evangelicals - have largely abandoned major aspects of the traditional Christian teaching on such crucial issues to the Gospel as the wrath of God, penal substitution, imputation, propitiation, etc. He takes us to the Scriptures and establishes their clear meaning on the very heart of salvation. He speaks in a moving and compassionate manner to our modern, ever-changing culture in terms of the changeless (and thus, ever fresh) Word of God written. His chapters on contemporary objections to God's having used "violence" in saving us through the death of Christ, and on the forsakenness of Christ by the Father are outstanding.

I shall be recommending this grand little volume to students in my classes, as it will be an important aid for those who wish to preach effectively the Gospel to our relativistic culture.'

Douglas Kelly, Richard Jordan Professor of Theology, Reformed Theological Seminary, Charlotte, North Carolina

'By writing an exhaustive and at the same time very readable defense of the centrality of the doctrine of the Cross in Christian proclamation and life, Paul Wells has performed a remarkable and necessary service for the 21st century church. He returns us bedrock, essential material. Taking on all the major opponents of the doctrine of the atonement, Wells answers their objections with convincing and balanced arguments. He looks at every possible aspect of this profound doctrine and lays out a credible exposition of the cogency and coherence of Scriptural teaching. Satisfying to your mind, this is also a text that will move you to tears and to praise.'

Peter Jones, Adjunct Professor and Scholar-in-Residence, Westminster Seminary in California, Escondido, California

'Paul Wells is emerging as one of the premier evangelical theologians of our day. *Cross Words* is at once accessible and erudite. One of Dr Wells' more timely gifts is putting deep things simply and winsomely. Considering the number of authors who have written about the atonement, and the small number of those which are straightforward and short on jargon, this make the present volume both rare and urgent for our times. The reader will be drawn into good doctrine, but, more importantly, into communion with the Saviour.'

William Edgar, Professor of Apologetics
Westminster Theological Seminary, Philadelphia, Pennsylvania

'This is a satisfying book about the atonement, written by a man of God who lives in the biblical text, and yet is in close touch with the real world and today's church. Paul Wells' friendly style cannot hide his theological rigour and obvious scholarship. He shows us how the cross is viewed today, why Christ's suffering was necessary, what it entailed and what it has accomplished. He deals honestly and robustly with views that do not do justice to the biblical data, and leaves us with a full mind and a humbled heart. Who can fail to profit from a book like this?'

Stuart Olyott,Pastoral Director,
The Evangelical Movement of Wales.

'With much admiration and appreciation I read this new book of the Aix-en-Provence dogmatist Paul Wells. The title *Cross Words* is well chosen: the 'great words' and pivotal notions of the gospel pass in review during the author's scrutinizing investigation into the meaning and significance of Christ's death. Wells stresses the importance and value of the substitutionary doctrine of atonement, and he rightly does so, contrary to the feelings of modern people or the constructions of theologians, who try to take away the scandal of the cross. The ideas of vicarious death and penal sacrifice are indispensable elements of the biblical message of salvation. This is a rich book, pious and scientific at the same time, written in an easy readable, pleasant style. I really hope this book will be read by many people, enriching their understanding and experience of God's mighty deeds in the death and resurrection of Christ Jesus.'

H. G. L. Peels, Principal,
The Theological University of Apeldoorn, Netherlands

Cross Words

The Biblical Doctrine of the Atonement

Paul Wells

CHRISTIAN FOCUS

For Valin and Jonathan

August 6th, 2005

'Meet me in Montana'

Copyright © 2006

ISBN 1-84550-118-7

This edition published in 2006
by
Christian Focus Publications,
Geanies House, Fearn, Ross-shire,
IV20 1TW, Scotland

10 9 8 7 6 5 4 3 2 1

www.christianfocus.com

Cover design by Alister MacInnes

Printed and bound by
J. H. Haynes & Co. Ltd., Sparkford

Contents

1 An Impossible Undertaking? 7
2 Scandal 13
3 Relations 27
4 Lordship 41
5 Love and Justice 55
6 Crime and Punishment 67
7 Violence 81
8 Shadows 93
9 Victor 107
10 Sacrifice 121
11 Penalty 137
12 Abandonment 153
13 Mediator 167
14 Peacemaker 183
15 The 'Three Rs' 199
16 Satisfaction 219
17 Grace 233
18 No More Cross Words 247
   Select Bibliography 253
   Index of Principal Subjects 255

ABOUT THE AUTHOR

Paul Wells teaches systematic theology and has lived in Aix-en-Provence in the south of France since 1972. After studying French at Liverpool University and a stint at Westminster Theological Seminary in Philadelphia, he became one of the founder members of the Faculté libre de théologie réformée together with Pasteur Pierre Courthial and Dr Peter Jones. His doctoral thesis at the Free University of Amsterdam, *James Barr and the Bible. Critique of a New Liberalism* was published by Presbyterian and Reformed Publishing Co. in 1980. Books in French include works on the doctrine of Scripture, the words of Christ from the cross, the Christian life, commentaries on the Lord's Prayer and the Apostles creed, and more recently a general introduction to the Christian faith for students (*La foi chrétienne en libre accès*, 2001). Paul Wells has been editor of *La Revue réformée*, a leading evangelical journal in French, since 1981. He is also responsible for Editions Kerygma, which has published Calvin's *Institutes* and New Testament commentaries in modernised French and new editions of classics such as the *Heidelberg Catechism* and the *Westminster Confession*. He is married to Alison who teaches adult English and they have three children who live in Spain and the English Midlands. Together they are involved in church planting in Gardanne, a mining town between Aix and Marseilles, where there is no other Protestant church. Their free time might find them walking in the Lubéron or, in winter, enjoying the beauty of the Mediterranean coast.

1

An Impossible Undertaking?

Atonement is about right relationships. Its past speaks of brokenness, alienation, and the death of love. Its present sees restoration, healing, and wholeness. Its future holds hope for deepening friendship and mutual confidence.

For human beings endowed with a sense of right and wrong, the question of how to repair broken relationships is a continual concern. Every day we run the risk of estrangement, hostility, and conflict. Sometimes they arise because of thoughtlessness; sometimes as the result of a calculated act. Something may be so attractive that we will endanger our standing with others to get it. They can suffer the consequences, and if we experience a certain discomfort…the end justifies the means.

Some issues of life and death lead to totally broken situations. Certain kinds of behaviour—lies, betrayal, and violence—are deemed irreparable by those involved and by society as a whole: nothing can atone for the wrong done, nothing return the counter to zero. There is no way back. Forgiveness is impossible. The cancer of resentment fosters anger and aggression, so that withdrawal seems preferable. A bad day at the office can be shrugged off, but if the problem involves a wrong that cannot be made good, how is it possible to go on? Can we live with the knowledge that things will never be the same again and nothing can be done about it? What value can life have, once ruined beyond redemption?

These questions bring the Christian message of atonement into sharp focus as good news. Business as normal can be resumed with God and our fellows. The abrupt start to Mark's Gospel illustrates how this message of hope breaks into situations of despair in a dramatic way: 'The beginning of the gospel of Jesus Christ, the Son of God…Jesus went into Galilee proclaiming the good news of God. The time has come. The kingdom of God is near. Repent and believe the good news' (Mark 1: 1, 14–15). It is not by chance that Mark's opening word, 'beginning', echoes the first words of Genesis: 'In the beginning God'. God's good news intercepts lives characterised by emptiness—deserts 'without form and void' (Gen. 1: 2, Mark 1: 2). Radical new beginnings are possible. Life can be recreated. The kingdom promise is return from exile to order and happiness.

The Christian good news majors in 're-' words: rebirth, redemption, reconciliation, renewal, and finally re-creation. Atonement is the process and the state of restoration. In a narrower sense, the appearing of Jesus—his person and work, his alienation in death—introduces a radical new beginning for human hopes. Jesus himself experienced the dregs of human brokenness. 'Despised and rejected, a man of sorrows and familiar with suffering', he was cut off from life (Isa. 53: 3, 8). But out of despair and defeat come new life and victory over death in resurrection. The focus of Christian experience becomes being raised from death to newness of life, which is renewal, entering into a life of different and positive relations. Salvation involves repair of past traumas, but it is also the personal and spiritual satisfaction of a transformed life. The end of Isaiah's fourth 'servant song' speaks about the joy issuing from suffering, when the victim sees his days lengthened and prosperous in the light of life (Isa. 53: 10–11).

This is just what our contemporaries do not want to hear. Taking the absence of God for granted, their overriding attitude is: 'I can get along very well without God, thank you. Problems are of human making and have human solutions. God is not the question or the answer; man is. So why should a relationship with God interest us? How could it help practically?'

All this fails to stand up to scrutiny, for the simple reason that modern man is bankrupt. Advanced modern knowledge, 'science', is incapable of curing humanity of greed, exploitation, violence, or its other ills. In fact, in some ways, the progress of knowledge makes the possibilities of manipulation and suffering more subtle and sophisticated. Spiritual values must come from somewhere other than from technical development.

Besides this, the attitude of 'man on his own' assumes there is some order in life holding things together and giving them meaning, whereas, without God, human experience is made up of the accidental and unexpected. Man is like a gambler in the casino of life, who keeps on betting without knowing where the chips are coming from. Win some or lose some is not the question. If the end product of seventy or so years' good or bad luck is nothing but oblivion, there is no atonement, and it does not matter.

Christianity is often tempted to turn its wine into water when faced with modern feelings about the absence of God. An effort is made to humanize God by underlining the higher power's proximity, love, compassion, and weakness. Forget the shadow-side of a deity expressing anger, jealousy, or judgment! God identifies with situations of suffering and need; he becomes a God of proximity—man's fellow-sufferer.

From this perspective, traditional doctrines of the atonement do not fare well. They are, we are told, closely related to their social background and have been formed by the mentality of their time. They might have been impeccably logical in their arguments, but they have become highly doubtful in a religious sense. So John Hick can say: 'It is hardly necessary to criticise the penal-substitutionary conception (of the atonement), so totally implausible has it become for most of us.' The idea that guilt 'can be removed from a wrong-doer by someone else being punished instead is morally grotesque.'[1] For the likes of Hick, traditional atonement theories no longer perform any useful function. They can be relegated to the antiques museum of historical theology.

Like all doctrines, goes the conventional wisdom, ideas about the atonement are socially constructed in different universes of meaning. There is really no classical, traditional, or 'church' doctrine of the atonement. No universal 'theory' can join together the various strands in the meaning of the cross. The story of the life and death of Jesus is not a universally applicable narrative giving details of a transaction in which God, Jesus, and humanity are involved. The most we can get from the New Testament are some hints that may contribute in a variety of ways to changing our outlook on life.

Reconstructions of the atonement that seek to glean fresh biblical insights and contribute to the transformation of human expectations are not particularly encouraging. The meaning of the cross is a lot more than 'the restoration of a reciprocal relation of love between God the Father and the human race.'[2] If the Father took the trouble of sending his Son and the Son accepted the mission, if he actually became man, then it is hardly too much to hope there might be more than simple hints in biblical revelation on the subject. As J. I. Packer stated: 'All our understanding of the cross comes from attending to the biblical witnesses and learning to hear and echo what they say about it; speculative rationalism (and I would add, under diverse guises) breeds only misunderstanding, nothing more.'[3] It is not hopeless optimism to expect there might be some coherence in the apostolic message of the cross.

The primary object of this book is, therefore, to look into why it was necessary for God in Jesus Christ to take on himself human nature, to redeem people from sin and death by dying for them in the flesh. To do this, we propose, in chapters two to six, to look at the situation existing between God and man that makes the cross necessary. What the cross discloses about God himself is as significant as what it accomplishes for man. God's nature is intricately connected to his way of salvation.

Chapters seven to twelve present 'cross words', which describe what the death of Christ entails, as seen through the preparation for the coming of Jesus, his life, and his death. The centre of the Christian drama is not the cross in itself, but the person of the crucified one and the unique way he stands between God and man as mediator. This is essential, as it closes the blind alley leading to an understanding of the cross that reduces it to a symbol of human suffering.

In chapters thirteen to seventeen the results of the work of the cross are examined. The finished work of Christ opens the way to freedom from sin and death, to new life in communion with God, characterised by obedience, love, and service. The atonement is more than just a change of direction—it leads to a relationship with a new master, it brings forth a new sense of belonging.

This undertaking as a whole is highly scandalous to the mentality of our day, within or without the church. We will therefore begin by navigating these reefs in the following chapter.

ENDNOTES

[1] J. Hick, *The Metaphor of God Incarnate* (London: SCM, 1993), 119 and his critique of R. Swinburne's *Responsibility and Atonement* (Oxford: Clarendon Press, 1989).

[2] M. Winter, *The Atonement* (London: Geoffrey Chapman, 1995), 2.

[3] J. I. Packer, 'What did the Cross achieve? The Logic of Penal Substitution' *Tyndale Bulletin* 25 (1974), 20.

2

Scandal

At the beginning of 1 Corinthians 15, the apostle Paul presents variations on the theme of resurrection, he summarizes the message he has received: 'Christ died for our sins according to the Scriptures, he was buried, he was raised again on the third day according to the Scriptures and he appeared to Peter and then to the twelve.' (1 Cor. 15: 3–5)

Quite apart from any preconceived ideas, the first statement, 'Christ died for our sins' is problematic. In dramatic circumstances it could be accepted that a person die to save the life of another, as happens in Louis de Bernière's novel *Captain Corelli's Mandolin*, when a fellow soldier protects the captain from a firing squad. But what would it mean for someone to die for another's sins? It seems implausible that sin, a moral quality, could be transferred from one person to another. Moreover, why should physical death serve as an antidote to sin, since death itself is the end and not a celebration of new life? What positive outcome could the death of someone possibly achieve? To say from a purely human perspective that one person could die for another, other than in the context of a good yarn, seems far-fetched.

Add God as a further actor in the situation where 'Christ died for our sins' and an already perplexing situation is made more complex. But this is precisely what the apostle does when he repeats that Christ died 'according to the Scriptures'. This is a way of saying Christ died as God predicted beforehand, and in such a way as to fulfil his plan. It could even be taken to mean that God had promised Christ would die for our sins. So Paul gets himself into even deeper water. Why should God deal with sin by demanding a life in the place of a sinner's life? How could it be morally justified? How could such an action on God's part be effective?

OFFENSIVE LANGUAGE

Such questions foster uneasiness among Christians. Since the time of the Enlightenment, various solutions have been proposed to make the meaning of the cross more palatable. Today even these compromises with humanism seem irrelevant. The question is: if such a thing as sin exists, and if there is a God, surely he would not have to go to these lengths to deal with a human problem? Voltaire must have hit the spot when he said God is bound to forgive, because that's the business he's in. God is a God of love, if he's a God at all, isn't he?

To speak about God, sin, and forgiveness, in relation to one person dying for another seems unnecessarily offensive to any normal way of thinking. The message of the cross has always been a scandal because of the way Scripture presents it. Its various aspects seem logically impossible if not ineffective. It should be no surprise that this is true today, even deep in the ranks of the church's best thinkers. The situation is little different from a century ago when B. B. Warfield remarked: 'Surely if hard words broke bones, the doctrine of the substitutional sacrifice of the Son of God for the sin of man would long ago have been ground to powder.'[1]

Two questions can be asked about the scandal of the cross. The first is, why would God chose a way of salvation that cannot be understood and is difficult to accept? In a sense the question is unanswerable because God has not disclosed the deep reasons for any of his ways of acting. And why should he? Martin Luther had a point when he repeatedly argued against Erasmus in his treatise, *The Bondage of the Will*, that God always does things in ways contrary to our human way of thinking and what seems reasonable to it. It is God's prerogative to demonstrate how different he is by doing things his way, not our way. In fact, if God's ways were set out in tabloidese and his reasons were perfectly evident to everyone, faith would have no essential function in man's relationship with God. Man could walk according to his own light. The truth that 'without faith it is impossible to please God' (Heb. 11:6) would be redundant. Faith is not contrary to reason, but its content certainly lies beyond demonstration. Having a receptive character that reason does not have, it expresses man's relationship with God.

Secondly, there is the nature of the scandal itself. Every age and culture has different reasons for finding belief in the God of the Bible problematic, reasons often related to the kind of human outlook prevailing in that day. Time was when miracles were a great debating point, then the Genesis creation over against evolutionism, and in the last century with its inexplicable wars, the problem of evil and the absence of God. Nowadays the problem is the meaninglessness of human life— why there is something rather than nothing. That any given description of the big picture of life must fail to satisfy is taken for granted. In the context of creeping relativism, the idea that one act could have an eternal value is implausible. The death of a man two millennia ago is of no concern to those who live surrounded by materialism.

SCANDALOUSLY DIFFERENT

The scandal of the cross, however, is different from these objections and seems to have a perennial nature, beyond considerations of time and place. The apostle Paul had a convert's acute awareness of the foolishness of the cross. In 1 Corinthians 1 he deals frankly with the apparently unacceptable claims about the death of Christ for his fellow citizens:

> For the message of the cross is foolishness to those who are perishing, but to us who are being saved it is the power of God. For it is written 'I will destroy the wisdom of the wise and the intelligence of the intelligent I will frustrate.' Where is the wise man? Where is the scholar? Where is the philosopher of this age? Has God not made foolish the wisdom of the world?…Jews demand miraculous signs and Greeks look for wisdom, but we preach Christ crucified: a stumbling block to the Jews and foolishness to Gentiles, but to those whom God has called, both Jews and Greeks, Christ the power of God and the wisdom of God.
>
> 1 Cor. 1: 18–25

Paul is acutely aware of the unpalatable nature of 'Christ crucified'. It goes against the grain of what his public would consider to be useful information.

For his Jewish compatriots, the idea that the awaited Messiah could suffer crucifixion belies expectations that the promised one would prove his pedigree by the powerful liberation of his people. Nothing could be more of a stumbling block to the expectations of Judaism than the idea of a Messiah humiliated by crucifixion.

For the Greeks, the chattering classes of the day, the message of the cross is no less offensive than for the Jews. Paul had encountered their wisdom in his brush with the thinkers of Athens and had felt the barbs of their wit (Acts 17: 32). Pagan thought left no place for a divine intervention in the cosmos that would disturb the regularity of human reasoning. The idea that the suffering of a cross could reveal something of divine wisdom cut against all their ideas about the noble and esoteric nature of speculative thought. That anything divine could be known from a Roman gibbet was totally unacceptable. Not only that, but the cross hardly provided subject matter for the high-flown discussions in vogue in their debating societies.

Paul was not one to try and make a silk purse out of a sow's ear. In 1 Corinthians 1 he makes a stark contrast between the wisdom of the world and the foolishness of God: 'The foolishness of God is wiser than man's wisdom and the weakness of God is stronger than man's strength' (1 Cor. 1: 25). The apostle makes no concessions to those who desire either signs of power or finely crafted arguments. We are talking about God, he says, and what God does at the cross leaves human power and wisdom at the starting blocks. God is not foolish, neither is God weak in what he has done; it simply appears that way in the light of the conventional views of wisdom and power held by Paul's contemporaries. In fact, if he had made any historic compromises with those thought systems, the cross would have lost its cutting edge (v. 17). Despite appearances, the message of the cross has hidden ways of convincing, resting on God's own power that human wisdom knows nothing about (2: 5–6).

No doubt the Jews and Greeks reject the cross as foolishness because of their inherent cultural ideas. But there is more to it than that in Paul's argument. What it tells us is that there is a human mind-set, a world-view to which all men naturally adhere, behind different cultural expressions. From any viewpoint that deals in what seems acceptable to human reason, the cross will always be a scandal. That it is folly, or in our own day, purely irrelevant, comes as no surprise. 'Shocking and ridiculous' is the natural man's reaction to the cross. It transcends human cultures and is expressed every time human beings are faced with the claims of Christ crucified.

ADAPTING THE SCANDAL?

It is often pointed out that 'our theological commitments with regard to atonement theology do not simply speak to our culture but actually grow out of it.' All our theological formulations, including those about the cross have an historical origin and are rooted in socio-historical processes.[2]

There is doubtless a modicum of truth in such observations. However, they are often used to put a particular slant on the question of the scandal of the cross. A current way of stating it goes something like this. Paul spoke about the scandal of the cross as an historical event. As the theology of the Church developed, the biblical statements about the atonement were interpreted to make them comprehensible for the needs of specific situations. Different models of what 'Christ died for our sins' means were proposed in line with their cultural contexts. In the rationalistic west, with its legal structures and individualism, the 'penal substitutionary model' came to monopolize the field in Christian preaching and hymnology.[3] Today the diversity of the biblical teaching about the cross needs to be recovered from the debris of this particular theory. All the more so because we live in an age where this model has gone past its 'sell-by date'.

In the light of what we have said about the scandal of the cross, however, such a line of argument only tells a part of the story. If 'Christ died for our sins' is properly explained, it will certainly not make it more palatable. The scandal will appear in its true light as the foolishness of the cross becomes more obvious to the eye of human wisdom. Clarity of explanation may well function in such a way as to make rejection of the message more likely, because its scandal becomes all the more unacceptable. To imagine receptivity to the cross can be heightened by cultural sensitivity is an illusion.

Historically speaking, it seems that since the time the Christian church began to interpret what happened at the cross, strenuous efforts have been made to make its meaning clear and to avoid normalising the scandal. This is not always the case with more recent interpretations, which often run the risk of modifying the message itself, in the interest of making it consumer friendly.

CROSS METAPHORS AND MODELS

Christ's dying for sin on the cross is presented in the New Testament in a variety of linguistic ways. It is not surprising that many of the 'cross words' we will examine in the coming chapters are of a metaphorical nature. The Bible is not a philosophical manual, its story is dramatic and metaphors open windows on the depth of its truth. It would be wrong to think the use of metaphorical language obscures the facts spoken about. Many times it serves to heighten their meaning. For a people who live in the desert is it more evocative to say, 'God is totally dependable' or to say, 'God is a rock'?

In Scripture a variety of language is found to describe what happened at the cross: the cultic language of sacrifice, the payment of ransom, punishment and acquittal, and that of victory. In these instances, the meaning of 'Christ died for our sins' is presented as an offering, a debt, a judgment, and the outcome of a conflict.[4]

The various forms of language in the New Testament have provided the material for different atonement models, which have been advanced as interpretations of what transpired at the cross. Some biblical metaphors lend direct justification to the model they suggest. Such is the case with the language of conflict and battle which gives rise to the victory of Christ model. Other models seek to incorporate the various forms of language and to harmonise them into a unified theory that does justice to their variety.

A great many models have been constructed in an attempt to shed light on the cross and provide a satisfying theory of the various aspects of the atonement. The plurality of models can be compacted to three main families:

- Victory: Christ emerged from the struggle of the cross as the victor who frees humanity from the power of sin, death and the devil (*Christus* or *Agnus victor*);
- Substitution: The model of substitution, and in particular penal satisfaction, proposes the cross be interpreted as an act in which Christ took the place of sinful man. He met the demands of divine justice and removed the judgment of God by his death;
- Example: Christ lived a life in harmony with divine justice and love. The cross proposes the ultimate model of what human nature ought to be. His example of self-giving inspires others to similar altruism.

Elements of these three models can be found in the New Testament corpus as a whole and in its individual writers. That there is no overarching doctrine of the atonement articulated in Scripture is often thought to be a disadvantage for the theology of the cross. Why should this be? For three reasons at least:

First, like all acts God performed in history, the atonement is a mystery. It concerns relationships between God, Christ, and the destruction of man's sin. We can get hold of the 'that', that God did this or that, but not the 'how', so as to be able to explain how or why God acted in this particular way. God's operational secrets belong to him alone. For this reason, it is not really a problem to find several complementary aspects of the same event presented in the Scriptures. The three models proposed all find support in the biblical texts and contribute to the understanding of the cross without ever exhausting it. The magnitude of the event is such that human language cannot get to the bottom of its mystery.

Secondly, the question of different models might be an embarrassment if it were thought the various forms of biblical language were contradictory, or the models were exclusive. However, this is not so, as each model in some way implies the others. For instance, the exemplary approach, which has an inspirational thrust, provides an encouragement precisely because a victory was won over evil. The victory of the cross is just that, because by exhausting the accusation of divine justice against sin, condemnation was abolished in its legal demand. Christ 'in our place' and his vicarious substitution was also a demonstration of God's love for sinners (Rom. 5: 8). By dying for us, victory was achieved in Christ's human nature over the power of evil. The complementarity is beautiful and convincing.

Finally, it might be asked whether or not one of the three models is foundational for the others, whether there is one class of biblical metaphor which, comparatively speaking, has more 'weight' than the others. In answer to this question, it seems to be feasible to think, despite what some 'experts' say, that the penal substitution model has a centrality other models lack and it can be held as fundamental in understanding the meaning of 'Christ died for our sins'. It is more complete and other atonement models dovetail with it nicely.[5]

SCANDALS BEYOND THE SCANDAL

The model of 'blood-bought redemption' had been viewed with increasing distaste for more than a century when Gustav Aulén suggested, incorrectly,[6] that the victory model of the atonement was the classical model of the Church in the first centuries.[7] The unpopularity of penal substitution was further aggravated when existentialism made the exemplary model fashionable once again, replacing legal categories in the discussion of the atonement by personal and relational ones. These were only the beginning of the woes for the penal substitutionary model in modern debate.

More recent criticism has centred particularly on whether 'Christ died for our sins' can be taken in the way the traditional models have taken it—at face value as a résumé of the foundational story of Christianity. Can a system of exchange, in which one life is given for others, be read out of the New Testament witness? Such an explication seems to be too neat and unreal in the light of what happened at Golgotha. Is not the cross rather an unmasking of the evil and violence in which the Old Testament legal and sacrificial systems, and the injustice of the oppressive Roman power, were steeped? Does not the point of the story lie in the innocence of the victim and the abusive nature of the structures of oppression?

In the light of these new and radical suggestions the model of penal substitution as an explication of what it means for 'Christ to die for our sins' comes under fire. The idea that payment for sin is a reason for forgiveness and that the anger of God is turned away because Christ pays the price for sin seems to involve an unjust rather than a just exchange. Forgiveness at a price appears less generous than unmotivated forgiveness. The requirement of payment for sin seems to imply that God goes to extreme lengths to be avenged. What Martin Luther deemed to be a 'glorious exchange' looks more like a murderous exchange for people today.[8]

FOUR CRITICISMS OF PENAL SUBSTITUTION

Four specific criticisms are levelled today against the scandalous belief that God's intention was that Christ should die for our sins. They have to do with sin and guilt, violence and sacrifice, debt and satisfaction, and the abuse of victims. Their goal is to dismantle the traditional model of penal substitution.

Sin and guilt

First of all, 'Christ died for our sins' has more often than not been taken to mean Christ died for us, that is, in our place. 'In my place condemned he stood, sealed my pardon with his blood', as the hymn goes.[9] Man owes perfect obedience to God's law but sin establishes guilt. According to the conditions of God's justice, retribution is unavoidable. Sinners are under condemnation and the penalty is death. Christ dies for sins and procures release from judgment. Sin > condemnation > death provides a simple structure to explain how Christ stood in the sinner's place to satisfy the demands of divine justice.

The criticism of this construction is that it weaves together several strands of thought that are not joined together in Scripture to form one picture of what happened at the cross. It fits them together like pieces in a jigsaw puzzle. The structure itself is not biblical, but a legal one and the pieces only fit because they are forced to. The problem is that the message of the cross is construed exhaustively in terms of legal relations. That is not the scandal of the cross, but one created by theorising along the lines of guilt and the penalty pronounced against sin.

The real challenge of the cross is not Christ dying for us but his being totally identified with us in human misery to demonstrate God's unconditional acceptance of us. Atonement, it is claimed, is not a legal fiction but the story of new life out of death. Retribution and death are unsatisfactory ways of describing it. They do not account for newness of life that comes from Christ's identification with us and God's demonstration of how he freely accepts man. Contemporary society is not interested in the message of Christ dying for sins because it is not even aware of sin as a problem.[10] Human suffering preoccupies us more than sin, and Christ's identifying with suffering brings him near to us in ways impersonal legal theories of representation and satisfaction cannot.

Violence and sacrifice

In the second place, one of the main reasons for concern about suffering is the preoccupation with violence perpetrated either by individuals or by oppressive groups and structures. The violence of the cross is the unacceptable face of Christianity, made visually impressive by films such as Mel Gibson's *The Passion of the Christ*. Parents would hesitate to let their children see that, and they certainly would not take them down the road to be a spectator at Golgotha. People often think along the following lines: God is good and all-powerful and yet he allows horror and violence in the world. That he even used violence in the death of Christ is a moral outrage. Is violence legitimate as a way to save from violence? Surely the idea that violence could be redeemed by violence is a myth. It is only a further act in a continuing cycle of violence. Traditional views of the cross do not deliver from violence but only perpetuate it.[11]

It is particularly offensive for modern sensitivity to speak of Christ's death as a sacrifice for sin. If Christ entered into a situation of suffering it was to unmask the folly of violence and break the repeated cycle of violence by ending sacrifices. He demonstrated that the victims of violence are innocent, not guilty. The answer to violence in human relationships is not more and greater violence, retaliatory violence, but non-violence and positive acts of mercy and forgiveness.

The atonement, contrary to appearances, shows that victory is by non-violence.[12] Christ, in a voluntary conscious act, absorbs in his suffering the effects of all human oppression, hatred and aggression. In so doing, he opens the prospect of a new kind of humanity freed from slavery to the myth that might is right. What God demands is non-violence, not sacrifice. If Christ dies in a sacrificial way it is to demonstrate that the mechanism of violence used to end violence does not work.

Debt and satisfaction

Thirdly, Anselm's contribution to atonement theology needs debunking. Archbishop of Canterbury at the start of the 12th century, he was responsible for the idea that the death of Christ was a satisfaction to placate divine honour. The idea of satisfaction was taken up by the Reformers and translated into a legal context, so the satisfaction was rendered to divine justice. The end product is a cross stripped of its dramatic and tragic reality. Rather than a place of personal crisis, it becomes an instance of a legal transaction. Just as the concept of debt to justice and sacrificial substitution are found wanting because they imply heartless retribution and violent revenge, so also satisfaction is improper because it means something is bartered to get something else. The life of Christ is given in exchange for ours on the cross. Transaction takes the love out of the cross and reduces the relationship of the Father and the Son to a commercial negotiation.

The parable of the prodigal son shows the contrary, or so we are told. No payment is necessary and forgiveness requires no negotiating. There is no retribution in this story, which is about radical acceptance—forgiveness granted without strings attached. There is without doubt a debit on man's side in his relationship with God, but the cross does not pay for it. God's love wipes the slate clean.

Abuse and victims

What appears to be too scandalous to be true about 'Christ died for our sins' is that the cross actually bears a victim. Behind this victim and the punishment lurks the shadowy figure of an unrelenting father. The satisfaction theories implied in Anselm's theology illustrate a sadomasochistic side of Christian teaching at its oppressive worst. For radical feminists, the cross is a form of 'divine child abuse'. Grace is really a polite way of expressing a sense of relief at escaping from the punishment of the victimising parent. This model is truly scandalous. Far from providing a healthy portrait of human relationships, it fosters abusive practices and the victimisation of the poor and weak. The punishment the Father meted out on the Son, the innocent sufferer, justifies other similar unwarranted injustices. The cross comes out of a macho-masochistic mentality and fuels pathological deviance.

Why is punishment necessary at all? Why should the powerful delight in it and the weak live in fear of it? Has not Christian theology, in its traditional models, proposed interpretations in which powerful oppression obscures self-giving love? The victims of this 'divine-child abuse' are women, children and anyone else in a situation of helplessness and weakness.

These four criticisms of the scandalous nature of traditional doctrines of the death of Christ have a common denominator. They reject a logic of exchange—payment for debts, substitution by sacrifice, giving to get satisfaction and punishment for grace—by a logic of gratuity, or a logic of excess.[13] God, it is said, loves against all opposition and continues to love in the face of violence, human injustice and rejection. Jesus demonstrates the ultimate lengths to which God goes to identify with his creatures in their suffering and with the consequences of evil. Jesus is 'more than a victim: when God receives and approves the condemned Jesus and returns him to his judges through the preaching of the Church, he transcends the world of oppressor-oppressed relations to create a new humanity, capable of other kinds of relations.'[14]

CONCLUSION

In and of itself, the idea Christ died for sins on the cross is a scandal for the natural man's reasoning. Recent interpretations have not generally found the same reasons for speaking about the folly of the cross as the apostle in 1 Corinthians.

No single traditional atonement model can exhaust the fullness of the biblical mystery of the cross. Even taken together, in complementary fashion, they fall short of an explanation of the mechanics of the atonement. However, 'that no single theory of the atonement has won universal acceptance does not show that the story is one that lacks power and relevance today. It is rather confirmation of the fact that the work the Church claims God accomplished in Christ is both complex and mysterious.'[15]

The contemporary critics we have mentioned tend to throw the baby out with the bath water. All too often, an element detached from its true context in one of the models of atonement is isolated from its broader perspective and put through the shredder. Attention is diverted from the real scandal of the gospel to a straw man existing in the minds of the critics.

The resulting confusion about the doctrine of the atonement is a valid reason for giving a fair hearing to the 'cross words' which cluster around this central event of human history. 'The need to work with the traditional models in new ways and to relate them in a culturally relevant fashion is always necessary, and in the case of atonement theology, we are emboldened to do so because the Church has consistently shied away from giving creedal affirmation to one particular model only.'[16]

ENDNOTES

[1] B. B. Warfield, 'Modern Theories of the Atonement' (1903), *The Works of Benjamin B. Warfield*, IX, (Grand Rapids: Baker Book House, 1981), 287.

[2] J. B. Green, M. D. Baker, *Recovering the Scandal of the Cross* (Downers Grove: IVP., 2000), 28.

[3] Ibid., 15–27.

[4] Green and Baker, Ibid., 25–29 list the language of the law (justice), commerce (redemption), personal relationships (reconciliation), worship (sacrifice) and the battlefield (victory). It has also been argued from a post-modern perspective that metaphors cannot be flattened out into concepts or models and that the atonement loses its power in theorising. *Cf.* K. Vanhoozer, 'The Atonement in Postmodernity: Guilt, Goats and Gifts' in C. E. Hill, F. A. James, eds., *The Glory of the Atonement* (Leicester: IVP., 2004), 371.

[5] A debatable point that will be dealt with in ch. 8–11. This is J. I. Packer's proposition in his important article 'What did the Cross achieve? The Logic of Penal Substitution', 20. See also H. Blocher, '*Agnus Victor*. The Atonement as Victory and Vicarious Punishment' in J.G. Stackhouse, ed., *What Does it Mean to be Saved?* (Grand Rapids: Baker, 2002) 90–1.

[6] G. Aulén, *Christus Victor. An Historical Study of the Three Main Types of the Idea of the Atonement*, 1931, (London: SPCK, 1970).

[7] Warfield, art. cit., has demonstrated that the model of penal substitution is as well attested as others in the writings of the Church fathers.

[8] Vanhoozer's expression in art. cit., 370

[9] P. P. Bliss, 'Man of sorrows, what a name'.

[10] T. Smail, 'Can one Man die for the People?' in *Atonement Today*, J. Goldingay, ed., (London: SPCK, 1995), 75 ff.

[11] *Cf.* The ideas of W. Wink, *The Powers that be* (New York: Doubleday, 1998) as used by S. Chalke, *The Lost Message of Jesus* (Grand Rapids: Zondervan, 2003), 122 ff.

[12] J. D. Weaver, *The Nonviolent Atonement* (Grand Rapids: Eerdmans, 2001). For Weaver the traditional theology of the 'satisfaction' of the cross is incapable of dialogue with black and liberation theology or feminism.

He proposes a theology of the victory of Christ, with a narrative approach to Scripture.

13 As Vanhoozer calls it, in art. cit., 394 ff.

14 R. Williams, *Resurrection* (New York: Pilgrim, 1982), 89 quoted by Vanhoozer, art. cit., 389.

15 C. S. Evans, *The Historical Christ and the Jesus of Faith: The Incarnational Narrative as History* (Oxford: Clarendon, 1996), 96–97.

16 H. Boersma, *Violence, Hospitality and the Cross* (Grand Rapids: Baker, 2004), 111.

3

Relations

A Royal Society for the Prevention of Cruelty to Animals superintendent who witnessed the ritual sacrifice of sheep by Muslims in the Paris region during the Eid El Kebir festival, said 'The animals are not being handled with respect and humanity before they are killed. They are not even being sacrificed in accordance with Islamic law as their throats are being slit in front of other sheep.'[1] On French television at the start of January 2005, commenting on the devastating effects of the tsunami which hit South East Asia, a sociologist aired the opinion that what was new about this disaster was that for the first time it was being considered from a planetary perspective and not just a human one.

Animals spoken of as if they were human and natural catastrophe considered on a level with human suffering. Such pearls that crop up in the media indicate uncertainty as to what humanness is. Animal or natural suffering is spoken of in a relational way similar to that of human beings.

So what does 'relational' mean, and are human relations something special? 'Relational' is often used in discussions about the atonement, and like a thermometer it gives a reading of the temperature between God and man, or between men. Without atonement, and all it implies, we are cold with regard to God and others; but the temperature can always rise.

In previous times, covenant theology used the word 'relational' in a vertical sense to speak of the relation between God and man, and to describe restored human situations.[2]

Recently, the word figures more frequently in a horizontal and existential perspective, to express the effects of the work of the cross from a human standpoint.[3]

The purpose of this chapter is to describe the need for the atonement from the perspective of the relationship between God and man, and how the concept of 'relational' functions in a covenantal sense.

RELATIONSHIPS AND PERSONS

As we saw in the preceding chapter, one fear concerning the traditional doctrine of the atonement, and in particular the concept of penal substitution, is that it trades living personal relationships with God for a system of exchange. The danger is thought to be that impersonal structures, particularly those that imply rigid ideas of law, eclipse a vital relationship between God and man, or between people. The living and personal aspect inherent in relationships disappears behind those structures and freedom is sacrificed—fixed rules tie God and man. This is contrary to the essentially personal dynamic disclosed in the biblical story of salvation.[4]

Abstract talk about the atonement makes it into a transaction in which the personal nature of sin and salvation is put into inappropriate categories. 'Guilt and punishment', it is argued, 'are not like fines, things that can be incurred by one person and settled by another. Intrinsically, by their nature, and morally by every rule of justice, they are inseparably attached to the person who, by what he or she does and is, has incurred them.'[5] This is said to be 'a valid insight into the way things really are', which describes things realistically and avoids the pitfalls of excessive legality.

Current wisdom says people's attitudes to their relationships make them what they are. Personal identity is made up of the way people react to circumstances: how they relate to those around them, toward themselves, the environment, and eventually to God. Personhood is made up of a series of criteria-based experiences in different facets of life.

Considered in this way, atonement is an experience of being restored to right relations with God, with others by forgiveness, to oneself through inner healing, and to the environment in ecologically correct attitudes. This new experience makes people more convivial.

But is personhood just about relations? Is it simply the way people relate and nothing more? We think not.

SELF-CENTRED INDIVIDUALISM

Relationships in and of themselves tell us little about what it means to be a person, a human being created in the image of God. Even the love most of us aspire to in our relationships 'ceases to be a demon only when it ceases to be a god'. It is capable of the best and the worst—pure self-giving or obsessive possession.[6]

Relationships today are seen as experiences that involve personal choice, without much regard for structure. You can make it any way you want it. Feeling good is what matters. Free improvisation in relations relies on intuition and instinct, and feelings motivate choices. Emotions get the upper hand over rational considerations of good and bad. Cool evaluation of the circumstances takes a back seat.

This, however, will not provide a real experience of what relationships are, can be, or ought to be. Modern individualism and sentimentality risk obscuring the real nature of what it means to be human. What makes people feel good may have little or no bearing on reality. The Christian gospel of the need for reconciliation with God because of the dire consequences of sin will invariably produce the opposite effect and people will reject it as undesirable. Sin, on the other hand, rarely seems disagreeable to those tied up in it, only becoming so in the light of consequences for oneself and others. The Bible repeatedly shows, from man's first acts on, how agreeable forbidden fruit is to the sinner (Gen. 3: 6), how the broad and easy way seems the right one (Matt. 7: 13–14), and how the way which is right in man's eyes leads to disaster (Prov. 14: 12).

The weakness of describing what people *are* by their relationships is that it assumes that they are inherently good, and whatever they choose to be or do must be right for them. That the primacy of feelings consistently leads to acceptable choices is a modern myth. The Bible speaks about the mind as being fallen and hostile toward God (Eph. 2: 1–3), but even a fallen mind, when functioning normally, has some hold on what is real and what is not. However, when emotions are no longer differentiated from the intellect, they inundate it, making it incapable of discerning decisions about the real world. When sentiment takes over from good and bad, from right and wrong, what God 'has made plain to man' is suppressed and he hands men over 'in the sinful desires of their hearts' (Rom. 1: 19). Man ends up 'serving created things rather than the Creator' (Rom. 1: 24–5). Even the capacity of the conscience to 'accuse or excuse' oneself (Rom. 2: 15) is dulled. If the conscience is seared and emotions take the wheel, who can anticipate what the outcome will be?

INESCAPABLE STRUCTURES

The apostle Paul speaks about a law that is 'written on the heart', a capacity to distinguish between good and evil (Rom. 2: 14–15). Something other than relationships makes people what they are, and that unavoidable something lies in the structures set up in creation by God's law. The universe is a moral entity with objective rights and wrongs, goods and bads, possibles and impossibles. Something deeper underlies relationships, without which it is difficult to grasp their meaning or to sustain them for any length of time. When this is missing, the lines become blurred. There is no way of justifying any personal preference over against anything else that might be chosen. This is why right and wrong are like water off a duck's back for many people today.

In the act of creation God progressively separated different aspects of reality from one another. These distinctions provide order and show the fundamental differences between things, according to their specific nature. Structure was established in creation. To neglect it is dangerous.

God first drew a line of demarcation between everything else and himself. Genesis 1: 1 tells of a creation out of nothing, into nothing, and with nothing. That makes a reality distinct from God who exists in himself, by himself, and for himself. 'From him, through him and to him are all things, to him be the glory, forever' (Rom. 11: 36).

At the heart of the created order is the qualitative distinction between God and everything else. This excludes the possibility of confusing divine reality with things that depend on God for their existence.[7] It also means man cannot know God directly through intuition, feeling, or experience. Knowledge of God can never be natural. It must be special, by divine revelation. From a biblical perspective this limits the kind of relations that can exist between God and man. It also implies that human relations get their meaning from divine authorisation, not human experience.

Creation continues in God's acts of separation: light and dark; sky and earth; sea and land; day and night; animals, according to their kind, and man, created distinct in the image of God as male and female (Gen. 1: 27). The seventh day is not itself a day of creation, but the conclusion of creation, as everything is 'blessed and holy' (Gen. 2: 3). In its harmony, it is 'very good'. Creation receives God's invitation to enter into his rest. In fact, rest is the result of respecting the structure of created reality. 'Holiness means keeping distinct the categories of creation. It therefore involves correct definition, discrimination and order.'[8] Unrest and confusion come from transgressing the lines of established order.

Disobedience consists in not observing the divine structure of the creation. Man, as the image of God, receives a specific commandment about how to work and respect the divine order: 'You are free to eat from any tree in the garden; but you must not eat of the tree of the knowledge of good and evil, for when you eat it you will surely die' (Gen. 2: 16–17). By this commandment another separation enters into man's experience, the one between the possibility of life and death. Three things can be noted: firstly, the wide area of liberty which God grants; secondly, man's liberty is structured by the frontier of prohibition, making man responsible to observe this order; finally, the warning that transgression of God's revealed order leads to dire consequences.

God's command makes man an ethical subject, with freedom and responsibility—his acts have consequences, that is death, whatever Adam understood death to mean. The pre-fall situation establishes that, in the nature of things, the relationship between God and man is conditioned by the structure of law that undergirds it. Nothing could show more clearly that relations are not just expressions of personal choice, but are ethically qualified by the divinely established order. Man's ability to understand this and carry it into action lies in his being made in the image of God.

Adam's situation is an open-ended one[9] and its outcome is determined by the existence of the divine commandment. Man is the apex of the creation and the divine order running throughout God's work must come to conscious expression in his willing obedience. He is called to interiorise the order existing externally in the creation as a whole by continued obedience. Conformity to the divine intention is the condition of a relationship of joy and peace with the Creator. Righteousness, justification, and life are determined by God's standards, not according to man's choices. Free improvisation leads man to sin, condemnation, and death.

GOD'S UNIVERSAL ORDER

God's law is the criterion that gives meaning to every relationship in which human beings are involved, whether with God, in inter-personal relations, or in the use of natural resources. As the human body needs the structure of the skeleton, human beings need the inescapable order of divine law to avoid becoming moral amoebae. A true sense of personhood is found not contra, but within proper structures, allowing for the development of responsible actions.

This is universally recognized as far as natural laws are concerned. Seeking to defy the force of gravity like Icarus who wanted to fly, abusing steroids to be a top athlete, or playing with mathematical possibilities by indulging in Russian roulette are not recommended pursuits for human beings. They lead to irreversible consequences. Much more difficult for normal sinners is to see is that cheating, for example, is wrong. Whether it involves the examination board, the wife, the taxman, or the expense account, it is fine as long as one gets away with it, even if it is another issue when one becomes the victim of such practices. Surely fallen man is blinkered and cannot see that what is self evident in natural law holds good in the realm of personal ethics. Nevertheless, despite current moral laxity, many people adhere to standards of honesty or faithfulness, at least in the ideal. From when sin entered the world, man knew the existence of evil. The separation between the two has been broken down and experience is a mixed grey.[10]

What does all this have to do with the atonement? The breaking of relations between God and man and between human beings is not just like a passing cloud that hides the sun on a summer day and shades relationships for a while. The world is a dark place because God's law–order structure has been overturned. More than a question of broken relationships, man's problem is one of the broken laws that structure them. Just as goodness has been undone in an ethical way, it must be repaired by perfect obedience according to criteria acceptable to God.

People may deeply desire a new and healthy relationship with God and with others, but how are they to achieve it? The biblical answer to this question lies not in vague speculation, but in the divinely established covenant order of revelation. Man's rebellion is atoned for by God, who sets the situation to right.

RELATIONS VIA REPRESENTATION

'It will not be denied or doubted that the covenant of grace is a larger category than the doctrine of the atonement. It is wider, comprehending the atonement within its provisions, affording to it also both explanation and support.'[11]

This bears thinking about. Many problems related to the idea of atonement arise because it is not seen within the covenant context. God's central word for man in the cross is heard in a vacuum—it is amputated from the body of God's dealings with men, which give it meaning. Perhaps this perspective is neglected because God's relationships with men presented in this way are considered foreign to the man-centred accents of modern individualism.

God does not deal with humans on a one-to-one basis. He relates to men in collective entities through representatives. His relationships with humans pass primarily through Adam, the first spokesperson for humanity, and through Jesus Christ, a new Adam, a second spokesman: 'a second Adam to the fight, who to the rescue came'.[12] Even though Romans 5: 12–20 is a very difficult passage of Scripture to interpret, this is what the apostle says there. 1 Corinthians 15: 22 puts it in a nutshell: 'As in Adam all die, so in Christ all will be made alive.' From a biblical perspective, all are identified with Adam in his relationship with God, which is one of spiritual death. This is how humanity as a whole stands with respect to God. Conversely, no one is identified with Christ who is not spiritually alive for God, and considered to be so by him.

God's two spokesmen were invested with offices or functions. Both are prophets, priests, and kings. The prophetic office is one of transmission and interpretation of divine truth in God's world. The priestly function is to represent others before God in obedience and worship. The kingly role is one of rule under God.

As man's representative, Adam came to grief in the three realms and in his case the qualifier 'false' can be added to the three functions. He listened to Satan's word, disobeyed his calling, and became the servant of a liar, rather than dismissing his overtures.

Jesus on the other hand, identified himself as the true priest, prophet, and king, by saying 'I am the way and the truth and the life.' He also affirmed his representative role in a definite way, adding 'No one comes to the Father except through me' (John 14: 6). Jesus could not have found a clearer way of indicating that he determines God's relationship to men and their relationship with God. All lines pass through this junction, in both directions. No other operators run side-lines to God.

This might seem an undemocratic way of organising relationships with men, but God is not a the head of a republic who seeks re-election. This is God's legislature and the form of covenant solidarity he instituted is equitable in every respect. Under divine government, man could not have had a better representative for his cause than Adam, nor a more effective mediator for his restoration than Christ.

JESUS CHRIST AND THE TRIPLE ORDER

The relationship between God and humanity, through representatives, has a historical and dynamic nature. It is disclosed in three different movements, which describe different states of the relationship. The best way of illustrating this is by starting with the historical person of Jesus, the incarnate Son of God, and working outward.

Why did Christ need to come among men as the God-man? Could not God just have decreed salvation? Puzzling questions! Perhaps, but they are also important ones. Christ came as a new representative, or spokesman, for the human race.[13] Paul expresses this with remarkable precision in Galatians 4: 4–5: '(a) When the time had fully come, (b) God sent his Son, (c) born of a woman, (d) born under the law, (e) to redeem those under the law, (f) that we might receive the full rights of sons.' Drawing the meaning out of this:

a) Christ becomes man at a time fixed in God's plan, not by impulse, but as part of a global strategy of salvation;

b) Christ comes in agreement with his Father, who sends him;[14]

c) The full humanity of Christ, with a human nature like ours, is united to his divinity in one unique person;

d) Christ is made subject to the natural and moral order of creation, with the same obligations as other human beings;

e) The purpose of his coming is to deliver those not able to deliver themselves. They are unable to obey the law and are under its curse because of disobedience—their condition is one of sin and death;

f) The result of Christ's work, salvation and life, is God's gift because of Christ. Receiving it, we become sons of God, like the son.[15]

The pertinent fact exposed by the apostle is that, as man, Jesus Christ occupied simultaneously a threefold role in relation to God's order. His triple function provides the key to how God operates with the human race.

Firstly, Christ became man. Like every other human being, he stood in a natural relation to God's moral order. He was obliged to fulfil the great command of love for God and neighbour by living a life of truth, justice, goodness, and love, in every aspect of his human constitution.

Secondly, Christ is not only under the order that regulates relations between God and man, he also 'redeems' others, showing he is their representative. The destiny of others and their deliverance depend on the success of what Christ did. A bond of solidarity links Christ to them and them to him. He is their 'federal' head. As such, his position is unique, for in no other case since the fall do the destinies of men depend on another acting for them in relation to God.

Thirdly, that Christ came to occupy this position as representative is to be attributed to the standing of human beings with regard to God's universal moral order. As sinners, men have gone beyond the line of obedience set by God. Their standing is penal and his law condemns them. Their relation to God is no longer as it was. As the apostle indicates in the third chapter of Galatians, Christ also came to occupy this position: 'Cursed is everyone who does not continue to do everything clearly written in the book of the law...Christ redeemed us from the curse of the law by becoming a curse for us, as it is written; "Cursed is everyone who is hung on a tree."' (Gal. 3:10–13).[16]

Christ, as a man, occupied a relationship to God in which the three orders came into play. His stance was natural with the obligation to obey the whole law as a man; representational, as he was called to act for others; penal, as he voluntarily placed himself under the curse of the law for their salvation. No other man or woman, since sin entered the world, has ever stood in this triple relationship with God. When man violates God's order, his relation to God is one of condemnation. Christ entered into a penal relation before God, not because of his own deeds—he was totally innocent, 'holy, harmless, and undefiled'—but freely, as the spokesman for others.

Before Christ came, only Adam had a relationship with God that was natural and representational (with regard to God), but through disobedience he lost the title deed to life. He passed into a new situation in which he discovered condemnation. The divine order defined his case henceforth, and all human beings after him, in terms of the negative, penal application of the law.[17] Like Adam, human beings are called to be representatives of true humanity, but all forfeit the possibility of entering into a real divine–human relationship because of sin.

> The penal relation to the law is that which instantly supervenes when the law is violated...the penal and federal relations to the law are mutually exclusive. The instant a moral agent incurs the penalty his federal relation to the law necessarily terminates because the end of that relation— that is his confirmation in a holy character—has definitely failed...Adam was created under the natural and the federal relation to law. When he sinned he continued under the natural, and passed from the federal to the penal, where his non-elect descendents remain for all eternity.[18]

As representative, Christ the second Adam acts in perfect conformity with divine order. His relation to God was not penal on his own account; he suffered for others. The condemnation of the cross was not personal, but covenantal. God had no anger against the person of his Son, but against sinners in the office Christ executed on their behalf. Christ's death establishes the covenant. The difference between Adam and Christ is not in the nature of their representative roles. It is that Adam's day as spokesman ended in failure, whereas Christ's representation is eternal, because of his success: 'Although he was a son, he learned obedience from what he suffered and, once made perfect, became the source of eternal salvation for all who obey him, and was designated by God to be a high priest (forever) after the order of Melchizedek' (Heb. 5: 8–10).

CONCLUSION

If atonement is restoring relations with God and has as its end communion with God, man cannot achieve it. He cannot know God and can only speculate what God might require of him. On these grounds, a personal relationship with God is beyond his reach. Furthermore, in his heart of hearts, behind the bluff and bravado, he knows he is a miserable sinner. His efforts are mere palliatives—a major operation is needed for his full return to health.

This is why only the biblical presentation of Christ as representative, according to the covenant conditions, can provide the basis for a personal relationship with God and with our neighbours. By ourselves we are incapable of making our way into God's presence, but Jesus as our spokesman represents man before God. He stands for us. His role is twofold: standing before God to restore creation to its proper end and standing for us, in our place, assuming the death of the cross.

The three atonement models we have considered, victory, penal substitution, and example, can be assessed as to their ability to account for full personal relationships between God and man.[19]

Christ as example of perfect humanity only represents something symbolically to man, and cannot account for a renewed relationship with God. No personal relationship either with God or with other human beings is established by it. The victory of Christ over sin, death, and the powers of evil does not refer to God either. On the contrary, it concerns the defeat of forces foreign to God's good creation. Victory over evil does not effectively reintroduce man into God's presence and establish the basis of a new relation.

When Christ dies for our sins as representative of man, divine justice is satisfied positively by his perfect obedience to the divine order and also negatively, as Christ suffers the consequences of the condemnation of man's sin. The reference of Christ's work is God-ward and the result of its acceptance is that man is brought back into communion with God. Not only so, but as representative Christ defeats the powers of evil and provides an example of holiness. The first two models of atonement are drawn into the orbit of the penal substitutionary model.

Christ is the spokesman for humanity before God and the head of the new covenant in which he administers God's grace for us. Faith in his person and work unites believers to him and opens a way to a new relationship with God, which is fully personal.

As was the case for Adam, Christ the representative stands at the origin of another open-ended situation. As the Omega, the end of creation, he leads his people into a new creation that is eternal: 'As was the earthly man, so also are those who are of the earth; and as is the man from heaven, so also are those who are of heaven. And just as we have borne the likeness of the earthly man, so shall we bear the likeness of the man from heaven' (1 Cor. 15: 48–9).

ENDNOTES

[1] *The Times*, March 29, 1999, 13.

[2] For instance in R. L. Dabney's *Christ Our Penal Substitute* (Harrisonburg, Va: Sprinkle Publications, 1985).

[3] The authors of *Atonement Today* get a lot of mileage out of 'relational'.

[4] On 'abstractionism' see J. Frame, *The Doctrine of the Knowledge of God* (Phillipsburg: Presbyterian and Reformed, 1987), 178 ff.

[5] T. Smail, 'Can one Man die for the People?' in *Atonement Today*, 78. Dabney already replied to most of these objections convincingly in the 19th century in *Christ our Penal Substitute*.

[6] C. S. Lewis, *The Four Loves* (London: Collins, 1960), 11.

[7] The distinction between God and man is of an ontological nature, which means that the relationship between them is not established in terms of similarity of being but through ethical considerations. This is one reason why Luther and Calvin were not interested in approaching God in terms of being and nature, but in those of person, by how God relates to man. Cf. G. Bray, *The Doctrine of God* (Leicester: IVP, 1993), ch. V.

[8] M. Douglas, *Purity and Danger. An Analysis of the Concepts of Pollution and Taboo* (London: Penguin, 1970), 67.

9   Reformed theology has seen the creation as placing man in an eschatological situation. See G. Vos, 'The Doctrine of the Covenant in Reformed Theology' in *Redemptive History and Biblical Interpretation*, R. B. Gaffin, ed., (Phillipsburg: Presbyterian and Reformed, 1980).

10 Genesis 3: 22, compare with 3: 4 and 2: 17.

11 H. Martin, *The Atonement in its Relations to the Covenant, the Priesthood, the Intercession of our Lord*, 1870, in A. A. Hodge, H. Martin, *The Atonement* (Cherry Hill, NJ: Mack, nd.), 1.

12 J. H. Newman, 'Praise to the Holiest in the height': 'O loving wisdom of our God;/ When all was sin and shame,/ A second Adam to the fight,/ And to the rescue came./ O wisest love! That flesh and blood,/ Which did in Adam fall,/ Should strive afresh against the foe,/ Should strive and should prevail.'

13 We use 'representative' whereas the older theology used the word 'federal'.

14 The famous Augustinian *opera trinitatis ad extra indivisa esse—the external actions of the Trinity are not done separately. De Trinit.*, XV.1. 4, 7.

15 This speaks about adoption, just as (e) speaks about justification. Both constitute conditions for union with Christ, which is the foundation of the covenant of grace.

16 C. Baxter, 'The Cursed Beloved. A Reconsideration of Penal Substitution', in *Atonement Today*, 56, is correct in saying that the notion of substitution of one for another is not always of a penal nature. The law can be spoken of in private, civil or penal senses. But in Scripture the idea of law is above all *covenantal*. In Galatians, if Paul is using the metaphor of redemption in terms of debt and civil law, it is obvious that the debt also has a penal nature.

17 Cf. F. Turretin, *The Atonement of Christ*, 1859, (Grand Rapids: Baker, 1978), 96–9.

18 Hodge, in A. A. Hodge, H. Martin, *The Atonement*, 39.

19 B. B. Warfield documents various theories of the atonement by considering on which person or persons the work of Christ terminates, in his article 'Atonement', *Works*, IX, 266 ff.

4

Lordship

What does Jesus' death on the cross have to do with the idea of God? The need for man to be represented to a divinity in this way, so right relations can be restored, is obscure to any form of thought that insists on man's intrinsic dignity. 'But isn't it infantilizing to think we can't speak to God for ourselves? Doesn't every human being have individual value?' How often have we heard things like, 'Jones was a good person, good enough for God,' or 'If anyone is in hell, I don't want to be in heaven'?

Objections like this, and several others, make it necessary to explain the relationship between the God of the Bible, the cross of Christ, and man's need. In this chapter we will consider how the lordship of God relates to the work of Christ. The following chapter will continue along these lines by considering the interrelation of God's love and justice. Subsequently, the need for the cross will be seen in the light of man's sin. In this way, it is hoped the standing of the cross at the junction between what God requires and what man needs will become clear.

A STRANGE GOD

The God of the Bible cannot be imagined even by the farthest stretches of human imagination. When men think about God, they often conclude it is impossible to say anything about him in relation to the reality they experience. If God exists, they think, he must be a reality so different from what is known and from everything else that he is beyond human knowledge. If this were not so, God would just be an aspect of all other known things. On the other hand, some people try to represent God by bringing him close to human experiences—what man can grasp. Human religions bear witness to a multitude of images men have made to represent the divinity. From this perspective, God is made to be just a little more than man, more powerful, more holy, more true, but essentially not totally different from what man is and experiences.

If God is transcendent, as in the first instance, then he cannot really be known as God. If he is immanent, as in the second case, he cannot be fundamentally different from other existing realities: a sense of the absoluteness of God is lost. The God who reveals himself in biblical revelation, however, is neither one nor the other, but both. The way God speaks in the Bible makes him totally different from us in his transcendence, yet present with us in his revelation to man. God is transcendent as a spiritual being, but immanent in identifying himself in a way that men, who are his creatures, can understand.

Biblical revelation presents a God who is strange in comparison with the gods of other beliefs. When Jesus met the woman of Samaria at the well, he brought both aspects of the question together: 'God is spirit and his worshippers must worship him in spirit and in truth' (John 4: 24). 'God is spirit' expresses that God lies beyond the material and visible world. Even so, the truth about God can and must be known. To be acceptable, true worship, as contact between the divine spirit and the human spirit, must be on the basis of this knowledge.

In his speech to the Greek philosophers at Athens, the apostle Paul said essentially the same thing as Jesus: 'As I walked around and looked carefully at your objects of worship, I even found an altar with this inscription: TO AN UNKNOWN GOD. Now what you worship as something unknown I am going to proclaim to you' (Acts. 17: 23). God needs nothing because he is transcendent. He himself gives all men life and breath and everything else; he is self-sufficient (v. 25). False worship of images made by man's design and skill, gets nowhere near to him (v. 29). In the past, God overlooked man's ignorance, but he now commands men to turn from their ways and to recognise his work in Jesus Christ who rose from the dead (v. 30–31)

The strangeness of the God of the Bible is seen at precisely this point. God is transcendent and immanent. He is the eternal spirit. Human reality cannot represent him, yet he can be truly known by what he has revealed about himself within that reality. God is a spirit; an eternal, invisible, and immaterial being. No human thought can represent him and man can make no models of what he is like. Isaiah said this repeatedly in his polemic against idols and the temptation to reduce God to the level of human reality: 'To whom will you compare God? What image will you compare him to?...To whom will you compare me? Or who is my equal? says the Holy One' (Isa. 40: 18, 25; 46: 5). God certainly does not live in 'temples made by human hands.' Nonetheless, the God who is spirit, the Lord of heaven and earth, is 'the God who made the world and everything in it' (v. 24).

Because of this surprising complementarity, there is no contradiction in the Bible between spiritual and material reality, between the invisible and the visible. 'By faith we understand that the universe was formed at God's command, so that what is seen was not made out of what was visible' (Heb. 11: 3). God, who is spirit, made the world in all its material aspects. What is more, God is involved in the material realm without it being either a part of himself or the same kind of reality as himself. When God created the totality of things we call the universe, he made it different from who he is, yet dependent on what he is. So Paul can also say to his audience at Athens, 'he is not far from each one of us. For in him we live and move and have our being' (v. 27–8). Created things are therefore different from God, though made so that God as Lord over all is intimately connected to them. This means that if God is totally different from things that are seen and known naturally, he is not distant from them as an absent or impersonal deity. God is related to his work of creation, and to men who live in it, as the upholder of life and good. As such, God is neither indifferent to events that happen in his world, nor to what man does in it.

There is a unity between God who is spirit and the world as a material reality. This unity can be thought of as God's purposes or intentions for his creation. When man, through a false use of his freedom finds himself in contradiction with God, then this unity of purpose is broken, and God intervenes to set the situation right. The relationship between the invisible

God and the visible created sphere is a moral and personal one. God upholds all things by his power, and reveals himself to man gone wrong not only as the creator God, but also as the Saviour in Jesus Christ, the Son: 'The Son is the radiance of God's glory and the exact representation of his being, sustaining all things by his powerful word. After he had provided purification for sins, he sat down at the right hand of the majesty in heaven' (Heb. 1: 3).

The spiritual nature of God, and his upholding presence in material reality, is ultimately the foundation for God's coming into his creation to redeem it in the person of the Lord Jesus Christ. In him, the fullness of God's transcendent spirituality and the material substance of human nature are joined together, so that he is at the same time true God and true man. Neither nature is mixed in with the other; both are held together in his person—really united, yet distinct. 'The word became flesh and made his dwelling among us. We have seen his glory, the glory of the One and Only, who came from the Father, full of grace and truth' (John 1: 14). Therefore, the spiritual reality of God and the material reality of human existence subsist in the incarnation, in a way that is comparable to the material reality of creation issuing from and upheld by the spirit of God.

Creation and incarnation are of a kind; the first cannot be understood without the second. Today, salvation is often reduced to an individual subjective experience, as it is isolated from the fundamental doctrines of creation and incarnation.

GOD AS LORD

All that has been said hitherto about God being both transcendent and immanent, implies God is Lord over all reality, both spiritual and material.[1] The Bible, however, does not speak about the lordship of God in an abstract way, but within the structure of the covenant with his people. Covenant can be defined in this way:

> A mutual promise and agreement between God and men, in which God gives assurance to men that he will be merciful to them...And on the other side, men bind themselves to God in this covenant that they will exercise repentance and faith...and render such obedience as will be acceptable to him.[2]

Even if the agreement of the covenant is mutual, God and man are not equal partners in the covenants of Scripture. God identifies himself as Lord in the covenant; man's position is that of God's servant to recognise the covenant terms and put them into practice.

The dual arrangement of the covenant is seen in the structure of some central biblical texts. For instance, the Ten Commandments of Exodus 20 are structured by the covenantal relationship between God and man.[3] In verse one, God identifies himself as the Lord and Saviour of his people: 'I am the Lord your God, who brought you out of Egypt, out of the land of slavery.' In the first four commandments, sometimes called the first table of the law, God specifies the kind of service that relates to his person. The last six, the second table, concern man's obedience and welfare in his created and social environment.[4] The way the commandments are set out indicate that man's obedience is first to God himself, and then to God's will in his relationships with others. This structure supplies the substance for Jesus' reply to the question concerning the greatest commandment of the law. Love to God is primary; love to man is of a similar kind and dependent on it (Matt. 22: 37–8).

When Jesus taught his prayer to the disciples, the covenant structure appeared again in the form of the petitions (Matt. 6: 9–13). Prayer is not only worship of God, but also service rendered to God in love. For this reason, the first three requests in the Lord's prayer concern God, recognition of who he is by his name, his rule, and his will. These are intimately connected; where God's name is honoured his kingdom comes, and when his kingdom comes, his will is done. The second set of requests concern man's life, which is dependent on God's goodness. Prayer concerning daily bread, forgiveness, and testing, concern man's well-being in its physical, psychological, and spiritual aspects. Man recognises his dependence on the goodness of God in all areas of his life. Because of its special form, Jesus' prayer binds together in one act of worship what is fitting to God and what is necessary for man—the divine and human sides of the covenant.

If the dual structure of the covenant indicates the complementarity of God and man in a common project, God's lordship is revealed by his name and his attributes. 'The biblical Lord is not just any other ruler…the basic concepts of hierarchy, rule and power are intrinsic to the lordship of God. To oppose the rule of God is to oppose his lordship altogether.'[5] Within the covenant God reveals his sovereignty over creation, salvation, and the life of his people constituted as a community. The divine power revealed in these three realms demonstrates his claim to be the Lord of the covenant, upon whom man depends for blessing and all that is good in human life.

GOD'S NAME AND ATTRIBUTES

In biblical revelation, God addresses himself to man in the first person singular: 'I am the Lord your God', 'Be holy as I am holy', 'I am the holy one among you.' These, and similar expressions, all indicate that God is first in the covenant as the one who establishes it and dictates its conditions. The lordship of God and his transcendence cannot be understood as an impersonal power. God always presents it in a personal way. Other religions have personal gods, which are not absolute. Other philosophies have absolute principles, but they are not personal expressions of power. God is absolute in nature and power, and personal in the way he identifies himself.

> In Scripture the personal is greater than the impersonal. The impersonal things and forces in this world are created and directed by a personal God…In the biblical view the impersonal reduces to the personal. Matter, energy, motion, time and space are under the rule of a personal Lord. All the wonderful things that we find in personality—intelligence, compassion, creativity, love, justice—are aspects of what is most permanent most ultimate. Only in biblical religion is there an absolute principle that is personal.[6]

When God encounters Moses at the burning bush that is not consumed, he also reveals his identity by a name, Yahweh: 'I am the God of your father, the God of Abraham, the God of Isaac and the God of Jacob…I AM WHOM I AM…this is my name forever, the name to be remembered from generation to generation' (Exod. 3: 6, 14–15). The name God gives to his people is not a statement about his inner eternity, although God is eternal.[7] It reveals his lordship in history, his power to intervene and save, as he did for Abraham and his descendents. It shows he remembers and fulfils the promises made to his people concerning their future. God's lordship extends over history in the past, present, and future. It is demonstrated by his power to save his people. 'God's name is not arbitrary, but God reveals himself as he is…God is that which he calls himself and he calls himself that which he is.'[8]

In the Gospels, Jesus takes the name of Yahweh for his own when he tells his scandalised listeners, 'Before Abraham was born I am!' (John 8: 58). In his 'I am' sayings in the gospel of John, he uses this expression to underline his oneness with God. 'I AM: the bread of life; the light of the world; the gate for the sheep; the good shepherd; the resurrection and the life; the way, the truth, and the life; and the true vine.'[9] This is no less than a claim to divinity on Jesus' part, and it is no empty claim. His authority as Lord is made good by the promise he attaches to each saying. He calls himself Jesus, and his lordship is made real to those who receive his witness and rest on his promises by believing in him. Just as Yahweh is the covenant head of his people, so also Jesus is the Lord of the new covenant community.

The New Testament identifies Jesus as the one who has a name that is 'over every name' (Phil. 2: 9), who is not only the Lord of his people, but is also the Creator and the Saviour God.[10] In his lordship, all power in heaven and on earth belongs to him (Matt. 28: 18). He is at the start and the end of all created reality: 'I am the Alpha and the Omega, says the Lord God, who is, who was and who is to come, the Almighty' (Rev. 1: 8). As Lord over all, Jesus addresses the seven churches of Asia Minor, using a covenantal form with threats and promises, and identifying himself with names that denote he is the Great King. He 'holds the seven stars in his right hand', is the first and the last, has a double-edged sword, is the Son of God, holds the seven spirits of God, is holy and true, and is the Amen.'[11] Each name defines the Lord's relation to each church, with respect to its situation and needs. What is true of Yahweh in the Old Testament is true of Jesus in the New. Now the love of God is revealed in a universal way to all nations, and because of Christ's lordship in salvation, 'God's covenant provides the blessings of common grace, the kindness of God to all his creatures.'[12]

God's names in Scripture are multiple, because they are related to his attributes as Lord. If God has many names, it is because his attributes reflect the greatness and glory of his infinite person. The attributes of God are also names by which he can be identified. He is therefore holy, and he is the Holy One, he is eternal and the Eternal One, he is mighty and the Almighty. The list is practically inexhaustible. The longest 'name' of God in Scripture is a list that combines several of his different attributes. God says to Moses:

> I will cause all my goodness to pass in front of you, and I will proclaim my name, the LORD, in your presence. I will have mercy on whom I will have mercy and I will have compassion on whom I will have compassion.
>
> The Lord came down in a cloud and stood there with Moses and proclaimed his name, the LORD. And he passed in front of Moses, proclaiming, 'The LORD, the LORD, the compassionate and gracious God, slow to anger, abounding in love and faithfulness, maintaining love to thousands and forgiving wickedness, rebellion and sin.'
>
> Exod. 33: 19; 34: 5–7

When God reveals himself in his name, either to Moses or in Jesus Christ, transcendence and immanence are joined. God is sovereign and free; he does not lay aside his transcendent power in revelation, but reveals it in an immanent sense by naming himself, in a way that is comprehensible to his people, as the God of love, mercy, and justice. In this way, the 'name by which God reveals himself' becomes the name by which we address him', and distinguish him as the true God over against all false divinities.[13] In this way the name of God in revelation preserves the absolute otherness of the Lord, and 'fixes' his identity in a human way, so his people can recognise and worship him.

The Westminster Confession of Faith says this:

> There is but one living and true God, who is infinite in being and perfection, a most pure spirit, invisible, without body, parts, or passions, immutable, immense, eternal, incomprehensible, almighty, most wise, most holy, most free, most absolute, working all things according to the counsel of his own immutable and most righteous will, for His own glory, most loving, gracious, merciful, longsuffering, abundant in goodness and truth, forgiving iniquity and sin.'[14]

Although this might sound a little crusty and abstract to modern ears, it essentially states there is only one God like this, who is spirit, characterised by perfections that belong only to his being, and who is not dependent on his creatures, but is independent in his lordship.

All God's attributes, however, are attested by his acts accomplished in the history of creation and salvation. It is only by what God does, and by the witness he bears to his acts in biblical revelation, that any of these things can be said about him. It is because God is active and intimately involved in the life and history of the world that human beings can say what God is like. None of his attributes can be extrapolated from earthly realities, or from human situations and culture. On the contrary, it is because God has entered into the arena of human affairs that God is confessed to be like this. Through God alone can God be known. God bears witness to himself:

> I, even I, am the Lord,
>   and apart from me there is no saviour.
> I have revealed and saved and proclaimed—
>   I, and not some foreign god among you…
> Yes, and from the ancient days I am he.
>   No one can deliver out of my hand.
>   When I act, who can reverse it?
>
> I, even I, am he
>   who blots out your transgressions
>   for my own sake,
>   and remembers your sins no more.
>
> Isa. 43: 11–13; 25

COVENANT CONDITIONS

The lordship of God does not crush human responsibilities; it provides the conditions in which God and man can prove to be faithful. The mutuality of the covenant as an agreement, or bond, and its conditionality, lie close together. 'Mutuality acknowledges that both parties of the covenant have responsibilities. Conditionality outlines the responsibilities that each party has towards the other. As first party of the covenant, God sets the duties that each party must fulfil.'[15]

It is not too much to say God has bound himself to man in the covenant. God has tied himself to his people in a way that demonstrates 'I will be your God' always remains true. He will be their saviour, protector, and partner. He will accomplish all that he has promised—blessings and threats. God will demonstrate his love and also his righteousness: 'I, the Lord your God am a jealous God, punishing the children for the sin of the fathers to the third and fourth generation of those who hate me, but showing love to a thousand generations of those who love me and keep my commandments' (Exod. 20: 4). The preponderance of the thousand generations over the three and four, whatever the judgment on the children might mean, serves to illustrate that the ultimate purpose of God is not to curse, but to bless his people. He will respect the condition of dwelling among his people. 'God is joined to us in such a manner that he wishes all that belongs to him and to us to be in common…the Lord has entered into covenant with us on the condition of undertaking our cause (and) he will actually fulfil it.'[16] God never makes promises that he cannot keep, either positively or negatively.

Man's reply to God, the first party of the covenant, is to recognise God as Lord, obey and serve him. Man's responsibility lies in these words: 'Now if you obey me fully and keep my covenant, then out of all nations you will be my treasured possession. Although the whole earth is mine, you will be for me a kingdom of priests and a holy nation' (Exod. 19: 5–6). The 'if' opens up for man the awful possibility of violating the covenant and falling under the Lord's judgment.

The question becomes acute when the character of God is fully understood. Can man live with a holy God? God's holiness pervades all his other attributes. It means he is wholly different from all his creation, including the people to whom he binds himself in the covenant: 'For I am God, and not man—the Holy One among you' (Hos. 11: 9). 'His holiness means un-approachability and marks the infinite, frightening distance between God and humankind. Its effect is that people bow down; they are tongue-tied, and convinced of their own futility.'[17] The holiness of God invariably defeats man, revealing how deeply he lacks conformity to the holiness of God. When the God of holiness relates to his people, he requires that they be holy, which means they must be completely dedicated to him. 'God is the One who is totally different, so the people who belong to him must be totally different as well.'[18]

This is why the Old Testament covenant of grace provides for forgiveness of sin through sacrifice—to restore the relations of purity existing between God and man. Ultimately, because man is unable to match up to the holiness of God, God must fulfil the covenant conditions for man. The covenant is unconditional on the divine side, as God will always be holy and will always keep his word, but on man's side it is conditional. If the people of God do not respond in holiness and obedience to the Lord, they will inevitably forfeit the covenant blessings. This points to the necessity for the coming of the Holy One, the true Israel, who will fulfil all righteousness (Matt. 3: 15), as Jesus accepts to do at his baptism. This is the act of the beloved Son, in whom God is well pleased (v. 17). In him the covenant conditions are fulfilled for his people, in his righteous life and in his sacrificial death.[19] Because of God's free forgiveness of sin, the holiness of God can be a subject of joy and rejoicing, as it was in the Old Testament for the expectant people of God.[20]

THE PROMISED ONE

A most remarkable thing is said about Jesus Christ in Revelation 13: 8, where he is called 'the Lamb that was slain from the foundation of the world.' John speaks of something that happened before the foundation of the world, as he refers to those purchased by the Lamb (5: 9), and whose names were written then in the 'Lamb's book of life' (21: 27, cf. 17: 8).[21] Jesus' teaching also revealed things 'kept secret from before the foundation of the world' (Matt. 13: 35), and he himself claimed to be beloved of the Father before the creation of the world (John 17: 24).

The covenant of grace fulfilled by Jesus reveals something about the lordship of God that is deeply rooted in his eternal purposes for humanity. God's lordship over history in the working out of his purposes is an aspect of his eternal lordship, which existed before time. God's plan involved much more than patching up a bad job made by man's sin. His purpose in Jesus Christ was already present in the divine mind in eternity. God's covenant not only contains Christ as its fulfilment, he is also from God's eternal perspective the foundation of the covenant. The covenant is the instrument by which God exercises his lordship over all things through Jesus Christ, his eternal Son.

From this perspective, as with the attributes of God, we can only reason backwards from the actual events of history to things that are secret and mysterious in God, as the biblical witness presents them. Things that happened in history fulfil a divine purpose that existed in God before time began and the world was founded.[22] We are told God promised faith and the hope of eternal life 'before the beginning of time' and brought this to light in the gospel of Jesus Christ 'at his appointed season' (Titus 1: 2–3). To whom was this eternal promise made? It can only have been to the Son in the role of saviour he accepted for those who would believe. Christ is also called the 'guarantee of a better covenant' (Heb. 7: 22). He can only stand in this function as the one who has accepted to be the 'priest after the order of Melchizedek' and as the one about whom 'the Lord has sworn and will not change his mind: You are a priest forever' (v. 17, 21). The promises of God, and Jesus as the divine guarantee, imply God has nominated Christ to occupy this function—a role he has undertaken to achieve on behalf of men for their salvation.

The biblical witness in general implies an agreement between the Father and the Son, in which the Son is sent into the world to accomplish a specific purpose, with the promise of God supporting him in his work of salvation.[23] Jesus' own word attests he has received and accepted this particular mission from his Father.[24] In his high priestly prayer, a high point in Jesus' understanding of his own mission, he claims the promised reward as his right: 'I have completed the work you gave me to do, now Father, glorify me in your presence with the glory I had with you before the world began' (John 17: 4–5). Before this, at the Passover meal, he had instituted the Lord's supper as a new covenant sign with these words: 'I confer on you a kingdom, just as my Father has conferred one on me, so that you may eat and drink at my table in my kingdom' (Luke 22: 29–30).[25] Christ's reward for his work is the kingdom inheritance, to which his disciples belong by his saving work—the breaking of his body and shedding of his blood on their behalf.[26]

CONCLUSION

The lordship of God in kingdom terms comes to its fullness in the finished work of Christ. The personal nature of God as a loving and just Lord, the faithfulness of God to his covenant promises, his holiness and sovereignty in redemption—all aspects of his lordship—come to their most complete expression in the person and work of Christ. The cross is the focal point where the attributes of God—his freedom, mercy, holiness, justice, love, wisdom, and truth—come to expression, in the light of his eternal purpose.

The final reasons for God's acts are found in his person and character, and are accomplished primarily for his own glory. His benevolence toward man in creation and salvation are secondary demonstrations of his lordship. Unacceptable as this may be to modern man, the Scriptures present us with a God who will not give his glory to another (Isa. 42: 8).

> The ultimate motive for the sacrifice of Christ must have been the divine glory, and not the effect intended to be produced in the creature. But glory is manifested excellence. And moral excellence is manifested only by being exercised. The infinite justice and love of God both find their highest conceivable exercise in the sacrifice of his own Son as the substitute of guilty man.[27]

ENDNOTES

[1] See J. Frame, *The Doctrine of God* (Phillipsburg: Presbyterian and Reformed, 2003), ch. 2.

[2] Z. Ursinus, *Commentary on the Heidelberg Catechism*, quoted in Golding, *Covenant Theology* (Fearn: Christian Focus, 2004), 85.

[3] O. P. Robertson, *The Christ of the Covenants* (Grand Rapids: Baker, 1980) gives many examples of how the covenants of Scripture progressively build on each other and the importance of this for the unity of revelation and salvation.

[4] M. J. Kline, *The Structure of Biblical Authority* (Grand Rapids: Eerdmans, 1972).

[5] Frame, *op. cit.*, 24.

[6] Ibid, 26–7.

[7] Ibid, ch. 3.

[8] H. Bavinck, *The Doctrine of God* (Baker: Grand Rapids, 1977), ch. 3.

[9] John 6: 35; 8: 12; 10: 7, 11; 11: 25; 14: 6; 15: 5.

[10] John 1: 10, Colossians 1: 16, Hebrews 1: 2, etc.

[11] Revelation 2: 1; 2: 8; 2: 12, 18; 3: 1, 7, 14. Cf. C. Vanderwaal, *Search the Scriptures*, 10, (St Catherines, Ontario: 1979), 79 ff. and his *The Covenantal Gospel* (Neerlandia, Alberta: Inheritance Publications, 1990).

[12] Frame, *op. cit.*, 34.

[13] Bavinck, *op. cit.*, 85.

[14] *The Westminster Confession of Faith* (1647), II.1.

[15] P. Lillback, *The Binding of God. Calvin's Role in the Development of Covenant Theology* (Grand Rapids: Baker, 2001), 169. *Cf.* Golding, *op. cit.*, ch. 4.

[16] Ibid.

[17] E. Peels, *Shadow Sides of God. God in the Old Testament* (Carlisle: Paternoster, 2003), 128. Cf. A.A. Hodge, *The Atonement*, 24 ff.

[18] Ibid, 136.

[19] To be considered in chapter 10.

[20] Peels, *op. cit.*, 130 ff.

[21] Cf. Ephesians 1: 4, 1 Peter 1: 20, Matthew 25: 34.

[22] This can be said without going as far as speaking about a fully blown eternal 'covenant of redemption' as reformed theology sometimes has done. Cf. G. Vos 'The Doctrine of the Covenant in Reformed Theology' in R. Gaffin, ed. *Redemptive History and Biblical Interpretation*, 245 ff.

[23] See, among other texts, Psalm 40: 7ss, Hebrews 10: 10, Galatians 4: 4, John 17: 4, 18, 1 John 4: 9–10.

[24] John 6 38–9, 10: 18.

[25] The word used for 'confer' here is *diatithemi* from the same word group as covenant, *diatheke*. Jesus is disposing the kingdom for his disciples by the terms of a covenant.

[26] John 17: 6, 9, 24 and Philippians 2: 9–11.

[27] Hodge, *op. cit.*, 24. *Cf.* E. Brunner, *The Mediator*, 470.

5

Love and Justice

What kind of action does man's salvation require of God? This question hides a further one. How are divine love and justice related in the work of salvation? Love must be at work, as salvation is God's intervention on man's behalf, but the question of justice is unavoidable. Man is being saved from something, namely sin and death, and a moral God cannot be indifferent to this.

Peter Abelard (1079–1142), the medieval theologian, is often better known for the tricky situation he got into with Héloïse's father than for his contribution to atonement theology. In contrast to his contemporary Anselm's idea that the sacrifice of the cross satisfied God, he proposed it be considered as a pure act of love. When the atonement is discussed from this perspective, the work of the cross tends to become an example of love, often to the exclusion of other considerations. 'God has fully bound himself to us by love; with the result that our hearts should be kindled by such a gift of divine grace and true charity should not now shrink from enduring anything for him.'[1]

Majoring in the love of God creates problems. The cross becomes a simple illustration of God's unbounded generosity toward sinners and Jesus' self-giving for others. No attribute of God, however, can be separated from others and considered in isolation. God's love is not God's love unless it is eternal, true, righteous, and all the other aspects of his nature that characterise him as God. In particular, as one of his ethical attributes, it can only be understood together with his holiness and justice.

Therefore, God's love is not like a changeable human emotion with ups and downs. It is a constant expression of his holiness and justice.

One problem with much talk about the love of God is it forgets he is also a God of justice. In this chapter, we will look at these two divine attributes together and see how they relate to the cross.

LOVE DIVINE

'Do you want me to tell you why and how one ought to love God? I reply briefly: the reason for which one ought to love God is God himself; and the measure of that love is to love him without measure.'[2]

Love requires two persons, even if a realistic view of one's own qualities needs a measure of self-love, which is not the same as egoism and narcissism. Love for God and one's neighbour constitute God's golden rule for human behaviour (Mark 12: 29–31). God himself is love; therefore, love is not only his gift to his creatures, but also a command and a duty. God alone can demand love from and of others because he alone is love.

The Christian confession concerning God is that God is a Trinity—three, not one or two persons—a seemingly insoluble problem for many people. How can this be understood? Surely to believe in one God is more intellectually satisfying? By confessing God is a Trinity, Christianity detracts neither from the oneness of God nor from his essential unity. On the contrary, the three persons of the godhead exist in perfect unity as one God. This concept is essential to the love of God, which Father, Son, and Holy Spirit experience simultaneously. The oneness of God is not a form of solitude; it exists in love expressed in the holy Trinity.

The love of God in Christianity is more personal and less monarchical than in other forms of monotheism, even than in Judaism.[3] The Holy Spirit who proceeds from the Father and the Son, and who is instrumental in creation and revelation, manifests the love that exists in God and the love of God.[4] 'The Holy Spirit proceeds from the Father and the Son and is the fruit of eternal and infinite love with which the Father and the Son love each other.'[5] Love is uncreated in God and the gift of the Holy Spirit creates it in his creatures.[6] Love binds the divine community together and is therefore the foundation of created human relations. Love in human beings is more than an affair between two people; created with man, love implies the presence of a third person, God himself.

The covenant between God and man is not something foreign he imposes upon man. Creation manifests God's love for realities outside himself, because love already existed within himself in a perfect way. He created humans in his image, not that their love might exist in a closed circuit, but in recognition that God is the source of their love. True love is not found in an ultimate sense in the relationship between two people, which can become an introspective end in itself. It flowers in relation to God, who as the source of love is not loved for what he does for us, but for himself, his own person and beauty. True love is precisely love of God for who he is, which runs deeper than loving him for what he does for us.[7]

The understanding of the cross as a marvellous example of God's love, and stimulus for human love, runs aground upon this reef. If love is the foundation of relations created between God and man, and between human beings, it is much more than an illustration. To make the cross an example of love is not only limiting as far as God is concerned; it is also unrealistic with regard to man's fundamental problem, which is not simply a lack of love.

THE BREADTH AND DEPTH OF GOD'S LOVE

The goodness of God, often called 'benevolence' in former times, looks at the love of God through a wide-angle lens. Zooming in on the subject, we see the love of God more precisely as God's grace, which gives a sharper theological image.[8] The Bible offers several complementary descriptions of divine love, which are not different kinds of love, but degrees of the same love.[9]

The goodness of God is made known in his actions of 'good will' to all his creatures. God alone is good (Mark 10: 18), and the fountain of life and light (Ps. 36: 9). His inherent goodness is manifested to all without discrimination (Ps. 145: 9–10, 14–17): rain and sun, springtime and harvest demonstrate the kindness of God to all. As Jesus says in the Sermon on the mount: 'He causes his sun to rise on the evil and the good, and sends rains on the righteous and the unrighteous' (Matt. 5: 45). God's common grace does not imply men have the capacity to see God at work in his kindness, or the inclination to give thanks. Only those who have the eye of faith can behold God in these works and be grateful.

By his compassion, God shows he loves sinners despite their sin. Perhaps in a strange way he 'feels for' them because of it. Divine compassion crystallises in the mercy or the pity of God toward those who suffer from sin and labour under its burden. God beholds those who suffer the consequences of their own injustice, or that of others, and their plight touches him. When Jesus saw the crowds as sheep without a shepherd, was he not moved to compassion? (Mark 6: 34). God is 'kind to the ungrateful and the wicked…Be merciful,' exhorts Jesus, 'just as your Father is merciful' (Luke 6: 35–6). In his pity, God is always prepared to receive those who turn to him and seek his mercy. God expresses his compassion in his welcome for suffering sinners; it is the antechamber of grace and forgiveness. All God's mercy is grace, but grace itself is more than mercy.[10]

The grace of God corresponds to man's guilt, just as his compassion corresponds to the sinner's suffering. Grace is God's mercy toward those unworthy of such favour. Grace is not shown to victors; only to the vanquished. Such is the goodness of God toward those who have relinquished the right to be loved and who, by their nature and their acts, merit only condemnation and judgment. The father of the prodigal son is the obvious biblical example of grace, and rightly so in the light of his son's behaviour (Luke 15: 21). Grace is shown in the deliverance that comes from the unmerited mercy of God. It is the source of all God's spiritual blessings granted to sinners. Ephesians 2: 4–7 is a fine example of how saving grace demonstrates the mercy of God:

> Because of his great love for us, God, who is rich in mercy, made us alive with Christ even when we were dead in transgressions—it is by grace you have been saved. And God raised us up with Christ…in order that in the coming ages he might show the incomparable riches of his grace, expressed in his kindness to us in Christ Jesus.

Mercy, love, grace and kindness are all aspects, at different levels, of God's saving work. Grace is the source, the accomplishment and the application of all that God is as saviour of sinners.

The love of God, as distinct from the goodness of God in general, is 'that perfection of God by which he is eternally moved to self communication. Since God is absolutely good in himself, his love cannot find complete satisfaction in any object that falls short of absolute perfection.'[11] But who can be loved of God, when the bench-mark is so high? God is love. He loves those who the Holy Spirit makes new in 'justice, holiness and love of the truth' (Eph. 4: 24, Col. 3: 10). God loves his children in a special, inalterable way and is pleased to bless them with his gifts and graces. As Jesus said to his disciples, 'The Father himself loves you because you have loved me and have believed that I came from God' (John 16: 27). The knowledge of God's love becomes a reality through the work of grace, calling forth a response of gratitude in return. 'How great is the love the Father has lavished on us, that we should be called the children of God! And that is what we are!' (1 John 3: 1). The grace God communicates to the sinner is the foundation of communion in love. The communication comes first; the communion in love is its result. God's love is specially revealed when Jesus Christ, his Son, declares believers to be God's children. When Paul says God has 'poured out his love into our hearts by the Holy Spirit whom he has given to us' (Rom. 5: 5), he indicates a settled state that is the consequence of a completed action.

A paradox appears in connection with the love of God. On the one hand, 'the love of God is not the complete truth about God as far as the Bible is concerned.' God is also just and righteous. Yet for believers, 'God is love is the complete truth about God as far as the Christian is concerned.' This is the case because 'God's love is an exercise of his goodness toward individual sinners whereby, having identified himself with their welfare, he has given his Son to be their saviour and now brings them to know and enjoy him in a covenant relation.'[12] The communion in love between God and the believer is possible because of the justice of Christ, which is the foundation of a change of life from darkness to light.

The love of God in Christ is not superior to the other forms of God's kindness that we have described. It is different since a particular form of this kindness is made known in and through Christ alone. The same light shines through the raindrops, but produces a rainbow. God is the instigator of the covenant of grace, which binds together his gift of love and the gratitude of his children, as the divine and human sides of the relationship.

GOD'S JUSTICE

'God's love is stern, for it expresses holiness in the lover and seeks holiness for the beloved. Scripture does not allow us to suppose that because God is love we may look to him to confer happiness on people who will not seek holiness or to shield his loved ones from trouble when he knows that they need trouble to further their sanctification.'[13] Hard words for folk who want their lives to glide along without questions! That is why it is easy to consider divine love and justice as mutually self-exclusive opposites, but biblical revelation does not present them in that way. They are complementary concepts: love demands justice and justice demands love. 'Mercy and justice do not need to be reconciled, for they are never at war. The true opposite of justice is not mercy but injustice, with which God can have nothing to do either in reconciliation or in any other of his works.'[14]

What is divine justice? It is essentially the same as God's righteousness. English expresses this by two words, but in Hebrew and in Greek a single word group expresses the two terms (*ṣedeq* and *dikaios*). God is just. He always acts in accordance with what is right; the final standards for his judgments are found in his person. Abraham recognised God's justice cannot be called into question, even when he was tested over the sacrifice of Isaac: 'Shall not the Judge of all the earth do right?' (Gen. 18: 25). Moses praised God for his integrity: 'All his ways are justice. A God of faithfulness and without iniquity, just and right is he' (Deut. 32: 4). The psalmist often praises the Lord because of his righteousness: 'The precepts of the Lord are just, rejoicing the heart' (Ps. 19: 8).

The idea of the justice of God can be summed up by linking justice, as it exists in God, with what God does. In an absolute sense, God is just and upright, true and good. There is no defect in God, no 'amoral subconscious', which might break out in unholy passion and evil. Scripture often calls God 'light', to indicate his perfect purity and righteousness, as in him there is no darkness at all (1 John 1: 5). God's life is light (John 1: 4–5). God maintains his righteousness in a positive sense by his acts of judgment, which define him as the one who is just in contrast with all that is unrighteous, sinful, and evil. God is perfect in all his ways and untainted by his knowledge of evil. His interventions in situations of injustice do not mean he is guilty by association. God is the 'fountain of life' and 'in his light we see light' (Ps. 36: 9).

Like the love of God, justice has several perspectives. Both are like a flower bulb with several layers to be peeled away before getting to the heart. When examined, the different aspects of divine justice will accord with the facets of God's love we have considered. To the general goodness of God corresponds what can be called his fairness in dealing with all his creatures; to his compassion for the suffering, his patience and forbearance; to his grace, the pardon of sins; and to his special love for his children, his holiness. Together, forbearance, patience, forgiveness, and holiness constitute a cluster of ideas that contribute to making God's justice what it is.

God's fairness, or equity, in dealing with all his creatures is the broadest aspect of divine justice. 'The Lord is righteous in all his ways and loving toward all he has made' (Ps. 145: 17). Because this aspect of divine righteousness concerns all men, it is often associated with God's rule: 'The Lord reigns, let the earth be glad...righteousness and justice are the foundation of his throne' (Ps. 97: 1–2). Those victorious over the beast sing the Song of Moses and of the Lamb:

> Great and marvellous are your deeds,
>   Lord God Almighty.
> Just and true are your ways;
>   King of the ages
> Who will not fear you,
>   O Lord and bring glory to your name?
> For you alone are holy.
>   All nations will come and worship before you.
> For your righteous acts have been revealed.

Rev. 15: 3–4

The fairness of God in his rule over his creatures is why many biblical texts speak of God being the hope of those who suffer, and against oppressors. Because the Lord reigns forever, and governs the world in righteousness and justice, he is 'a refuge for the oppressed and a stronghold in times of trouble' (Ps. 9: 7–9). The Lord is attentive to the cries of the righteous and his face is set against those who do evil (Ps. 34: 15–22). He 'defends the cause of the weak and the fatherless and maintains the rights of the poor and oppressed' (Ps. 82: 3–4). Because of God's concern for justice for the oppressed, the righteousness of God is not only a way of governing the world, it is also a reason for his intervention in saving acts. So God's deliverance and salvation work together as justice and righteousness (1 Sam. 12: 6 ff.).

A second aspect of divine justice is God's patience or longsuffering with those who oppose his rule. God's concern for the oppressed seems to contradict his lack of immediate intervention to end situations of injustice. God is not hot-tempered and hasty in his reaction against sin. He is the opposite of impatient and lets things run their course. Many times we are told God is 'slow to anger'.[15] 'The Bible makes much of the patience and forbearance of God in postponing merited judgements in order to extend the day of grace and give more opportunity for repentance...The patience of God in giving 'space to repent' (Rev. 2: 5) before judgment finally falls is one of the marvels of the Bible story.'[16] God's waiting patiently (1 Pet. 3: 20, 3: 9) serves to illustrate how his attributes are different from human emotions and passions. God's reply to unrighteousness is not a 'gut reaction' as when humans swoop for revenge, but a measured and just judgment that is as certain as it is true.

God's justice reaches a new point of development when it is revealed as forgiveness. A kind of grace is at work already in the fairness and patience of God, but in pardoning sinners his act of grace in justice comes to the forefront. Who is a pardoning God like this? God's people went into exile because of their disobedience to the covenant and as a punishment for their sin. Nonetheless, God's grace abounds in forgiveness, because sins are covered and God passes over them. The message of Isaiah is, 'Comfort my people...proclaim to Jerusalem that her hard service has been completed, that her sin has been paid for [pardoned]' (40: 1–2). Israel must recognise her covenant responsibility by turning to the Lord, who is merciful: 'Seek the Lord while he may be found...let the wicked forsake his way...let him turn to the Lord and he will have mercy on him and to our God for he will freely pardon' (55: 6–7).

It is not by chance that at the end of the Lord's Prayer Jesus commented on the petition 'forgive us our debts, as we forgive

our debtors': 'If you forgive men when they sin against you,
your heavenly Father will also forgive you. But if you do not
forgive men their sins, your Father will not forgive your sins'
(Matt. 6: 14–15). Jesus knew how difficult it is for us to exercise
forgiveness. The bigger the prejudice experienced, the harder
it is to accept others and to pardon them. But God forgives
the most grievous 'debt' of all, that of man's rejection of his
righteous rule. Jesus also knew existentially what this means
when he suffered rejection. He was 'despised and rejected of
men, a man of sorrows and familiar with suffering' (Isa. 53: 3).
It is surely wonderful that at the moment Jesus' enemies were
nailing him to the cross, he was able to forgive them, despite
excruciating pain. In the first word from the cross, Jesus echoes
the Lord's prayer: 'Father, forgive them, for they know not
what they do' (Luke 23: 34).

Jesus' prayer and action reveal the mechanism of forgiveness.
Strange though it may seem, we need God to forgive us so we
can forgive others. 'Forgive us our debts, as we forgive also…'
Only when we know how great is God's mercy in forgiving us,
do we realise how small our forgiveness is toward our fellows.[17]
Surprisingly, God has opened the way to forgiveness by acting
himself. He forgives us at great personal cost, removing our
sin by accepting his Son in our place: 'He was wounded for
our transgressions, he was crushed for our iniquities; the
punishment that brought us peace was upon him, and by
his wounds we are healed' (Isa. 53: 5). Genuine forgiveness
implies repair of wrong done. This is one condition of healing
in relationships. God provided the means of healing our sins
when Jesus took our place in suffering the condemnation and
death of a wrongdoer. This is strange justice, but justice that
makes for divine forgiveness.

Finally, God's holiness is an expression of justice; it is
the very heart of his righteous judgments. It speaks of God
acting in conformity with his character in his relationships
with human beings. God's justice is holy justice, because it is
according to his righteous standards. 'Holiness speaks of God's
transcendence and separation from finite and sinful creatures.
But it also speaks of how God draws them to himself, making
them holy.'[18]

When Isaiah had his vision of God in the temple and heard
the seraphs worship, 'Holy, holy, holy is the Lord of hosts,' he

knew he stood condemned by God's holiness: 'Woe is me…For I am a man of unclean lips…and my eyes have seen the Lord, the Almighty' (Isa. 6:5). Isaiah is right in his understanding of the situation. Because he is justly condemned in the light of God's holiness, he needs purification for God to accept him. So before hearing God's call to be a prophet, a live coal from the altar symbolically purifies his lips—a sign his sin has been judged and he is now clean.

THE LOVING JUDGE

To speak about the justice of God implies that God as Lord is the judge of all things. His justice, however, is inseparable from his love. One cannot be understood without the other. But what would it imply to say God was a loving judge? That sounds like a contradiction in human terms.

The different aspects of God's character are interrelated. Consequently, attributes with the same names have different meanings with regard to God and to human beings. God's goodness is fair for all without prejudicial preferences, his compassion is longsuffering and patient, his grace is shown in forgiveness, and his love in relationships of holiness. In these respects, God as Lord acts as the loving judge of his creatures. When God acts as judge, he is always true to himself, but also to the contractual relationships he has with his creatures.

If God's love, expressed in forgiveness and holiness, is not too difficult to understand, it is another case when we speak of God's love in judgment and condemnation. Here love is limited by justice; it is expressed in the perfection of God's judgment. His judgments are entirely equitable, executed according to justice, and their rightness expresses his love. He does not judge as humans might, in hatred or for reasons of revenge because he has been offended, but by what is right and good according to his holy laws. His judgment is not intuitive. Even in judgment, God can have compassion for those he judges. Yet, for reasons superior to those considerations, and despite his compassion, he can decide to carry through the sentence with genuine pity.[19]

Paul's statement about God's way of handling the Jews and the Gentiles illustrates this: 'Consider the kindness and sternness of God; sternness to those who fell, but kindness to you, provided that you continue in his kindness. Otherwise you also will be cut off' (Rom. 11: 22). The 'provided that...' followed by the 'otherwise' is an important proviso. It shows God has been very kind to the Jews (Rom. 9: 4) and given them many signs of his goodness, which they have neglected by falling into unbelief. But at some point, God ceases his generous actions to those who have spurned them. Behind divine goodness stands a threat of severity in judgment if that goodness is rejected. Even here, love and justice are joined in a mysterious way and there is no middle ground. Right and wrong imply one or the other.

CONCLUSION

Only atonement theologies that fully account for the interrelated nature of the justice and the love of God at the cross can be fully biblical and therefore satisfying. They must reflect both aspects of the divine attributes united in the supreme work of Christ at the cross.

Why did Christ have to die the death of a sinner? Surely not for anything that could be found in him. Was he not being subjected to divine condemnation in a way that was foreign to his nature? For God to be just with regard to Christ, he should not have died. But if God was acting, as always, in a perfectly right fashion, there must have been a reason for his death that lay outside himself as a person. It was precisely in this way that God showed the greatness of his love—the just was standing for the unjust: 'Christ died once the just for the unjust, to bring you to God' (1 Pet. 3: 18).

In the person of Christ, God's love and justice join. Because of his presence in history and his perfect righteousness, God continues to show his common grace to men in daily blessings, his patience and compassion in delaying judgment, his grace and forgiveness, and his holy love in the salvation of sinners. Because of Jesus' obedience in life and death, 'God is good to all in some ways and to some in all ways.'[20] Salvation is near to those who receive Christ for what he is:

> Love and faithfulness meet together;
> righteousness and peace kiss each other.
> Faithfulness springs forth from the earth
> and righteousness looks down from heaven.

Ps. 85: 10–11

ENDNOTES

[1] Quoted in J. B. Green, M. D. Baker, *Recovering the Scandal of the Cross*, 137–38.

[2] Bernard of Clairvaux, «Traité de l'amour», in *Œuvres mystiques de saint Bernard* (Paris: Seuil, 1953), 29.

[3] In this respect J. Moltmann is right in underlining the communal character of the Trinity in *The Trinity and the Kingdom of God* (London: SCM Press, 1981), 16–20. Cf. G. Vos 'The Scripture Doctrine of the love of God' in R. B. Gaffin, ed., *Redemptive History and Biblical Interpretation*, 425–57.

[4] J. Edwards, *Charity and its Fruits* (Edinburgh: Banner of Truth, 1969), ch. I.

[5] Augustine, *In Epist. Joan.*, 105, 3 quoted by G. Combès, *La charité d'après Saint Augustin* (Paris: Desclée de Brouwer, 1934), 50.

[6] Augustine, *De Trinit.*, XV, 19, 37.

[7] Edwards, *op. cit.*, 5.

[8] Frame, *The Doctrine of God*, 414 ff.

[9] F. Turretin, *Institutes of Elenctic Theology*, I, 242, speaks of a threefold love of God. He loved us before we were, as we are, and for what we are as the image of Christ. He is speaking of election, redemption and reward and for this reason his analysis is different from ours.

[10] R. L. Dabney, 'God's Indiscriminate Proposals of Mercy', *Discussions: Evangelical and Theological*, I, (Edinburgh: Banner of Truth, 1980), 282ff.

[11] L. Berkhof, *Systematic Theology* (Edinburgh: Banner of Truth, 1958), 71.

[12] J. I. Packer, *Knowing God* (London: Hodder and Stoughton, 1973), 108, 111.

[13] Ibid, 110.

[14] J. Denney, *The Christian Doctrine of Reconciliation* (Carlisle: Paternoster Press, 1998), 22.

[15] Nehemiah 9: 17; Psalm 86: 15; 103: 8; 145: 8; Joel 2: 13.

[16] Packer, *op. cit.*, 149.

[17] Cf. D. M. Lloyd-Jones, *Studies in the Sermon on the Mount*, II, (Leicester: IVP, 1960), 74 ff.

[18] Frame, *op. cit.*, 29.

[19] As Dabney argues in art. cit., 284 ff. 'The pity may have been truly in God, and yet countervailed by his superior motives, so that he did not will to exert his omnipotence for that sinner's renewal.'

[20] Packer, *op. cit.*, 147.

6

Crime and Punishment

That Jesus had to die as he did raises a difficult question. The answer may seem obvious to many Christians: it was because of sins committed against God. This, however, does not explain the link between the cause, our sins, and the effect, which is the shameful and painful death of the cross. The problem and the solution seem disproportionate, if not inappropriate. Could not God have chosen a more cost-effective method?

Some attempt must be made to define the relationship that exists between one and the other. Why was it appropriate for God to choose this way of dealing with sin? What is it about sin that requires this particular solution? What makes the cross a proper way of dealing with it? When these questions are asked, it becomes clear that the relation between our sins and the cross is complex rather than simple and straightforward.

SIN TRIVIALISED

To explain the reason why the cross was needed to deal with sin is all the more pressing in light of the trivialisation of sin in the contemporary mentality.

The hoarding over the road from my house in France sometimes advertises a table wine called Vieux Papes (Old Popes) with the slogan 'a little sin every day'. The pleasure of certain 'sins' is used to sell such diverse products as perfume, cars, or lingerie. Advertising presents what is 'bad' as being good and desirable. A newspaper supplement article on sin was even entitled 'Are you sinning comfortably?' It stated that people do not avoid sin any more because sin does not exist as a serious idea in modern life, apart from as a way to make life more exciting. The idea that such acts may be insults to God, it is said, seems to be lost forever because 'God' is my own god with whom private deals can be made. The only real sins are those committed against oneself and one's self-realisation, or those extreme cases everyone condemns, such as abusing others through harassment. Modern man with his own private deity has nothing left to sin against. Acts are not good or bad in themselves, but only to the extent they have good or bad consequences. There is no God above to judge, we are told, no heaven to reward or hell to punish; there is only this life.[1]

This mentality seems like an impenetrable jungle for the Christian message of sin and forgiveness. Where does the problem lie? Not primarily in the question of sin and how it might be defined, but in who God is and why he does not accept sin. The fundamental issue is *who* defines what sin is. The popular idea is that God is a benevolent deity and if he exists, he will make things well in the end.

> A benevolent God, yes: men have framed a benevolent God for themselves. But a thoroughly honest God, perhaps never. That has been left for the revelation of God himself to give us...a God who deals honestly and conscientiously with himself and us. And a thoroughly conscientious God, we may be sure, is not a God who can deal with sinners as if they were not sinners. In this fact lies perhaps the deepest ground of the necessity of an expiatory atonement.[2]

Sin can only be trivialised when the holiness of God is treated lightly; when God is made less than he really is, sin becomes of no consequence. 'If we have not much to be saved from, why, certainly, a very little atonement will suffice for our needs.'[3] This is why after knowing God, the most important thing for a correct understanding of the need of atonement is understanding what sin really is.

WHY IS ATONEMENT NEEDED AT ALL?

Of course it is often denied that there is any need for atonement and there is no real relation between the sins of men and the death of Jesus. If God is a God of love, so the argument goes, suffering must be offensive to him; any other reason for the cross, apart from the demonstration of love, loses its meaning. Christ's suffering is an example destined to melt hearts through sympathy, or a dramatic display of God's love in opposition to sin.

Despite its plausibility this idea is self-defeating. If God is purely and simply benevolence, surely he would have rejected the cross altogether as being incompatible with his love? The love of God is the strongest indication that the suffering of Christ on the cross must be an expression of judgment and justice. Moreover, if it is taken seriously and given its full weight as *love*, the existence of misery and suffering in the world must be related to justice and judgment in the overall scheme of divine providence. Otherwise his allowing them to exist has no meaning, unless of course God were thought to be powerless to do anything about it.[4]

Another approach to the relation between sin and the cross is to say God *could have* imagined other ways of salvation. For instance, he could have given all men a change of heart through showing every human being their need of salvation. Yet, for reasons beyond us, he chose the cross, even though he could have accomplished salvation in some other way. The way of salvation through the cross depends on God's wise decision, although it is not obligatory for God himself, or as a reply to man's dilemma.

The strong and the weak point of this idea is that with our limited intelligence and knowledge of God, we cannot speculate about what is possible for God and what is not. So in a sense, we do not know that the cross is the best way of dealing with sin. There is something arbitrary about saying it is simply a case of God deciding that salvation was to be accomplished in this fashion. Doubtless, the way of salvation is a result of God's decision and we can trust that in God's wisdom his decisions are the best ones, but it is possible to be more specific.

A final way of looking at the need for the death of Christ on the cross is to consider both the nature of God and also what sin is. The relation between the two explains how God acts to accomplish salvation. Given who God is, what sin is, and the opposition between them, Christ's death was not just the best way of salvation, it was also the only way. Contrary to appearances, this does not imply God was forced to act in a way that limited his liberty. By deciding upon and implementing salvation in this way, God was being faithful to his character.

It is natural and moral for men not to attempt to fly like birds, as to do so would mean suicide. They must build planes if they want to fly. For God it is natural and moral to deal with sin as he did, because he is completely holy and just. He cannot, as almighty God, simply leave sin alone; it constitutes a principle of opposition to his holy will in the universe he rules. As the expression of a will foreign to God's, the power of sin and the holy power of God repel each other like two magnets.

In his holiness, God must reject sin to be consistent with himself. God's judgment is his statement as to what is unacceptable because he is a righteous and a holy God. Judgment occurs when the holiness of God and sin meet up. Even human governments seek to eliminate forms of behaviour opposed to the laws of the state. Sin being what sin is, God could not do otherwise than seek its elimination. This is not something imposed on God. It is the free and spontaneous expression of his righteousness, holiness, and purity. With regard to sin, God must act in a way that expresses his freedom of decision and action.[5]

Christ's death on the cross is the result of God's decision to save man. It is also what his holiness required him to do against sin, in a way that is in harmony with his own freedom. The apostle hinted at as much when he stated that God demonstrates his justice in such a way as to be 'just and the one who justifies those who have faith in Jesus' (Rom. 3: 26). The rationale of the death of Christ on the cross is that God is at the same time holy and righteous in his justice—the one who makes men righteous by faith. The work of Christ expresses God's justice and his judgment against sin in salvation.

SO WHAT ABOUT SIN?

When it comes to saying what sin is in its fundamental nature, we run into another problem that goes beyond the modern trivialisation of sin. It is easy to slip from talking about *sin* to talking about *sins*, and so to limit ourselves to specific problems that can easily be sorted. Sin, however, is singular before it is plural and concerns man's fundamental situation in life. Sin is not primarily what we *do*, but what we *are*.

Moreover, looking at sin is like trying to see the bottom of a muddy pond. It is murky and incomprehensible. 'Man worships at an altar of a stagnant pool and when he sees his reflection he's fulfilled.'[6] Why should we sin, and why do we sin again? Such questions underline the folly and irrationality of sin.[7] The enigma is that nobody finds sin naturally disagreeable but enjoyable and satisfying—at least until its toxic waste starts to pollute the atmosphere of life.

The reasons for sin are enigmatic and inexplicable. Attempts to locate its essential nature in a fundamental attitude such as pride, laziness, or self-centredness run aground on the mysteriousness of sin. Nonetheless, its negative orientation cannot be doubted, as day by day we suffer from it, because of our own nature as sinners and that of those around us. Man's sinfulness is real evil, which shows the reality of his problem. It exists first in relation to God, defining the state of man's present relationship with him: 'Against you only have I sinned and done what is evil in your sight' (Ps. 51: 4). This is surprising, as David's sin was against Uriah and Bathsheba, whom he had wronged, but he sees it primarily as a break of relations with God. Man's sin offends God. He is the first victim, because the creature's sin opposes his will and desire.[8]

That sin is against God also underlines that it is not known in a natural way through our experiences or intuitions; sin is only known in its fundamental nature by God's judgment on it. Knowledge of sin, like knowledge of salvation, must be revealed. If man can know that all is not well and amends must be made, only Scripture can tell us that the covenant is broken and what sin is, as opposition and rebellion against God. The reality of sin is known not through vague guilt feelings, but because of what God says about it in his revelation. Sin is recognised as part of the gospel and belief that we are sinners is the negative side of the good news (Rom. 3: 19, 1 John 1: 8). Knowledge of what sin is goes with repentance, faith, and forgiveness, just as belief that Christ died for our offences goes with belief that he was raised for our justification (Rom. 6: 5–11).

Three conclusions can be reached with regard to the nature of sin in the light of this. Firstly, sin is specific and fundamental to fallen human nature. It lies at the root of everything and is an attitude of heart that determines man's fundamental direction in life. It misses the mark as far as God is concerned, turning all man's existence in a wrong direction. Secondly, sin expresses an attitude of rejection and revolt against God's goodness. It consists in a refusal to accept moral obligation as defined by God (1 John 3: 4). A form of depravity of human nature, it shows openly that man is inclined to evil because of an inner condition at the source of all his dispositions. Finally, if it is a negative attitude towards God, it also involves pollution of the person and of social relationships. Pollution is its positive manifestation and sin's consequences multiply as milestones on the road to death (Rom. 6: 23).

To say man needs saving from sin means he needs to be saved from himself. Only God can supply the solution to sin.

GOD AND SIN

'Christ came into the world to save sinners' (1 Tim. 1: 15). In the New Testament, Christ's coming into the world, and his death, are repeatedly presented in relation to sin. Without sin there is no rationale for either. 'Absent the sin of Adam and its universal repercussions, there is no need for the last Adam… sin is the plight, Christ the solution, particularly his being obedient to death even the death of the cross (Phil. 2: 8).'[9] But sin is more than man's plight:

> Above all sin is theocentric; it is primarily against God and then, derivatively, against human beings, including the self. (Rom. 1: 18–32, Eph. 4: 17–19) As such, sin is both relational and judicial, and it is the one only as it is the other. Sin is relational in that it is essentially rebellion against God, the image-bearing creature's effective renunciation of God as creator…Sin is idolatrous…All told, it is deeply rooted hostility, particularly to God. Sin is also illegal. It is that, not in addition to its being relational, but as it is relational and it is relational only as it is illegal…Sin…does not accord with God's will or law.[10]

In its relational aspect, sin is enmity and rebellion against God. In its judicial aspect, it involves all that is illegal for God. An enslaving power, it renders man helpless and spiritually dead with regard to God. Sin, rather than God, has become man's lord and master; the sinner is a slave, in bondage to sin.[11]

Is God *angry* with sin? Certainly, and to use this word is not too strong, even if it most disagreeable to think God is angry with us. God is angry precisely because he is personal and sin is not just harm done to humanity, but an affront to God and his goodness. 'This injury is not mere damage to property, it is an injury done to the divine person himself. In accordance with this personal sin is the personal reaction of God: that is the wrath of God...God is angry because he is personal, because he really loves.'[12] To reject the idea of God's anger is also to reject the love of God. Efforts to create a god who does not react to sin render God less than personal, and at the same time make a true understanding of his love for *sinful* man, in its breadth and depth, impossible. God's love appears in its true light only in the context of man's sin and misery, and his rebellion against God. God hates sin.

THE LIABILITY OF SIN

On the basis of these considerations, classic theology presented a view of sin not always considered today. It indicated that in relation to God sin has three dimensions. These provide the context for the restoration of man by the intervention of Jesus Christ. Sin constitutes a triple block to the relationship between God and man because it involves a debt to God, alienation from God, and crime against God.[13]

In order to understand this, it is not superfluous to introduce the distinction between *potential and actual guilt*. What makes sin sin? The only answer to this question is that sin is wrong according to the standard of a holy God. 'Like God himself and reflective of his person, the law is holy, righteous and good (Rom. 7: 12)...Sin as relational is inherently illegal, the violation of God's will as revealed in Scripture and creation.'[14] Between what is right and what is wrong stands the standard of God's law, which is his criterion of judgment. The law of God, written on tables of stone in the Decalogue, or on the table of man's heart through conscience (Rom. 2: 15), either excuses or accuses man. 'Through the law we become conscious of sin' (Rom. 3: 19–20). The law is therefore what mediates between right and wrong. As God's standard, it indicates what is potentially right and good, and what is wrong and merits punishment. Man is warned of the dangers of disobedience, which become real when sin is actually committed. Actual guilt arises from disobedience because of transgression of the law and is expressed as divine condemnation and penalty, according to the law's conditions. The criminal knows stealing is wrong and it makes him potentially guilty. Guilt becomes concrete and visible when the judgment is rendered as the penalty on crime.[15]

Scripture often uses the word 'sin' as a metonymy for actual guilt, for instance in Jeremiah 50: 20: 'at that time, declares the Lord, search will be made for Israel's *guilt* but there will be none, and for the *sins* of Judah but none will be found.' Sin as guilt is the judgment of God against it. Likewise the remission of sin is the putting away of the sinner's guilt, which is the penalty of sin. So when Paul writes 'all have sinned and fall short of the glory of God' (Rom. 3: 23), he is saying that all stand under the declaration of divine judgment because of sin. So 'every mouth is silenced and the whole world held accountable before God' (3: 19).[16] Romans 1: 18–3: 20 shows all men stand before God not just as sinners, they are also under *the penalty of divine judgement* as condemnation, or actual guilt.

If sin is guilt incurred by the penalty of divine judgment its threefold relation to God becomes clear. 'It is the personal relation between a sinning agent and the sovereign will of God which legislates the penal statute.'[17] Personally, man stands before God as a *debtor* by the divine judgment; as a sinner, he is in a situation of *alienation* before God; and as a *condemned criminal*, he has transgressed divine law. Compare this with human justice: before a criminal has been sentenced, he is only in a position of potential guilt until proven guilty, even if he has committed the crime. He may be in custody or he may still be running free. Either way he is still only potentially guilty and not actually guilty. When the sentence has been passed, then his state is that of a debtor. The condemnation takes into account the transgression of the law and indicates that the criminal's behaviour is in opposition to the right conduct that it demands. He has to pay the penalty according to the nature of the offence committed under the law.

The divine judgment makes clear that man is a debtor to God's law and righteousness. Subjectively, man is enslaved by sin, 'sold under sin' (Rom. 7: 14), and objectively he has contracted a debt by the distance that separates him from the law. He cannot make up this debt—only increase it. The condemnation takes into account that objectively the sinner is guilty by God's standards as well as being alienated from God in a subjective sense. The breach made with the law of life, and the rejection of divine government, means the penalty for sins is death: 'the soul that sins shall die' (Ezek. 18: 4).

From man's side of the divine–human relationship, man is in debt to God (Matt. 6: 12). His transgression puts him in opposition to God (Col. 1: 21) and his sin calls forth the penalty that sanctions this fact (Rom. 3: 19). From God's side of the relationship, God is the 'creditor' to whom man has to pay the price for his disobedience. God is the offended party against whom the sinner has sinned, the judge and ruler who judges according to righteousness.

> On the day of God's wrath, when his righteous judgment will be revealed, God will give to each person according to what he has done. To those who by persistence in doing good seek glory, honour and immortality, he will give eternal life. But to the self-seeking, to those who reject the truth and follow evil, there will be wrath and anger. There will be trouble and distress for every human being who does evil…but glory honour and peace for everyone who does good.
>
> Rom. 2: 5–10

The threefold situation of man as a sinner appears like this:

Subjective sin	Sin as guilt	Sin in relation to God
Enslavement	Debt	God is 'creditor'
Enmity	Alienation	God is offended party
Pollution	Crime/rebellion	God is judge

As a sinner, man is for the present under the sentence of death, having a suspended sentence from the final judgement, but a real sentence in view of his spiritual inertia. Despite his apparent vitality in the physical sense, like a prisoner awaiting the electric chair on death row, he is a dead man walking. 'According to Scripture, death is related to sin as its just reward. The Bible everywhere views human death not as a *natural* but as a *penal* event. It is an alien intrusion into God's good world (and) is seen as a divine judgment on human disobedience.'[18]

WHAT SIN REQUIRES

'Though sin may have a natural birth it does not die a natural death; in every case it has to be morally sentenced and put to death.'[19] How can this be? Not by a vague notion of sinners entering God's presence to ask forgiveness for themselves.

If sin as guilt is man's debt, estrangement, and a crime against God, the removal of sin must be seen as debt being paid, reconciliation replacing alienation, and the crime eliminated. The *must* is essential as these conditions exist because man's sin against God bears upon his essential attributes—holiness, righteousness, and justice. Atonement for sin requires a satisfaction demanded by these attributes if the relationship between God and man as sinner is to be restored. God, by his very nature, cannot wipe the slate clean. For him to do so would be a denial of his character and principles of law. If the personal relation between God and man is to be renewed, a solution must be provided, which corresponds to man's need and God's demands.

The New Testament witness is that Jesus meets the needs of this situation: 'There is one mediator between God and man, the man Christ Jesus, who gave himself as a ransom for all' (1 Tim. 2: 5–6). Since man is helpless in his slavery to sin, God must provide the mediator and this was done in Christ's coming to occupy that function. The mediator must really represent man, which is indicated by the insistence on the humanity of Christ—'the man Christ Jesus'. The debt is met by Jesus giving his life as a ransom for all.

The guilt of man is his debt that must be condemned; the condemnation expresses the alienation between God and man, and the power of sin lies in its enslaving character, which makes man a stranger to the life of God. 'The guilt and power of sin are not co-ordinate. It is its guilt which gives it power. Its guilt alienates us from God, and it is in virtue of this alienation that sin reigns in us. Hence to be reconciled to God is the sinner's primary need.'[20] God deals with the problem of the guilt and condemnation of sin, of its alienation and enslaving debt, through Christ's death and resurrection. It can be summarised as follows:

Sin as guilt	Sin in relation to God	Christ the Mediator
Debt	God is 'creditor'	Pays debt of sin
Alienation	God is offended party	Makes peace
Crime/rebellion	God is judge	Condemned in our place

As mediator between God and man, Christ, in his person and work, meets perfectly what God requires for his justice to be satisfied, and what man needs to be forgiven, reconciled, and freed from sin.

Christ pays the debt for sinners: 'At the right time when we were still powerless, Christ died for the ungodly…God demonstrates his own love for us in this: while we were sinners, Christ died for us' (Rom. 5: 6–8).

Christ makes peace: 'If when we were God's enemies, we were reconciled to him through the death of his Son, how much more having been reconciled, shall we be saved though his life!' (Rom. 5: 10).

Christ condemned in our place: 'Since we have been justified through his blood, how much more shall we be saved from God's wrath through him' (Rom. 5: 9).

'Christ's death does for sinners what they cannot do for themselves; it clears them from the just punishment of death issuing in eternal destruction.'[21] Not only this, Christ's resurrection completes his death as what is needed for sinners to be freed from their enslavement. His being 'raised to life for our justification' (Rom. 4: 25) means the resurrection annuls the penal condemnation of death, which was still in force while Christ was in the tomb. The resurrection justifies and liberates Christ, and with him, those who belong to him.[22]

Paul adds 'if Christ has not been raised, your faith is futile; you are still in your sins' (1 Cor. 15: 17). Why should this be so? If Christ is not raised then those who believe in him are still under the condemnation of the law, which remains in force. The resurrection demonstrates that the problem of the guilt of sin has been dealt with so as to satisfy the demands of divine justice, and in a way that wholly corresponds to the plight of man as a sinner under the divine condemnation.

The result of the work of Christ in his death and resurrection is the remission of sin. There is no atonement without the remission of sin, and no remission of sin without atonement. As the author of salvation, Christ makes remission of sin by his death, by shedding his blood on the cross, and removing the liability of the guilt of sin.[23] 'The law requires that nearly everything be cleansed with blood, and without the shedding of blood there is no forgiveness' (Heb. 9: 22). Christ redeems from the curse of the law by becoming a curse for us through his death on the cross (Gal. 3: 13). The work of Christ in his death and resurrection having put sin away, there is now forgiveness of sin, which frees sinners from its guilt and power. The sinner's plea, his claim to justice and acceptance by God, can only be the cross of Christ that it may 'be of sin the double cure, cleanse me from its guilt and power.'[24]

SIN MORE THAN SIN?

Some claim that sin is much more than debt to God, which must be paid. The reign of sin is vast. It is experienced in many forms such as anxiety, unfaithfulness, pride, desire to possess, self-justification, cruelty or blasphemy, and so on.[25] The effects of sin paralyse human life and in the light of our present experience of sin, the idea that sin is guilt before God is limited. It smacks too much of an economy of exchange that reduces sin to one of its aspects. Moreover, it is foreign to our mentality.

The shame of sin, it is argued, is more complex than the guilt of sin, which relates to specific acts and their consequences. Shame is associated with a feeling of being impure or defiled, in need of restoration by the removal of the dirtiness of sin and forgiveness. Only restoration and renewal can heal shame, not the idea of the payment of a debt.[26] The shame of the cross was the tragic moral pain endured by Christ, who became identified with us in the shamefulness of evil. The revelation of God's love for us holds out the possibility of emerging from the shame of sin to a new life; it heals alienation from God and removes shame. 'Shame,' it is claimed, 'alienates and destroys relationships, but on the cross Jesus responded with forgiveness. God removes the alienation of shame through love.'[27]

There is an element of truth in this, but it is not clear why love should remove the alienation of shame, by a demonstration of forgiveness, any more than it should remove the cause of shame, debt toward God because of guilt. In addition, the legal aspects of the death of Christ have their full meaning in the structure of the covenant between God and man.

> In the context of God's covenant with Israel, the law served the purpose of regulating relationships, both within the covenant community and between the covenant community and God. From a biblical perspective, God's justice is a

matter of his preserving right covenant relationships, and of doing so with integrity (as a holy, just and loving God).[28]

This insight allows us to distinguish between the function of the law in the foundation of the covenant and in its right regulation of relationships. If the cause of alienation between God and man is that the covenant has been broken, then restoration must be made according to the law of the covenant. The cause of guilt has to be dealt with, before the results of sin—anxiety, guilt feelings, or shame—the consequences of alienation in the realm of subjective sin. 'The atonement makes things 'right', to be sure, but this rightness is legal *and* interpersonal, objective *and* subjective.'[29] The healing of sin in the subjective sense supposes the establishing of a ground upon which it can work. That ground is that Christ has endured the 'shame of the cross' in our place and for us. (Heb. 12: 2) Surely the knowledge that Christ did this as 'author and perfecter of our faith' (Heb. 2: 10) is sufficient to deal with subjective shame and sin, and to liberate those who look to Jesus.

CONCLUSION

As the divine-human Son of God and mediator between God and man, Christ participates in our sinful nature to bear the weight of guilt and condemnation that separated man from God. He did this by an act of substitution, in which he suffered on behalf of sinners: 'Christ died for sins once for all, the righteous for the unrighteous in order to bring us to God' (1 Pet. 3: 18). The result is the restoration of relationships between God and sinners, objectively through Christ, and subjectively through the healing work of the Spirit working through faith, hope, and love in believers' lives. The atonement displays the justice, mercy, and love of God for sinners in a way that is true to God and true to sinners' needs.

'The law indeed demands that the person who sins shall suffer; but the gospel, through the fatherly kindness of God declares it meet that there shall be a substitution; that it suffices to punish sin, and let the sinner go free.'[30]

ENDNOTES

[1] 'Is Sin Good?' *The Sunday Times Magazine*, April 11, 2004, 18.
[2] B. B. Warfield, 'Modern Theories of the Atonement', *Works*, IX, 296.

[3] Ibid, 297.

[4] See J. W. Wenham on the goodness of God and retribution in *The Goodness of God* (Leicester: IVP, 1974), ch. 5. R. L. Dabney develops this point fully in *Christ our Penal Substitute*, ch. 7.

[5] On the necessity of the cross see F. Turretin, *Institutes of Elenctic Theology*, II, 418–22.

[6] B. Dylan, 'Licence to kill', *Infidels*, Columbia, 1983.

[7] G. C. Berkouwer, *Sin* (Grand Rapids: Eerdmans, 1971), ch. 5.

[8] See ch. 7.

[9] R. B. Gaffin, 'Atonement in the Pauline corpus', in C. E. Hill, F. A. James, eds., *The Glory of the Atonement* (Downers Grove: IVP, 2004), 145.

[10] Ibid, 145–46.

[11] Ibid, 149.

[12] E. Brunner, *The Mediator*, 478.

[13] Categories developed by Turretin, *op. cit*, 418–22 and his *The Atonement of Christ,* 17–24.

[14] Gaffin, art. cit., 147–148.

[15] Dabney, *op. cit.*, 10–11.

[16] This is unavoidably legal or forensic language as D. A. Carson points out in 'Atonement in Romans 3.21–26', *The Glory of the Atonement*, 120.

[17] Dabney, *op. cit.*, 11.

[18] J. Stott, *The Cross of Christ*, 64–65, quoted by C. Baxter, 'The Curse Beloved' in *Atonement Today*, 65. *Cf.* J. Denney, *The Christian Doctrine of Reconciliation*, 275, who says that death belongs to the moral world and the natural necessity of it must be morally significant.

[19] Denney, *op. cit.*, 198.

[20] Ibid., 191.

[21] Gaffin, art. cit., 158, referring to J. Murray on reconciliation in *Redemption Accomplished and Applied* (Edinburgh: Banner of Truth Trust, 1970), 33 ff.

[22] Ibid., 160.

[23] H. Martin, *The Atonement*, ch. 9.

[24] A. M. Toplady, *Rock of Ages*, 1776.

[25] J. B. Green, M. D. Baker, *Recovering the Scandal of the Cross*, 203 ff.

[26] Ibid., 155 ff.

[27] Ibid., 167. The solidarity of Christ with us is sometimes called vicarious identification. Green and Baker are no friends of penal substitutionary atonement and consider that in it God has to kill his Son, which is something he would rather not do. For them the imposition of Western cultural values on the biblical narrative determine God's nature and actions, *op. cit.*, 169. The latter claim is far from being substantiated in their argument.

[28] K. Vanhhoozer, 'The Atonement in Postmodernity', in *The Glory of the Atonement*, 380–381.

[29] Ibid., 381.

[30] Turretin, *The Atonement of Christ*, 55.

7

Violence

Violence is the great affliction of humanity. It leaves in its wake victims of physical or psychological abuse perpetrated by individuals or institutions. It can take the form of perverse attrition or strike with the lightning efficiency of a terrorist attack.

Since Jesus warned that 'all who take the sword will die by the sword' (Matt. 26: 52), is not non-violence the ideal reply to aggression? 'Non-violence is fundamental to the gospel message, because its basic tenant is the absolute value of love... Love is the antidote to violence.'[1]

If there is no other remedy for human violence, does God counter violence with non-violence? The problem is that the suffering of Jesus, his unjust trial, and vindictive liquidation, seem to be one with situations where violence escalates out of control. If this is so, why did God choose this way to save man from sin and evil? If, contrary to appearances, it is not the case, then a new non-violent interpretation of the cross has to be spun out. The sacrificial and bloody nature of the cross raises such unavoidable questions.

One most hackneyed objection against Christianity is that its God never really shook off the shackles of Old Testament barbarity. God even seems to torture his Son at Gethsemane and Golgotha, the most horrendous form of violence of all. Following this lead, western Christianity became, through Augustine's teaching about forcible conversion and just war, an oppressive religion. Allied to political power, it used instruments of inquisition for its dismal ends.[2] Was not revenge the motive behind the killing of Jews in the past on Good Fridays in Poland?

Criticism of the barbarous Christian God is often broadened so as to make religion the mainspring of violence. Exclusive truths justify the use of violence, often against others who hold different opinions.[3] But religious groups do not have the monopoly of violence; it can rear its ugly head whenever man sees his neighbour as a rival and seeks to get the better of him by forcible means or by guile.

IS GOD VIOLENT?

A preliminary superficial reply would be no, because of the divine attributes. God is the source of light and life. In him is no darkness at all (1 John 1: 5). His goodness and love mean evil is contrary to his person and plans. There is, however, more to it than that, particularly regarding the origin of violence and its first victim.

A striking aspect of the modern worldview, owing to the influence of the theory of evolution, is the censure of references to creational origins. 'Man is fallen man…there is no other man than fallen man. At the start there is the fall.'[4] In this scheme of things there is no original righteousness, no covenant in creation or with man, and no historical passage from good to evil. Violence *is* the fall and original sin. Sin should not be seen in an individualistic way as personal disobedience to God. This makes little sense to modern people. Sin is violence against others, arising from the desire to dominate.[5]

In Genesis 1–3, however, man does not become conscious of violence as he climbs the rungs of the evolutionary ladder. God himself reveals the mystery of origins, original goodness and innocence, the first covenant, the appearance of sin and evil in transgression, and the first sacrifice.

The prohibition concerning the tree of good and evil (Gen. 2: 17) is not restrictive in its intention, but indicates a positive destiny for the creature. Man is *neither a double nor an equal* of God, but the image of God. The divine commandment reveals God's nature as Lord, and eliminates the possibility of rivalry. Man's life cycle is directed to what is good.

The prohibition indicates, negatively, the integrity of man as image of God, male and female. Order in creation includes balanced relationships with Creator, neighbour, and ecosphere.[6] In this situation, the first and great command, the original law, is to love the Lord, fellow humans, and the creation. Obedience concretized through love excludes sacrifice, which appears only after the fall, because of sin and the need for restoration.[7]

How is man's disobedience to be understood? In Genesis 3, God's ironic reply, 'man has now become like one of us, knowing good and evil' (v. 22), is the counterpart of Satan's bait, 'you will be like God knowing good and evil' (v. 5). Man's fallen state corresponds to the situation described prophetically in the divine threat, 'when you eat of the tree of the knowledge of good and evil you will surely die' (2: 17). Prohibition, temptation, desire, transgression, acquisition, opposition, and curse constitute the matrix of human rebellion. Original sin, as the transgression of divine law and goodness, is an act of sacred violence *directed against* God. Presumption and pride are the root of sin and violence. Man aspires to power and control.

God is in no way violent. Man introduces violence and aggression into the good creation by overturning God's order. Relationships with the Creator, fellow creatures, and the sub-human world fall out of kilter.

THE IDENTITY OF THE VICTIM

But *who* exactly is the victim of sacred violence? God is not the instigator of violence, even though the curse introduces sanctions and death into a creation pronounced to be good (Gen. 3: 15–16). Appearances are misleading.

God is the object of human violence in Eden, because man's desire to be like God makes him a rival and an obstacle. Lawbreaking overturns God's rights in a strange role reversal and as a result, man acts as if he were a god. God is not recognized as rightful owner and is dispossessed of his property rights by a squatter.

Contrary to all expectations, God is the primary victim of human violence. Victims are generally considered as such because of their defencelessness. God is victim in an ethical sense, as man's move pre-empts his authority and turns the tables on him by introducing evil into creation. God is not powerless, as the continuation of the story shows, but he cannot un-ring the bell that man has rung. Ironically, God, the injured party, becomes the accused, the 'scapegoat' of history, butt of man's rejection and barbs: 'God made man in his image and man gave it back.'

Alienation from God leads man to try to dodge the implications of his guilt, as the first couple did when they hid in the garden (Gen. 3: 8). Then they sought to avoid it by shifting responsibility. When challenged, guilt is transferred from Adam to Eve, and from Eve to the serpent (vv. 12–13). The Creator is cast as the guilty party. After all, who created man, woman, and serpents? This is typical of the mechanism that kicks in when people do wrong and try to find an excuse for it. A tactic of evasion is deployed in which the fault is transferred onto others who are made to carry the buck.

THE BEGINNING OF GRACE

God's reply to man's shifting of guilt is equally surprising. The link between the sinful act and death is established because God brings into effect the death threat stated in the divine prohibition (Gen. 2: 17). The leaves of the vegetable world are insufficient cover for what man has done and a blood-victim from God's own good creation is killed to cover his nakedness (Gen. 3: 7, 21). God deals with human guilt and allows man's life to continue by an act corresponding to man's fallen state and need.[8]

It is not primarily man who needs to be reconciled to God, but God, the offended party, who reconciles himself to man and provides for him.[9] By an unexpected act of grace, God is not the violent avenger, but the Saviour who makes peace. Sin is dealt with in a graphic way by a sacrificial death, and because of it, life continues.

In a similar way, the sacrificial system of the older testament, later instituted by God, hides his identity as the real victim of violence. At the same time it reveals the divine reply to sin.

> In other modes of conceiving it, sacrifice may represent the reaching out of man towards God; in its expiatory conception it represents the stooping down of God to man. The fundamental difference is that the one case rests upon consciousness of sin and has reference to the restoration of a guilty human being to the favour of a condemning God; in the other it stands outside of all relation to sin and has its reference only to the expression of the proper attitude

of deference which a creature should preserve towards his
Maker and Ruler.[10]

So God's rejoinder to human violence is not more of the same,
but pardon and grace through a substitute that represents him
as the injured party. The Mosaic covenantal code establishes
law and sacrifice as a way of approaching God. Violence is
contained and purification of sin through substitution restores
right relations with God.[11]

The multiplicity of human religions jostling with each other
is not the *cause* of antagonism and aggression. It is the *result*
of rebellious sacred violence against the one true God. False
sacrifices and innocent victims express man's rejection of God's
creational blessings of life and peace, and his vain struggle to
create a way back to God. 'Man cannot get rid of the burden of
sin by himself. Man tries, *first*, either to pay for his sins himself
by masochistic activity, a futile process, or *second*, to make others
pay for them through sadistic activities. Both alternatives lead
to sick lives and sick societies.'[12] Man needs to repair wrong
by paying himself or making others pay—works religion—the
opposite of the grace God institutes. Religions springing from
the human heart are deadly and essentially idolatrous. 'The
human righteousness of religion, of *pious* man, of phariseeism,
the man-made righteousness, is nothing other than irreverence
and insubordination.'[13]

By contrast, the primal divine law of love and justice is
resumed in the words of Jesus: 'Love the Lord your God with all
your heart...Love your neighbour as yourself.'[14] The Creator's
intention for life and fellowship in a good creation was nothing
other than love ordered according to the laws of divine nature,
which man forfeited when he put his own pseudo-power in the
place of God's. As a fallen creature created in the image of a
righteous God, suffering from tension in his inner being, man
now needs justice before love. God's cure for human violence
is not *homeopathic*—treating violence by counter violence,
but *allopathic*—healing violence by restoration to normality.
Not vengeance, but justice and forgiveness. But how is this
accomplished?

IS THE CROSS VIOLENT?

It is impossible not to reply to this question affirmatively. Christ was killed in a most terrible way, in a surrealistic atmosphere characterised by rare intensity of abuse—physical, verbal and psychological. But there is more to it than that.

Can we claim Jesus' mission was to unmask the forces of human aggression? Does his non-retaliatory attitude represent victims of abuse as innocent? Does Jesus achieve the neutralisation of wickedness by meeting violence with powerlessness?[15] Is non-violence the antidote to violence? Can pure and simple love cure the ills of humanity? Is the 'primary saving effect of the cross a disclosure of religious violence—not a sacrificial transaction that appeases divine wrath'?[16] If this were so, the cross of Christ would be effective to change the world, the power of its example stimulating similar acts of non-retaliation. The example of Christ's love is without doubt supremely compelling, but the power of the cross does not reside in its being an example. In the end, this leaves man to complete the work of salvation himself.

The Old Testament sacrifices, which God instituted, served to restore fellowship between God and man by the shedding of blood. They were a divinely appointed way of demonstrating that only God could provide man with a way out. Moreover, sacrifices showed that God intervenes through a victim and in doing so restores relationships. Sacrificial victims point to the one final and unrepeatable event in which sin against God, the cause of all violence, is uprooted. The cross is violent because God assumes the conditions of human existence. God's involvement does not introduce a change from violence to non-violence by way of example, but puts an end to sin. Christ is the end of sacrifice in the sense that all that precedes him finds its final and perfect expression in him.[17]

'For Christ's love compels us, because we are convinced that one died for all and therefore all died. And he died for all, that those who live should no longer live for themselves but for him who died for them and was raised again' (2 Cor. 5: 14–15). This is sacrificial language. The 'because' is important since it indicates the reason why the love of Christ is compelling. Violence, sin, and death have been brought to a conclusion at the cross, whose finality is revealed in the life that comes to light in the resurrection.

The final sacrifice has been made and there will be no repetitions. Jesus Christ is the victim, and in him God provides a sacrifice that needs no repeating, because it puts paid to man's rebellion against God. Lives caught up in the karma of human wickedness are liberated, having died with Christ to their former life, just as Paul had done. Imitation of Christ takes the place of sinful rivalry and one-upmanship against God and neighbour. In the community of the new humanity in Christ, all are crucified with Christ, all are sacrificial victims with him, but all are brothers and servants, as he was before them (Rom. 12: 1–2).

Romans 3: 21–6 indicates God is the instigator of this strange work. 'God presented him as a sacrifice of atonement…He did this to demonstrate his justice' (v. 25). This probably does not refer to the scapegoat sent into the wilderness on the Day of Atonement, but to the paschal lamb and the offering presented by God for the safety of his people (*cf.* Ezek. 43: 20; 45: 21ff). The primary sense of this lies in the divine act. God chose this to represent the meaning of exodus from slavery.

In Hebrews 5: 1, a classical statement about the nature of the sacrificial institution, priests are 'appointed to represent men in matters related to God, to offer gifts and sacrifices for sins'. That the appointment is of divine origin and the sacrifice is offered to God and not to man:

> God alone can make this sacrifice…Over and over again it is forgotten that it is God Himself who expiates, who provides the sacrifice…Thus in the New Testament the cross of Christ is conceived of as the self-offering of God. It is God who does it, God himself who suffers, God who takes the burden on himself…This act of expiation is real. God *does* something.[18]

The work of the cross, as a suffering sacrifice, functions in two directions at once. First, it is the offering of the Son presented to God and accepted by God. It is also an act accomplished by God that represents something to man. The cross establishes peace between God and man once more.

When, in 2 Corinthians 5: 19, the apostle says, 'God was in Christ reconciling the world to himself' we can add, 'through the sacrifice of the cross'. Paul qualifies this with 'not counting men's sins against them'. God accepts the victim of human rejection fully and completely, abolishing the reality of sin by his death. The surprising fact of Golgotha is that the innocence of the one who is just deals with the violence of the unjust. The substitution of Christ is objective.[19] To be saved 'by the blood of Christ' means by his death. Blood, in the Old Testament in particular, invariably implies violence.

'GOD DOES SOMETHING'

The desire for a non-violent atonement is understandable. The idea is to put as much distance as possible between God and human violence and to avoid accusations of involvement in evil. This can only be done by making the love of God the main thing demonstrated at the cross, and by playing subtle hermeneutical games to subvert the teaching of large sections of biblical revelation.[20]

The reality of the coming of the Son of God onto the world scene is much more than a demonstration of non-violent love, however attractive that might be. It means God gets his hands dirty in the fallenness of human existence. Just as Christ did not 'despise the virgin's womb', so also God in Christ became intimately involved in the violence of human life.[21] God did not enter a world of pure love and perfect justice, but one where havoc and ruin reign. In this kind of world 'it is impossible to extend acts of hospitality without at the same time being involved in some kind of violence. In Jesus Christ God steps into a world that is already beset by violence, injustice and inhospitality.'[22]

Nonetheless, God's involvement with violence is not a negative one. Unlike the violence of our fellow humans, so often gratuitous, irrational, and spiteful, God's violence is *warranted violence*. As victim of man's rejection, God does not act in a vengeful way. The sacrificial system provides a symbolic transfer of guilt to another victim, a non-human one, which becomes the focus of sin and animosity. God's own Son, not another human being, bears and abolishes the consequences of sin. The victim on the cross hides the real victim, the God on whose behalf he acts, with reconciliation as the goal.

God's way of salvation is a beneficent way. Sacrifice is an act of hospitality, attended by violence, in which God extends forgiveness to those in sinful revolt against him. God takes the sin and violence of man to himself, distils it in the suffering of the cross, and abolishes it in love and forgiveness. This is not a 'myth of redemptive violence' in which a further violent act seeks to annul a previous one. It is evil assumed and love coming forth in one act, good overcoming evil in restoration.

We continue to live in a world gone wrong, where violence escalates out of control. Man's ability for self-destruction seems to grow, along with the sophistication of technology. What can it mean to speak about the cross as the end of violence when violence itself continues unabated?

First, God in Christ brings an end to the reason for the hostility between man and himself. The obstacle between God and man, created by sin and rebellion, is removed. Secondly, Christ says his 'kingdom is not of this world and if it were, his servants would fight' (John 18: 36). The association of this world and fighting indicates the struggle will continue as long as Christ's kingdom has not yet appeared. Pure hospitality will exist when the results of Christ's work bear fruit in the final coming of his kingdom. For the moment, 'put provocatively, God's hospitality in Christ needs an edge of violence to ensure the (future) welcome of humanity and all creation.'[23] Violence does not win out, nor will it have the last word.

FROM EXCLUSION TO INCLUSION

Exclusion, mental, physical, or geographical, is a litmus test for the presence of violence in human situations, including religious ones. The apostle Paul provides a good case of how Christ terminates violence. His mentality changed from one of persecuting Christians to one of embracing what he formerly despised. The transformation centres on his encounter with Christ, which put an end to his former life. Paul was obliged to lay down his arms at the foot of the cross. He accepted that in Christ, Jews and pagans form a reconciled body, apart from any conditions of the law or ritual practices, such as circumcision, Sabbath observance, or *kosher* purity. It constituted a sea change of 180° because what had been unimaginable for him became the rallying point of a new humanity.

Galatians 2: 20 describes this graphically. Before his conversion, Paul interpreted the cross as being scandalous in the light of his understanding of the law. In his new situation, Paul has followed the path of Jesus and is dead to the law: 'through the law I died to the law, so that I might live to God' (v. 19). In this respect he can say: 'I have been crucified with Christ and I no longer live, but Christ lives in me.' Paul is dead to the old life, with its violence, because he is one with Christ, whom he had formerly persecuted (Acts 9: 5). Now he 'lives by faith in the Son of God, who loved me and gave himself for me.' The reason for his new life is the 'giving' of Christ's for him and the love it demonstrates. Paul has died to the system of exclusion he sought to advance, by becoming one with the crucified victim, the sacrificed Son of God. It was as if Jesus had said to Paul, 'Why are you still persecuting me and trying to put me to death when I am alive?' The new life of Christ is beyond the reach of human violence. It transcends the conditions of violence and exclusion that hold sway in the world.

CONCLUSION

There is a profound difference between mythology and biblical faith. The first tells the story from the point of view of the dominant power, from a position where violence has the upper hand. The Bible, however, demythologises the structures of religious violence by telling the story from the victim's point of view.[24] God and Christ are victims of acts of religious violence. The Creator was spurned and became the victim of man's rebellion, before the Redeemer suffered the same fate. God gets involved in this situation of enmity by making sacrifice the way of abolishing sin. He prepared the ultimate defeat of violence through the suffering and dying of the Son.

In a mysterious way, God uses what he has become at the hands of man, a victim, to deal with man's sin. By doing so, sacrifice becomes a demonstration of God's love in forgiveness. God cannot be shielded from the violence of the cross because it is his way of taking man's violence on himself to abolish it.

The proto-evangel of Genesis 3: 15 speaks of enmity between the offspring of the woman and the serpent. When God says the woman's offspring 'will crush your head, and you will strike his heal,' the curse on Satan is also the blessing of salvation: this promise casts the shadow of the Messiah to come across the pages the Old Testament.[25] We see *a person* in the seed of the woman; *suffering*, in the prediction that his heel will be bruised; and *victory* because he will crush the serpent's head. The victor will be David's greater son, the shepherd and king of God's people. He will also identify with the exile and curse of God's disobedient people as the suffering servant of God, the sacrificial lamb of Isaiah 53. He will be unveiled as the beloved Son, sent to manifest the love of God.

In a certain respect, Genesis 3: 15 expresses the three major historic atonement models in a nut-shell: the example, the substitute, and the victor. They have in common the mysterious fact that each involves God in a situation of violence, because of his own promise. As sacrificial lamb, Christ is thrust into the world of suffering and is injured, though not mortally. He will gain the victory over the adversary and inflict a mortal defeat on him. In his person the glorious love of God will shine forth as he submits to death and radiates new life in the resurrection.

ENDNOTES

[1] R. G. Hamerton-Kelly, *Sacred Violence. Paul's Hermeneutic of the Cross* (Minneapolis: Fortress, 1992), 14.

[2] Augustine speaks of the rod of temporal punishment in an erroneous interpretation of Luke 14: 23. Cf. *Epist. 185, ad Bonifacium*, §21, 24.

[3] French anthropologist René Girard considers exclusion to be the test of religious violence. *Je vois Satan tomber comme l'éclair* (Paris: Grasset, 1999) presents a good introduction to his thought. English translation, *I see Satan fall like Lightening* (Orbis Books, 2001).

[4] R. Girard, *Celui par qui le scandale arrive* (Paris: Desclée de Brouwer, 2003), 141. For Girard the first murder of Abel by Cain is the start of human history and a culture of violence.

[5] M. Alsford, 'The Atonement and the Post-Modern Deconstruction of the Self', in *Atonement Today*, 217.

[6] C. Gunton, *Christ and Creation* (Paternoster: Carlisle, 1992), 99 ff.

[7] This explains why obedience and sacrifice are constantly contrasted in Scripture. 1 Samuel 15: 22, Ecclesiastes 4: 17, Hosea 6: 6, Amos 5: 21 ff., Matthew 9: 15; 12: 7. Proverbs 21: 27 says 'the sacrifice of the wicked is an abomination.' Cf. Hebrews 10: 5, 8 and Psalm 40: 7–9.

[8] Genesis 3: 21 does not speak of expiatory sacrifice. Cf. G. Vos, *Biblical Theology* (Edinburgh: Banner of Truth, 1975), 155–56. The word used for 'covering' here is not the technical term used in the law for covering of sin. Neither is it necessarily God who kills the animal and there is no hint of sacrificial institution. Some interpreters, following Augustine, see a reference to the link between sin and death. The death of the animal must have had some significance for Adam and his offspring, as God's acceptance of Abel's offering rather than Cain's in Genesis 4 serves to indicate.

[9] F. Turretin, *Institutes of Elenctic Theology*, II, 181 ff., as over against C. Baxter's comments on B. B. Warfield and reconciliation in *Atonement Today*, 164. R. A. Peterson indicates that the concept of reconciliation of God to man is already present in Calvin, *Calvin and the Atonement* (Christian Focus: Fearn, 1999), 96.

10 B. B. Warfield, 'Christ our Sacrifice' in *Works,* II, 407–8.

11 M. Douglas, *Purity and Danger*, 13, states that rituals of purity are positive contributions to atonement.

12 R. Rushdoony, *The Politics of Guilt and Pity* (Thorburn Press: Fairfax, 1978), 17.

13 G. C. Berkouwer, *The Triumph of Grace in the Theology of Karl Barth* (Grand Rapids: Eerdmans, 1956), 27.

14 Leviticus 19: 18, 34, Deuteronomy 6: 5, Matthew 22: 37–8.

15 M. Winter, *The Atonement*, 80 ff., describing the position of R. Girard. Cf. R. Schwager, *Must there be Scapegoats? Violence and Redemption in the Bible* (New York: Harper and Row, 1987) and *Violence renounced: René Girard, Biblical Studies and Peacemaking*, W. M. Swartley, ed., (Kitchener: Pandora Press, 2000).

16 Hamerton-Kelly, *op. cit.*, 79

17 This will be dealt with in greater depth in chapter 10.

18 E. Brunner, *The Mediator* (London: Lutterworth, 1934), 482–83.

19 L. Morris, *The Atonement* (Leicester: IVP, 1983), 55. Morris says that of the 362 times where 'blood' is mentioned in the Old Testament, 203 refer to violent death.

20 J. D. Weaver in his book *The Nonviolent Atonement*, 71–4, admits departure from the traditional models of atonement as they imply divine involvement in violence.

21 *Heidelberg Catechism*, q. 37.

22 H. Boersma, *Violence, Hospitality and the Cross*, 36 and on the impossibility of 'pure hospitality', 92–4.

23 Boersma, *op. cit.,* 93.

24 Girard, *Je vois Satan tomber comme l'éclair*, 14 ff.

25 Cf. A. Edersheim, *The Temple. Its Ministry and Services at the Time of Jesus Christ* (New York: James Pott, 1874), 97.

8

Shadows

The parable of Gottlieb Lessing (1729–81), *Nathan the Wise,* is very much up to date. A magic ring conferred on the bearer the power to be loved by God and man. The owner found himself in a quandry, since he had three sons. Two copies were made and after his death each son had a ring. No one could ever know who had the real ring. A wise man advised that each son should act as if he had the original, without ever being sure that he had. So it is with the three monotheistic religions—Judaism, Christianity, and Islam.[1] Which one of them has the truth? We will never know. The important thing is that each religion act in a spirit of love for God and man. Perhaps, one day, their differences will be transcended in a universal religion of love.

Like any parable, this one can have several levels of meaning. A popular one nowadays would be that religious truth is elusive and it is no use fighting to prove who has the original true ring. What is important is sincerity and acts of love that it can stimulate. Every person can find the way to truth by showing love and tolerance for their fellows, and this is the true way to serve God. The golden rule is more important than any dogma.

The problem for the Christian faith, and for other faiths that appears in this story, relates to their claims of uniqueness. Can any religion have a monopoly of the truth? Is there only one way to God? Can an exclusive interpretation of the cross of Christ be credible in the light of world religions? The global context in which we live today makes such questions unavoidable, and important for the Christian doctrines of incarnation and atonement. What is to be made of the *shadows* of the one way of salvation found in other religions and in the Old Testament?

WHY RELIGIONS?

The Christian faith takes its lead from the Old Testament concerning the meaning of belief in God. Its fundamental fact is found in the confession of Israel: 'The LORD our God the LORD is One. Love the LORD your God with all your heart and with all your soul and with all your strength' (Deut. 6: 4). There is only one God. God is unique and for this reason he alone is worthy of undivided commitment and love. In fact, because God is one, he can command love—something no other person can do.

The unique nature of God is the starting point of the biblical doctrine of creation. This is nowhere better expressed than in Paul's debate with the philosophers of religion at Mars Hill in Athens. Contrasting the biblical view with paganism's many gods:

> The God who made the world and everything in it is the Lord of heaven and earth...he is not served by human hands as if he needed anything, because he himself gives all men life and breath and everything else. From one man he made every nation of men, that they should inhabit the whole earth; and he determined the times set for them and the exact places where they should live. God did this so that men would seek him and perhaps reach out for him and find him, though he is not far from each one of us. For in him we live and move and have our being.
>
> Acts 17: 24–8

In the beginning, there were no *religions* in the plural. There was one God and one faith. Man's rebellion against God is the origin of the many religions by which men seek God. The multiplicity of religions, forms of devotion, sacrifices, and creeds have at their heart the fall of man.

When Cain and Abel brought their offerings to God, they did so in two different ways, one of which was acceptable to God and one that was not (Gen. 4: 3 ff.). The result was the first murder. What the story underlines is not the conflict between two ways of life, the pastoral and arable, but the contrast between two different religious attitudes, 'uncovering for the first time the deadly antipathy of carnal religion to spiritual.'[2] As far as God is concerned, man in his fallen state has a sectarian nature. Harmony with God and the neighbour is broken and the multiplicity of religions is an expression of this reality in man's search for God.

For Christian revelation, religions are the expression of what man seeks to know about God based on his own spiritual capital. They can only be mere shadows of the truth God has made known in his revelation to humanity—across the divide of the fall and rebellion against God. In his religious aspirations, religious man does not like revelation, and he will react like this: 'what mattered most of all was my deep-seated hatred of authority, my monstrous individualism, my lawlessness. No word in my vocabulary expressed deeper hatred than the word *interference*. But Christianity placed at the centre what seemed to me a transcendental interferer.'[3]

Revelation is the opposite of even the noblest religious aspirations and the most pious worship. Only when the penny drops does the light begin to shine. 'The evidence for the historicity of the gospels is really remarkably good…Rum thing that stuff about the dying God…it almost looks as if it had really happened once.'[4] Incarnation (God becoming man) and atonement (God dying for our sin) did happen once, and because God did it, once was enough. All other religions are but shadows on the other side of this remarkable event, as are their sacrifices, priesthoods, and salvations.

MORE THAN MONOTHEISM

It may be argued that Judaism and Islam along with Christianity have a different ethos from other religions. Even if all religions have their sacred texts, in a special way these three are 'religions of the book' to which they owe their specific character. The book is an expression of divine revelation that makes known the name of God. It also recounts the foundational story that provides an historical explanation of the origins of God's dealings with men. Laws to be observed and theological explanations make explicit the consequences of knowing God in faith and life.

Is Christianity just another 'religion of the book' or does it have some other more specific claim to our attention? One difference is that the Christian scriptures complete the Old Testament and go beyond it. The Koran, written five centuries after the New Testament was penned, claims to be a final prophecy that is the key to the preceding ones. Islam is derivative of Judaism and Christianity, and for this reason some scholars consider it a sectarian offshoot from them.

However, apart from historical considerations, another fundamental factor distinguishes the Christian revelation from Judaism and Islam. The central reality of the New Testament is not an event that brings about a change of circumstances, but a *person*. Biblical history terminates in the historical figure of Jesus, his life, passion, death and resurrection. Jesus put the seal on his ministry on the cross when he pronounced that all had been accomplished (John 19: 30). On two occasions, after his resurrection, to the couple on the Emmaus road and then to the company of disciples, he interpreted his work as a personal accomplishment of what had been written previously in the Old Testament:

> Everything must be fulfilled that is written about me in the Law of Moses, the Prophets and the Psalms. The he opened their minds so they could understand the Scriptures. 'This is what is written: The Christ will suffer and rise from the dead on the third day and repentance and forgiveness of sins will be preached in his name to all nations beginning at Jerusalem. You are witnesses of these things'.
>
> Luke 24: 44–8, *cf.* 25–7

The historical and personal perspective is specific to the New Testament witness, which is not a collection of moral principles or wisdom for initiates. Nobody claims Mohammed fulfilled the Koran or Buddha the Upanishads, and no one claimed to fulfil the Old Testament but Christ. Orthodox Judaism still awaits the coming of the promised Messiah who will bring in the rule of God and save his people. For Islam, Jesus Christ is not the ultimate prophet but one of a line. The peculiar claim of Christianity is that it is founded on a revelation fulfilled by a person. For this reason, the Christian faith is more than a 'religion of the book' or another form of monotheism.

'*Everything must be fulfilled that is written about me in the Law of Moses, the Prophets and the Psalms.*' Jesus indicates by this that he is present in the whole of the older testament—the Torah, the historical prophets, and the writings. What is written in the parchments concerns the personal reality of the one who stands before the disciples as risen Lord. Nor are there any leftovers not completed by his life, death, and resurrection. Christ's fulfilment of Scripture means firstly that the sacred texts were in themselves incomplete and were invitations to look to a future moment for their finality. They are as a seed planted, when the form of the flower to come is yet unknown. The Old Testament is characterised by a dynamic that reaches its conclusion in the death and resurrection of Christ.

In addition, the fulfilment of Scripture in Christ means he embodied, in his person and work, realities described in a vague way by the types, rites, and institutions of the Old Testament. The various forms of Jewish worship prefigured his coming and required completion by his presence. But when the flower appeared, the full beauty enclosed in the seed was seen as never before. Finally, the fulfilment of the sacred texts by Christ meant that not only did he complete the promises of salvation; he did so in perfect conformity with the laws and precepts of the previous revelation. The seed and the flower reveal that they belong together.

What Jesus taught his astonished followers was that he was the centre of Scripture. How can this peculiar feature of biblical revelation—that a person fulfils a text—be understood?

GOD'S MOVE

At the end of a game of chess when one player says 'check mate' the pieces on the board are frozen in their final position. If the game were followed from start to finish, on a computer for example, all the chessmen could be observed in their successive positions leading up to the outcome. In a similar way, throughout Old Testament revelation God positions his revelation in moves that lead up to the finale when Christ appears for the closing battle against the powers of Satan, evil, and death. The last act has been envisaged and prepared for all along, even though it alone is the deciding one. God has been at work in various times and different ways precisely because of this moment on which hangs the fate of all history. 'In the past God spoke to our forefathers through the prophets at many times and in various ways' says the writer to the Hebrews, 'but in these last days he has spoken to us by his Son, whom he appointed heir of all things, and through whom he made the universe' (Heb. 1: 1–2). What was preparatory has now become irreversible and definitive.

Just as in the chess game the moves progress to the dénouement, so from the time of God's first promise in Genesis 3: 15, everything converges slowly but surely toward the unexpected event that will happen in a Bethlehem stable. God's promises, which are continually renewed, and his acts to save his people, are like links in a chain that culminate in the Saviour's coming into the world. On the basis of his saving acts, God forms a people whom he calls and with whom he makes his covenant. First of all the family of Abraham—'in you all the nations of the earth will be blessed' (Gen.22: 18) and then a people—'I am the Lord your God who has brought you out of the house of slavery' (Exod. 20: 1). The special people of God are placed in an uncomfortable situation, with a calling to holiness—'be holy even as I am holy'—which resounds through history as the condition by which God's promises will be fulfilled. Disobedience has dire consequences—'You only have I known of all the families of the earth: therefore I will punish you for your sins' (Amos 3: 2). The contrast between God's perfect holiness and the constant failure of his people to live up to their privileges, calls for the intervention of the one who will bring the divine plan of salvation to its climax.

Representatives are established as leaders from among the people, with varying importance according to the stage of development of God's plan. 'The Lord's power-presence is revealed in his Spirit with a view to fulfilling a variety of goals in redemptive history. He not only carries individuals beyond their normal physical capacities; he gives them abilities that extend beyond their native wit. Thus he distributes gifts for statesmanship and craftsmanship.'[6] In the Old Testament there are three offices of leadership, all of which are blessed with divine unction:

- *priests* represented the people in the realm of the worship of God; they offer sacrifices for the cleansing of sin, necessary for acceptance with God and life in his presence;

- *prophets* announce God's word and are messengers of the covenant; they recall the conditions of obedience and proclaim the blessings or judgments of God;
- *kings* are 'shepherds' of the people; their responsibility is to assure justice and protection for the people and show an example of righteous leadership.

No one individual could accumulate the three offices.[7] If David was endowed with a prophetic spirit and anointed to lead God's people, he could not be a priest, and the nearest he got to it was the unauthorised act of eating the consecrated bread on the altar (Matt. 12: 3–4). Saul had prophetic gifts and had been anointed the first king of Israel, but he lost his kingship when he disobeyed God by going against Samuel's word and offering a priestly sacrifice (1 Sam. 13: 11 ff.). The message is that no human being could be the complete representative of God's people and accomplish their salvation.

What the Old Testament spokesmen had not been able to do, Jesus claimed to have done completely. He referred to these three offices to demonstrate his messianic authority. Obviously, he did not bear the honorific titles officially, but he exercised the functions in such a way that his personal charisma broke the bounds of institutional structures.

As *priest*, Jesus is 'more' than the priests of the Old Testament and even more than the temple where they presented the offerings: 'Haven't you read that on the Sabbath the priests desecrate the day and are yet innocent. I tell you that one greater than the temple is here…The Son of Man is Lord of the Sabbath' (Matt. 12: 5–8). 'Destroy this temple and in three days I will build it again' (John 2: 19).

As *prophet*, Jesus compared himself with Jonah, the unwilling prophet the Lord sent to Nineveh, renowned for having received fishy hospitality for three days. The people would reject Jesus; he would die and rise again to complete his prophetic mission. No sign would be given to the unbelieving Jews other than the sign of Jonah (Matt. 16: 4):

> The men of Nineveh will stand up at the judgment with this generation and condemn it; for they repented at the preaching of Jonah and now one greater than Jonah is here. For as Jonah was three days and three nights in the belly of

a huge fish, so the Son of Man will be three days and three
nights in the heart of the earth.

(Matt. 13: 40–41)

As *king*, Jesus' glory puts that of the most magnificent of the
Old Testament kings, Solomon, in the shade: 'The queen of
the south will rise at the judgment with this generation and
condemn it; for she came from the ends of the earth to listen
to Solomon's wisdom, and now one greater than Solomon is
here' (v: 42).

Matthew 12 shows that Jesus is prophet, priest, and king,
and at the same time something far greater. The reason for this
is, as Matthew hints in the same chapter (vv: 17–21), that Jesus
fulfils each of these offices in a *messianic* way, as the promised
deliverer. Not only will he be the deliverer of his people, but he
will establish justice and be the hope of the nations: 'Here is my
servant who I have chosen, the one I love, in whom I delight;
I will put my spirit on him, and he will proclaim justice to the
nations...In his name the nations will put their hope.'

Jesus personalises each of the offices that represent the hope
of salvation for God's people. They are types and shadows
of the higher reality he embodies. The various aspects of life
under the old covenant find their point of convergence in him.
Jesus is the perfect leader of his people and the one who saves
them.

MORE THAN EXPECTED

The question concerning shadows of Jesus' person and work
in the Old Testament can be seen from another angle. Imagine
Jesus had never been born in Bethlehem, had never lived for
thirty-three years in Palestine, had never died on the cross
or risen again. Would we be able from the variety of Old
Testament types and prophecies to construct an identikit
picture of his person and work? Nothing is less certain.

From the Old Testament could we imagine a person who
would be at the same time great high priest, the sacrifice, and
the temple? Yet that is how the New Testament presents Jesus.
The shadows of previous revelation now become the reality of
flesh and blood. How could we reconcile the idea of kingship
with the stable at Bethlehem or with the itinerant ministry on
the dusty tracks of Galilee, to say nothing of the crucifixion,

even if the sign on the cross reads 'king of the Jews'? Again, does the view of the fulfilment of prophecy lead naturally without a quantum leap to the 'Word made flesh' of John's first chapter? What prior prediction would be sufficient to reconcile the contrasts represented by the power of Jesus' miracles and the suffering of the passion? No computer programme could take the Old Testament data and produce a picture of a virtual Christ with his two natures, divine and human; his two states of suffering and glory; and his three offices, prophet, priest, and king. 'The story of Jesus does not begin with the fulfilment of the promise, but with the promise itself, and with the acts of God that accompanied his word. As we go back to the beginning of the story, we find much that the New Testament does not tell us, because we have already been told.'[8]

At the same time, when we move forward from the Old Testament, we find the wonder of the fulfilment is far greater than anything that could be imagined from that perspective. The glory of Christ breaks forth like a daffodil from a bud. The personal reality of the Word of God incarnate resumes all the seemingly irreconcilable contrasts and goes beyond the wildest prophetic dreams in glorious fulfilment.

As representative of his people, Jesus takes on all the features of the covenantal relationship between God and man to bring them to their necessary culmination. Jesus is a prophet, like Moses and Jeremiah, a freedom fighter like Joshua, a king like David and Solomon, a priest like Melchizedek and Aaron. He is also the water that springs from the rock in the desert, the manna that comes down from heaven, the sacrificial lamb who removes sin, and Samson who dies when he gives his life to defeat his enemies and save his people. Jesus is the true Israel of God, the son called out of Egypt (Matt. 2: 15), the one who defeats Satan in the desert, before leading the new exodus from Jerusalem (Luke 9: 31). In calling his disciples he lays the foundation of a new Israel, upon which the people of the new community will he constructed. He is the new Adam who enters the new creation, and his people with him, because of his obedience. He is not just the king of Israel, but the Lord of history (Matt. 28: 20), who leads everything to its conclusion. 'All of history unfolds to complete the story of Jesus, until the day he comes again.'[9]

Incomparable Jesus Christ! Prick the surface of the biblical stories and we find he is the life-blood flowing through the whole *corpus*. In God's revelation he is active everywhere.

THE FINISHED WORK OF CHRIST

Shadows and reality, promise and fulfilment, incomplete and complete—such expressions serve to indicate that Jesus in person brought God's purposes to their saving conclusion. This was part of his own understanding of his experience in life and death. If history prepares the way for divine salvation, and if Jesus lived this out to the full in and through his humanity, there is also a divine intention involved. God is completing his plan.

In Gethsemane before his trial, Jesus declares in his high-priestly prayer 'I have completed the work you gave me to do'[10] (John 17: 4). The sixth word of Jesus on the cross is also one of completion: 'It is finished' (John 19: 30).[11] These expressions convey that Jesus had a sense of having perfectly and successfully completed his mission on earth, according to the plan of God. In fact, the whole of his life had been to do the Father's will and to 'complete the work' (John 4: 34) that had been entrusted to him (John 5: 36). The word of fulfilment from the cross is the ultimate act that seals the agreement between the Father and the Son, made for the salvation of men 'before the world began' (17: 5).

What Jesus fulfilled in his life and death is what the prophets had anticipated in the holy Scriptures. Jesus in his prayer spoke of bringing glory to the Father 'on the earth' (17: 4). Looking back on the same event Peter, one of the prime witnesses, wrote:

> Concerning this salvation, the prophets who spoke of the grace that was to come to you, searched intently and with the greatest care, trying to find out the time and circumstances to which the Spirit of Christ in them was pointing when he predicted the sufferings of Christ and the glories that would follow.
>
> 1 Pet. 1: 10–11

What can be known of how Jesus understood his final accomplishment at Golgotha? Not much by speculation, but enough by revelation.

The words 'It is finished' in a sense contain all Jesus' other words on the cross in germinal form, since in one way or another they all depend on the effectiveness of the fulfilment.[12] It has three fundamental orientations. As a declaration that Jesus made before God, it concerns his witness to himself. It is also offered to the scrutiny of men. Thirdly, to his heavenly Father as an attestation of the nature of his finished work. In these three respects, Jesus has fulfilled prophetic Scripture. He is conscious that his work is complete:

With regard to himself: 'After the suffering of his soul, (my righteous servant) will see the light and be satisfied' (Isa. 53: 11). 'You have made known to me the path of life; you will fill me with joy in your presence, with eternal pleasures at your right hand' (Ps. 16: 11).

With regard to the scrutiny of history: 'I will declare your name to my brothers: in the congregation I will praise you…For he has not despised or disdained the suffering of the afflicted one; He has not hidden his face from him, but listened to his cry for help' (Ps. 22: 23–4).[13]

With regard to his heavenly Father: 'Therefore let everyone who is godly pray to you while you may be found; surely when the mighty waters rise, they will not reach him. You are my hiding place; you will protect me from trouble and surround me with songs of deliverance' (Ps. 32: 6–7).

In his profound agony—beaten, bruised, scourged, wounded, disfigured almost beyond recognition, and executed—Jesus confesses before God and man that *this* is his perfectly completed work. The Lord comes as servant to make good the promises of his own word.[14]

Fulfilment of Scripture and perfect atonement are inextricably connected as the warp and woof of divine salvation. Christ declared in his sixth word that salvation has been accomplished *de jure* and soon it will be so *de facto*.[15]

NEW WRITING

How exactly did Jesus complete all that was said about him beforehand in the Old Testament writings? Luke 24: 44 refers to the law of Moses. Jesus had brought this to fulfilment not by abolishing it, but by embodying what obedience to it means: 'Do not think that I have come to abolish the law and the prophets; I have not come to abolish them but to fulfil them'

(Matt. 5: 17). The apostle Paul speaks in many and varying ways about the relationship between the law and the cross. 'Christ is the end of the law so that there may be righteousness for everyone who believes' (Rom. 10: 4). Here the word 'end' is used, as in John, in the sense of completion. Jesus fully and totally obeyed the law and the cross establishes perfect justice for believers, as Christ's death effaces the negative consequences of disobedience to the law.

In Galatians Paul also refers to the cross of Christ as a new form of text, comparable to the Old Testament in its authority: 'Foolish Galatians! Who has bewitched you? Before your very eyes Jesus Christ was clearly portrayed as crucified' (Gal. 3: 1).[16] The apostle carries the metaphor a little further in Colossians 2: 14, where he speaks of God forgiving sins and making us alive with Christ 'having cancelled the written code, with its regulations, that was against us and stood opposed to us.' The first of these texts speaks of Christ crucified as if he were a new written text that completes and puts a new complexion on the already existing law of God. In the second case, Colossians 2: 14, 'Christ crucified' assumes the accusation made against us, in this judgment and death. This cancellation of the act against us is another new act of writing. The perfect obedience of Christ in suffering and death are the heart of the work of the cross according to the perfect righteousness the law demanded.

Together, these give us a key to the meaning of 'it is finished'. In his life and death Christ 'fulfils all righteousness', as he said at his baptism (Matt. 3: 15). He fulfils the law by removing its accusation and establishing a new form of righteousness that comes by faith. Jesus is the perfect embodiment of victory over sin and death, and in uttering these words, he proclaims his triumph.

CONCLUSION

'It is finished' confronts us with the amazing fact that the sacred texts of the Old Testament with their laws, prophecies, history and types, are fulfilled in *a person* and specifically in his death on a cross. Jesus is neither a religious leader nor a swami whose teaching and example form part of the spiritual heritage of humanity.

Jesus completes one history and opens up another. That history is *our* history, as Peter remarked when he spoke about the prophets desiring to look into the things concerning the suffering and glory of Jesus: 'It was revealed to the prophets that they were not serving themselves but you, when they spoke of the things that have now been told you by those who have preached the gospel to you by the Holy Spirit sent from heaven' (1 Pet. 1: 12). The shadows are there in God's prior revelation so that we can fully understand the glory of the cross by way of contrast and comparison. How great is the glory of the cross, the suffering for sin, the victory, and the perfect example of righteousness Jesus provides in fulfilment of all that was written!

Salvation is for us, and what was written is also for us: 'Everything that was written in the past was written to teach us, so that through endurance and the encouragement of the Scriptures we might have hope' (Rom. 15: 4). *For us!* 'These things happened to the forefathers as examples and were written down as warnings for us, on whom the fulfilment of the ages has come' (1 Cor. 10: 11).[17] And Christ is at the centre of everything.

ENDNOTES

[1] Monotheism means the belief in one God. Monotheistic religions trace their source to Abraham and are often called 'religions of the book' as a divinely inspired text is essential to their belief in God.

[2] D. Kidner, *Genesis* (London: Tyndale Press, 1967), 75.

[3] C. S. Lewis, *Surprised by Joy* (London: Collins, 1959), 139.

[4] Ibid., 178 f.

[5] S. Ferguson, *The Holy Spirit* (Leicester: IVP, 1996), 21–2.

[6] It could be argued that Abraham and Moses occupied the three positions, but without the title.

[7] E. P. Clowney, *The Unfolding Mystery. Discovering Christ in the Old Testament* (Leicester: IVP., 1988), 15.

[8] Ibid., 202.

[9] 'finishing the work' = *to ergon teleiosas,* (*teleioo*, to make perfect complete, effective, successful, of a work as in James 1: 4) not just in the sense of making an end of it but that of completion and success as to results.

[10] *Tetelestai* (*teleioo*) is a perfect passive, which expresses the idea that an act done in the past has consequences in the present: 'it has assuredly been accomplished'.

[11] R. Stier, *The Words of the Lord Jesus*, VIII, (Edinburgh: T.&T. Clark, 1873), 25–7.

[12] Cf. Hebrews 2: 10–13; Isaiah 52: 13–15.

13 Clowney, *op. cit.*, ch. 9.
14 A. W. Pink, *The Seven Sayings on the Cross* (Grand Rapids: Baker, 1958), 103.
15 Paul uses the word *telos* for 'end' in this verse.
16 *proegraphe estaurômenos* = traced as if in writing as crucified; Colossians 2: 14, speaks also of cancelling the written code which was against us. (*chairographon tois dogmasin*)
17 'The end of the ages'—*ta tela ton aionion*.

9

Victor

In a remarkable novel by Chaim Potok, a young hassid alienates the Jewish community by painting a work entitled *Brooklyn Crucifixion* in which he portrays his mother as the one who suffers for the sake of Judaism. The artist, Asher Lev, considered the cross to be an appropriate if shocking symbol·to plumb depths of human anguish.[1]

This illustrates how far removed the cross of Christ seems at first glance from the idea of a victory. In and of itself the cross of Christ has none of the marks of triumph, nor does the crucified one appear to be a victor. Quite the contrary. The circumstances of the crucifixion leave only an impression of injustice, humiliation and degradation followed by the final dereliction of death. No wonder it has become a symbol for human suffering and not a sign of conquest. The defeat of the forces that lead to the death of Christ appears only in the resurrection as the sequel to the crucifixion. Without the resurrection, the cross is without effect, as the apostle Paul said, 'If Christ was not raised your faith is futile; you are still in your sins' (1 Cor. 15: 17). It is in the resurrection that Christ appears as the triumphant Lord.

The cult of the underdog who wins out against all possible odds plays a prominent role in the popular imagination because of the influence of Hollywood and block-buster fiction. The cross of Christ has also been cast as the struggle of a remarkable person against injustice, suffering, and finally death. If, however, the gospel records evoke the dignity of Christ in accomplishing his work on earth, it can hardly be concluded, in so far as the cross is concerned, that he was a heroic example of success against the odds or of courage in adversity.

CHRIST THE VICTOR

In discussions about the atonement the victory model has gained renewed popularity today. It provides an attractive alternative to what is considered an over-accentuation in the past on penal and legal interpretations of the work of the cross.[2] The presentation of the cross as a victory is dramatic and demonstrative; it has the advantage of a longstanding historical pedigree. Furthermore, it appeals to a mentality that values the notion of personal achievement through courageous decisions and actions.

In the Old Testament God is presented as a victor who vindicates himself and triumphs over evil forces opposing his rule. Victory is spoken of almost exclusively as the defeat of external foes resulting in physical peace and security for God's people.[3] Its end is the reign of God. It is interesting, however, to note that in the Old Testament, victory is also related to the righteousness and justice of God, who punishes evil and rewards good. It almost seems to be a synonym of righteousness. Victory demonstrates God's righteousness and vindicates his truth and justice (Deut. 11: 26–8). 'The *Christus Victor* theme provides continuity with a main Old Testament theme: that of YHWH as the champion of righteousness who overpowers his enemies. 'Who is the King of Glory? YHWH strong and valiant, YHWH valiant at war' (Ps. 24: 8).'[4]

In the New Testament, even if the confession that Jesus is Lord (1 Cor. 12: 3) has a polemic reference to the rule of Caesar, the victory of God is not spoken of in a material sense, as the defeat of evil manifested in political, social, or economic ways. It is primarily a mastery over spiritual forces opposed to God and his reign. The present victory of Christ over evil belongs to the realm of spiritual discernment, even if it also has eschatological implications for the future defeat of the powers of evil that oppose Christ.[5]

The concept of the spiritual victory of Christ over the forces of evil existed early in the Christian tradition. It represented an attempt to account for the reason why Christ had to die and to explain the result of his death. For Irenaeus, bishop of Lyons in the second century, Jesus represented men as the new Adam in the struggle against sin and evil. He resisted and conquered the devil, restoring humanity by his victory. It was only natural in this context that the idea of ransom should come to the fore. Ransom was part of everyday experience with slavery and payment for the release of prisoners. Moreover, Jesus himself stated: 'the Son of man came to serve and give his life as a ransom for many' (Mark 10: 45).

So the obvious question was, to whom was the ransom paid? Origen of Alexandria, in the third century, supplied an answer that seemed to be feasible. It could not be paid to God, who required no ransom, so it must have been offered to the devil. 'The devil accepted the deal, but according to Origen, the goodness of Jesus was too much for the devil. He could not stand having Jesus in his grasp; this was torture. He let go and lost his ransom payment after having already given up his prisoners.'[6]

Gregory of Nyssa (330–95) developed the idea of victory over the devil by the payment of ransom, in a way that has often been deemed as inappropriate, as it seems to involve the idea that God played Satan at his own game of deception and trickery. Satan was lured into accepting the ransom of Jesus' death for the liberation of those whom he held captive. He was, however, unaware of the divinity of Christ and his power, hidden under the appearance of his human nature. 'The deity was hidden under the veil of our nature, that so, as with ravenous fish, the hook of the Deity might be gulped down along with the bait of flesh, and thus, life being introduced into the house of death, and light shining in darkness, that which is diametrically opposed to life and light might vanish.'[7] So the devil got his come-uppance; God defeated him and the power of death. In modern parlance, the end justified the means, and the means were appropriate because the devil got what he deserved by being shown up as the deceiver.[8]

All this is bizarre to a modern way of thinking, which finds it difficult to think of evil other than as a symbol for impersonal powers. It is however the concept of victory that G. Aulén proposed in the first part of the last century as the 'classical' or the 'dramatic' model. It was a 'clever tactical move on the part of Aulén, as such a label lacks proper warrant from the texts!'[9] In his influential work *Christus Victor*[10] which claims to be an historical study, Aulén proposed that the importance of the victory motif was compromised by 'latin' juridical ideas. Later it was eclipsed by western 'legal' theories of the atonement, because of the influence of Anselm of Canterbury. An exception to this is found in Martin Luther, whose contribution to the doctrine of the atonement did justice to Christ as the victor over sin, death, and the devil. But now, claimed Aulén, 'a door stands open, which has been closed for centuries, for the classic idea to come to the fore.'[11]

Aulén indicated five strands of thought that sustain the idea of Christ as victor.[12] God is the actor in the victory over the powers of evil that are opposed to him, and his work is essentially one of grace rather than of justice or satisfaction. His victory is triumph over sin, which is essentially personal enslavement rather than a transgression of the law. Its result is salvation, the victory brought into the experience of believers by the Holy Spirit as justification, which brings the atonement into the present. It is God who accomplishes the victory through the work of Christ incarnate and God who reconciles the world to himself. The atonement is not a negotiation between God and Christ in an exchange, but it is God's love cancelling out his anger against sin and his triumph over the powers of evil. 'The result of this is an entirely non-penal understanding of the cross: it is not punishment but victory that removes judgment and achieves reconciliation.'[13]

This aspect of the victory theory is especially attractive to contemporary thought. 'Love is stronger than death. The God of love takes the powers of darkness and evil on their own terms and wins. There is hope in the universe...Without the resurrection the cross is impotent, a symbol of failure and defeat. Before the resurrection Jesus was just another victim of the ultimate method of exclusion—death itself.'[14] Of course the cross is never seen apart from the logical and historical sequel of the resurrection in the New Testament witness, but that is not the point. If Jesus was no more than 'just another victim', why are not all victims of violence raised to new life from the dead? If Jesus' suffering and death is just an exposure of the myth of redemptive violence,[15] a demonstration that violence is futile and we must repent of it, why does it find its outcome in the resurrection? Surely there must be something particular about the death of the cross that justifies the resurrection, the suffering of the cross itself must have its own intrinsic value. To limit it merely to an unmasking of the powers of evil and a victory over those powers is not enough.

THE CROSS AND VICTORY

If Christ is the victor, what did he defeat? It may come as a surprise after the preceding paragraphs that one of John Calvin's favourite themes of the atonement is Christ as the victor who conquers all the foes of his people.[16] Calvin was a master of renaissance rhetoric and his way of presenting the nature of Christ's victory is highly dramatic. Commenting on Christ's 'descent into hell' in the Apostle's creed, he wrote:

> Christ had to conquer that fear which by nature continually torments and oppresses all mortals. This he could only do by fighting it...This was no common sorrow or one engendered by a light cause. Therefore, by his wrestling hand to hand with the devil's power, with the dread of death, with the pains of hell, he was victorious and triumphed over them, that in death we may not now fear those things which our Prince has swallowed up (cf. 1 Pet. 3: 22).[17]

The victory of Christ defeats the power of the devil, who uses as his instruments the torments of death and the pains of hell to hold men in the thrall of mental slavery. 'The god of this age has blinded the minds of unbelievers, so that they cannot see the light of the gospel of the glory of Christ, who is the image of God' (2 Cor. 4: 4). This is Satan's main objective, but how does he do it? By the fear of death. This makes men want to hold on to the present as though it were the be all and end all. Without Christ and hope it is all they have and they cling to it for dear life. This does not necessarily mean they are aware that over-investment in the passing world and under-investment in spiritual things is a sign of fear, because they are blinded to the real cause of their obsession. Christ shared in our humanity 'so that by his death he might destroy him who holds the power of death—the devil—and free those who all their lives were held in slavery by the fear of death' (Heb. 2: 14–15). The fear of death is the constant anxiety of losing the only thing that one has—life, and all that goes with it.

There can be little doubt that it was at the cross that the power of the devil was destroyed. 'Having disarmed the powers and authorities, Christ made a public spectacle of them, by triumphing over them at the cross' (Col. 2: 15). This was the purpose for which he came into the world, to 'cast out' the prince of this world and bring about his undoing (John 12: 31, 16: 11). He explained that his power to free men and women from the hold of evil was a result of his mastery of it—'If I drive out demons by the finger of God, then the kingdom of God has come among you' (Luke 11: 20). This saying is explained by a parable. A stronger man enters the house of the strong man and overpowers him, stripping off his armour and tying him up. Then he plunders his goods (Luke 11: 21–2; Mark 3: 27). In similar manner, Christ has entered the world, where Satan holds sinners in his sway, to vanquish Satan and reduce him to powerlessness.

Christ has overcome the foes that held men in the vice of sin. His victory over them liberates the powerless. He 'divides the spoil of the strong' (Isa. 53: 12): 'Christ as a valiant and illustrious general triumphed over the enemies whom he had vanquished...he subdued death, the world and the devil.'[18]

What does the expression 'stronger man' hold for our understanding of the victory of Christ? First of all, in entering into the arena of combat for men, Christ clothed himself with their human condition and weaknesses. It was in the weakness of human flesh that he was crucified (1 Pet. 3: 18) and his humanity has an important place to play in the victory over the devil.[19] One of Adam's race had to acheive the victory for it to be a victory for human beings. The victory of Christ was the triumph of his humanity over Satan in his sinless perfection, spiritual, mental, and physical. It was also the triumph of his divinity, for only as true God could Christ overcome human death.

> It was his task to swallow up death. Who but the Life could do this? It was his task to conquer sin. Who but very Righteousness could do this? It was his task to rout the powers of world and air. Who but a power higher than world and air could do this? Now where does life or righteousness or lordship and authority of heaven lie, but with God alone? Therefore our most merciful God...made himself our Redeemer in the person of his only-begotten Son (cf. Rom. 5: 8).[20]

SATAN'S TACTICS

The victory of Christ takes on its true perspective when his strategy against the power of Satan is considered. What manoeuvres did Jesus undertake on the battlefield of spiritual combat to disarm the power of his adversary? What was the power of Satan?

The tactic of the devil is essentially seen in that he exercises his power against God as a force of opposition against divine truth and justice, and against all that is good in creation. This he does by temptation and accusation, by using sin, death, the flesh, and the world to his own advantage. To these Christ replied with obedience and trust in God to disarm and defeat the power of evil.[21]

'Tempter' is a common designation for Satan in Scripture. It refers to his activity against God from the beginning of the creation. The devil is a truth-twister from the start as 'the father of lies' (John 8: 44). His method is deception and he uses enticements whose results are contrary to what he promises (2 Tim. 2: 26; Eph. 4: 14). He works under the guise of an 'angel of light' (2 Cor. 11: 14–15) as a manipulator of truth. As such, he is a seducer who exploits men's weaknesses to draw them into his sway.

In and of himself, Satan has no positive power, his only weapons are negative, as forces of opposition against God. Without Christ, antichrist cannot exist; without God, Satan cannot accomplish his ends. Where God proposes a rule of righteousness, justice, and truth, Satan perverts and undermines them with the rule of disobedience, injustice, and error. Satan is essentially a sham, a parody, and a counterfeit of God's perfection. His operations are aided and abetted by habit and patterns of behaviour that hold men captive to their sin:

> The Tempter's power is reinforced by the developments of human nature and human society. Once one has yielded to temptation, the force of human habit works in favour of further sinning. Believing the lie further binds individuals who can no longer recognize the true shape of things. Sin settles in and produces that law in our members that frustrates the wishes of our consciences (Rom. 7: 23)—the flesh as an associate of the devil and a dimension of our bondage. And then human solidarity...gives sinful behaviour a contagious power. The lies of seduction, to which the

lies of self-justification are soon combined, grow into the symbolic system of a culture, which moulds the mind of every member from childhood onward. Groups behave like proud and cruel bandits and succeed in enlisting the noblest of passions in the service of oppressive or idolatrous ends. Such is the 'world', whose friendship is enmity toward God (Jas. 4: 4) and which 'lies in the evil one' (1 John 5: 19) or under Satan as *archon* (John 12: 31).[22]

It would be difficult to find a better résumé of the tactics of Satan than this! Satan works by dissimulation and seduction to engineer a world-system subjugated to his power. Men are under the impression that they are free and even that they are acting in the best interests of all. The victims of 'progress' all too often suffer because 'the kindest acts of the wicked are cruel' (Prov. 12: 10). The outcome is turmoil and affliction for those trapped in a system of oppression and lies.

The evil one is also the 'Accuser', as in Revelation 12: 10, 'the accuser of our brothers, who accuses them before our God day and night.' Satan is the adversary, not only the master of lies, but also the one who can use truth itself as a weapon against men. 'If Satan's opposition to the Lord were a matter of mere power, the rebel's finite resources would equal zero confronted with infinity. But the Accuser can appeal to justice. He may also indulge in slander, but his force resides in the rightness of his accusation.'[23] Strange though is may seem, Satan's power depends again on something that belongs to God—his law. The law was given as a way of life, as the apostle says: 'the law is holy, and the commandment is holy, righteous and good.' Nevertheless, 'if the law is spiritual', Paul has to add, 'I am unspiritual, sold as a slave to sin' (Rom. 7: 12, 14). On this basis, the accusation of Satan against us can only be proper, because we are obliged to admit: 'I cannot carry it out' (v. 17).

So Satan is formally right in his accusation, even if his intention is evil in procuring the condemnation of sinners. Such is Satan's lust for power and love of death that as Accuser he strives for our undoing. 'The power of sin is the law' (1 Cor. 15: 56). 'The law of God, precisely because it is good and holy, separates us, condemned sinners from our good and holy God, and we fall prey to agencies of wickedness. Satan's major weapon, as he enforces his rule, is thus divine law and justice. He is the relentless Accuser, day and night.'[24]

THE NATURE OF THE VICTORY

If the goal of Satan as the Tempter is to drive a wedge between God and man, to stimulate disobedience through unbelief, he is totally disarmed when his lies are rejected. The victory of Jesus is a victory of obedience, the triumph of truth over lies. Satan is rendered powerless simply when God's truth is received, honoured, and obeyed. The recognition of God's word is the best defence and the best attack.

In his perverted intelligence the great liar understood this perfectly. The temptation of Jesus in the desert was Satan's greatest attempt to divert Jesus from his mission. In this first engagement of conflict with the one who had just been invested with the Spirit, Satan chose a distortion of Scripture to attack Christ and turn him away from obedience (Luke 4: 1–13). He invited Jesus to display his power as the Son of God (v. 3, 9) in a fraudulent way, in opposition to God's word. His three temptations were: 'Live your own life, don't be hungry, turn the stones into bread. Take what belongs to you now, recognize me and I will give you all the power you want. Show that you really believe in God by trying him out.' In each instance, Satan invites Jesus to a false use of messianic power in relation to the created order. 'Work your magic, fulfil your political ambitions, use your freedom to see if it really works!' Jesus' reply is patience and trust in God's providence, recognition that God's glory and service come first, and the conviction that God is not to be tested but to be trusted. In his replies Jesus shows explicitly that his mission can only be accomplished by practical obedience to God's word. One word of truth from the Lord is enough to repel the devil's overtures. And so Satan 'left him until an opportune time' (v. 13).

Although we can surmise but little about the inner life of Jesus, the 'opportune time' seems to have been Jesus' moment of anguish in Gethsemane and on the cross. This time the attack was not direct, as it was after the forty days of fasting, but through his own anguish when faced by his passion and death. Jesus exhorts his disciples twice to pray so as not to fall into temptation and he uses the same method himself (Luke 22: 39–46). Jesus was experiencing intense heaviness of heart: 'my soul is overwhelmed with sorrow, to the point of death' (v. 44; Mark 14: 34). He is deeply 'distressed and troubled' and cannot avoid the fear of death, which Satan uses as his weapon against sinners.

Jesus, it would appear, shares in humanity even to the extent of experiencing mental oppression at the prospect of death (Heb. 2: 14–15). The power of the devil is destroyed by his prayer, in which Jesus submits himself entirely to his Father's will: 'Father, if you are willing, take this cup from me; yet not my will but yours be done' (Luke 22: 42).[25] The Son is praying the prayer he gave to his disciples, sharing in their suffering and obedience to God to accomplish his mission: 'Your will be done on earth as it is in heaven.' This is the bread from heaven that sustains him for the day and opens the way to the coming of the kingdom (Matt. 6: 9–11). If there is no direct reference to Satan in the garden scene, this is his hour, 'when darkness reigns' (Luke 22: 53). Does Jesus remember how he rebuked Peter when his disciple rejected the idea that he must die and rise again? 'Get behind me Satan! You are a stumbling block to me; you do not have in mind the things of God but the things of men' (Matt. 16: 22–3). Jesus must stay on course to win the victory and that can only be accomplished by submission to God's will and obedience to his word.

At Golgotha too, Satan is the strategist behind the mocking insults of the crowd—'He saved others; let him save himself if he is the Christ of God, the Chosen One.' 'If you are the king of the Jews, save yourself.' And the dying thief echoes the same satanic temptation, 'Aren't you the Christ? Save yourself and us' (Luke 23: 35–6, 39). The king of the Jews is crowned with the thorns of the *ifs* of his tormenters. But this 'defeat' is victory, victory over the Tempter in perfect conformity to the will of God. 'If Jesus had accepted any of the devil's proposals, we would have been lost forever.'[26]

Satan is also the Accuser. But he has nothing to accuse Jesus of. Jesus announces his death to his disciples: 'the prince of this world is coming. He has nothing in me, but the world must learn that I love the Father and that I do exactly what my Father has commanded me' (John 14: 30). Here is perfect conformity to the law of God, perfect love, demonstrated in a sinless life and in death for the sin of others. His death had to be a perversion of human justice, as his accusers could find nothing against him and condemned him on trumped-up charges. Pilate found no basis for charges against him and Jesus knew where the real seat of power lay: 'You would have no power over me, if it were not given you from above' (John 19: 6, 11). He could be unjustly accused by men, but no accusation can be brought against Jesus in the heavenly court. By his life and death in obedience to God, Jesus abolished Satan's powers of accusation because he made them null and void with regard to himself and also to those for whom he gave his life. The devil was deprived of his powers through the death of Jesus (Heb. 2: 14).

Jesus gained the victory over the powers of evil at the cross. The means to this end is the defusing of Satan's weapons of temptation and accusation. This is accomplished because Jesus gave his life as a ransom for the sins of others, paying the debt for them. The shedding of his blood obtained the remission of sins and removed the grounds of accusation. So Christ 'was sacrificed once to take away the sins of many people', and now as the one who pleads their cause 'he entered heaven itself, now to appear for us in God's presence' (Heb. 9: 22, 24, 28). Satan can no longer be the accuser when Christ is the advocate. This goes to show that the victory of Christ is intimately connected with his death for his people and depends on it for its effectiveness. At the cross 'man's sin has been dealt with, atoned for, washed away, forgiven; and thus, to put the whole in terms of the spiritual warfare, the power of sin over men's lives has been broken.'[27]

CONCLUSION

Because of his victory, Jesus is the one who has the power to confer the statute of sonship on those who believe on him (John 1: 12). He exercises his power over the world and its history following his resurrection and ascension (Matt. 28: 20). His resurrection is the manifestation of his divine power, as he has been 'declared with power to be the Son of God by his resurrection from the dead' (Rom. 1: 4).[28]

In Paul's letters, in particular, the victory of Christ comes to light in believers who are transformed according to the image of Christ by the Spirit and who live in hope.[29] Communion with Christ empowers believers in spiritual conflict against the powers (Eph. 6: 12), which are already subject to the authority of Christ.[30] If these 'principalities and powers' have an influence in the affairs of the present world, they have a spiritual and a supernatural character that transcends human institutions.

The ultimate issue of the present age will be the final victory of Christ over these powers and over Satan.[31]

The victory of Christ is past, continuing, and future. It is made real in the daily life of the believer in victory over the world. This is accomplished through the rule of the word of God and the appropriation of the benefits of Christ's victory on the cross. Paradoxically, in the case of the believer as in that of Christ, the power of God is known best in human weakness (2 Cor. 12: 9). This thought is what most inspires trust in God's word and his promises in situations when temptation knocks.

ENDNOTES

[1] C. Potok, *My Name is Asher Lev* (Harmondsworth: Penguin Books, 1972).

[2] As well as G. Aulén, and owing partly to his influence, scholars such as J. B. Green and M. D. Baker, H. Boersma, J. D. Weaver and N. T. Wright are attracted by the victory motif, as their recent publications show.

[3] Joshua 1: 15; 2 Samuel 23: 10; Psalm 20: 5–6; 69: 14; 106: 47; Jeremiah 23: 6.

[4] H. Blocher, '*Agnus Victor*. The Atonement as Victory and Vicarious Punishment', in J.G. Stackhouse, ed., *What does it mean to be Saved?* (Grand Rapids: Baker, 2002), 71.

[5] Revelation 5: 5; 6: 2, 19: 11 ff.; 1 Corinthians 15: 22–8.

[6] J. B. Green, M. D. Baker, *Rediscovering the Scandal of the Cross*, 122. Cf. Origen, *In Matt. xvi.8.*

[7] Ibid, 123, quoting Gregory of Nyssa, *The Great Catechism*, 24.

[8] For some critical comments, see H. Boersma, *Violence, Hospitality, and the Cross,* 191–192.

[9] H. Blocher, art. cit., 74.

[10] G. Aulén, *Christus Victor. An Historical Study of the Three Main Types of the Idea of the Atonement* (London: SPCK, 1931).

[11] Ibid, 144. Aulén referred also to Barth and Brunner in this respect, although the development of their thought, as he admits in the case of Brunner, can hardly support his advocacy of the *Christus victor* model. Cf. G. C. Berkouwer, *The Triumph of Grace in the Theology of Karl Barth* (Grand Rapids: Eerdmans, 1956), ch. V, on reconciliation in Barth.

[12] Ibid, 144–154.

[13] Cf. H. Boersma, *op. cit.,* 186–187, and H. Blocher, art. cit, 73 ff, for a criticism of Aulén's positions.

[14] S. Chalke, *The Lost Message of Jesus* (Grand Rapids: Zondervan, 2003), 187, 192.

[15] Ibid, 125 ff.

[16] R. A. Peterson, *Calvin and the Atonement* (Fearn: Christian Focus, 1999), ch. 5. *Cf.* H. Blocher, 'The Atonement in John Calvin's Theology', in *The Glory of the Atonement,* C. E. Hill, F. A. James, eds., 289–92.

[17] J. Calvin, *Institutes of the Christian Religion,* II. xvi. 11, J. T. McNeill, F. L. Battles, eds., (London: SCM, 1960), I, 517. *Cf.* Peterson, *op. cit.,* 76.

[18] J. Calvin, *Commentary on the Book of Isaiah* (Grand Rapids: Eerdmans, 1948) 129.

[19] C. Gunton, *The Actuality of the Atonement* (Edinburgh: T. & T. Clark, 1988), 57 ff. The divine victory is also a human one because of the obedience of the Messiah.

[20] J. Calvin, *Institutes*, I. xii. 2, 466.

[21] Cf. H. Blocher, art. cit., 78–86, to which I am indebted for this section.

[22] Ibid, 80,81.

[23] Ibid, 83.

[24] Ibid, 84.

[25] To say that Jesus 'does not want to be alone with his God. He is evidently afraid of him' as J. Moltmann does in *The Trinity and the Kingdom of God* (London: SCM, 1981), 76, seems purely speculative.

[26] Ibid, 85.

[27] C. A. M. Hall, *With the Spirit's Sword: The Drama of Spiritual Warfare in the Theology of John Calvin* (Richmond, Va: John Knox, 1970), 105, quoted by Peterson in *op. cit.*, 76.

[28] 1 Corinthians 15: 25; Philippians 2: 8–11.

[29] Romans 1: 16; 1 Corinthians 1: 18; Ephesians 1: 19–20; 2 Corinthians 3: 18; 13: 3–4; Romans 15: 13.

[30] Ephesians 1: 20–2; 4: 8; 1 Peter 3: 22.

[31] Revelation 5: 5, 12; 6: 2; 11: 15–18; 19: 11–20: 3.

10

Sacrifice

In a religious sense sacrifices are acts designed to change the relationship between God and man.[1] An offering set apart for the purpose is consecrated and presented in a ceremony that may involve death. In this way obstacles to communion and blessing are removed from an individual or a community. Sacrifice is different from other religious ceremonies, such as worship and prayer, in that it involves offering something to make things right with the divinity.[2]

Whether sacrifices began in homage and worship as gifts of communion, or as acts to appease God because of man's sin, is a point discussed by anthropologists. Sometimes the difference between the sacrifices of Cain and of Abel (Gen. 4) is considered in this light. In Israel's religion, however, there can be little doubt that the accent fell on the sinners' need to be restored to a right relationship with God. The destruction of the victim and the shedding of blood were of great importance.

Blood-sacrifice is repugnant to modern man and has long been the object of scorn on the part of critics of Christianity. Sometimes the immoderate language used to describe the cross has provoked this. H. G. Wells' mockery of William Cowper's hymn, 'There is a fountain filled with blood, drawn from Immanuel's veins', in his novel *Tono Bungay*, is a case in point.

If in the ancient world the idea of sacrifice was a fact of life it has become increasingly distant from every day experience. Modern man sees no break of order in the world, no need for revelation from God, or for a solution for removing man's 'guilty stains'. Sacrifice implies man's imperfection, and need for cleansing is anathema to humanism.[3] The idea of a *human* sacrifice, of someone dying for others on a cross, as well as being revolting, is the sign of a sick mind. Add to this the distaste for gratuitous violence and bloodshed, and it becomes even more difficult to talk about the cross as sacrifice. It seems to portray an irrational and sadistic god who, instead of healing human aggression, provides a justification for continuing acts of violence against others and fosters a victim mentality.[4] Because of these problems, some theologians, particularly in recent years, have sought 'non-sacrificial' or 'non-violent' interpretations of the cross, or have at least tried to downscale the blood factor in sacrifice as just one of many elements in the biblical materials.

Looking at things from another perspective, it is interesting to note that as street lights go out at dawn, wherever Christianity went, blood sacrifices ceased to be offered.

> The death of Christ, of this there can be no doubt, made an end to blood sacrifices in the history of religion…The instinct which led to them found its satisfaction and therefore its end in the death of Christ…His death had the value of a sacrificial death; for otherwise it would not have had the power to penetrate into that inner world out of which the blood sacrifices proceeded.[5]

This is a strong argument that early Christianity considered the death of Christ to be a sacrifice. Not only that, it put an end to any further need for sacrifice, because it was complete and final. As the sacrifice to end all sacrifices, the cross and its message suffered from its own success as the meaning of sacrificial acts was lost in the mists of time. The centrality of the sacrificial nature of the cross was maintained in the context of Christendom, but later when the gospel was increasingly marginalised in the western world, it became more and more implausible.

WHY SACRIFICES?

The notion of sacrifice is a central one for the Christian faith in two respects. Firstly, it is closely linked to the idea of revelation. If God is only truly known because he reveals himself to man, in a similar fashion he can only be properly approached through sacrifice. The great gulf between God and man, which makes revelation necessary, also exists in the other direction, from man to God. For there to be a relationship between God and man, one that corresponds to their situations, not only must man know who God is, but also how he can be approached.

Hebrews 11:6 talks about knowing God and seeking him: 'without faith it is impossible to please God, because anyone who comes to him must believe that he exists and that he rewards those who earnestly seek him.' Believing and seeking, knowing God by faith and approaching him go together. So the question is not simply one of knowing God, but also of how it is possible to come into his presence. Without the biblical revelation of God, no need will be felt for the biblical way of approaching him, which implies sacrifice. In ancient religions, sacrifice may have been an act of worship with a powerful mystical content, but in biblical revelation its context is the gulf that separates sinful man from a holy God.

> It is sacrifice for sin, and not a sacrifice in a vaguer sense. Its value is that somehow or other it neutralises sin as a power estranging man from God, and that in virtue of it God and man are reconciled...All sacrifice was sacrifice offered *to God*, and, whatever its value, it had that value *for him*. No man ever thought of offering sacrifice for the sake of a moral effect it was to produce on himself. If we say that the sacrifice of Christ was an atoning sacrifice, then the atonement must be an objective atonement. It is to God it is offered, and it is to God it makes a difference.[6]

The primary effect of sacrifice is that of putting away sin and restoring a situation of rightness necessary for true fellowship with God. God revealed to his people that this was the way into his presence.

Secondly, sacrifice is also a central concept for atonement theology in the way it works. Does it bridge the gulf between God and man because of its effect on God or its effect on man? If it is thought of as bearing upon God in the sense of 'objective atonement', as stated above, then its value must be considered in relation to who God is and what he requires. Its effectiveness will be deemed to provide satisfaction of what God demands in his law and justice. Sacrifice will be considered as enacting a punishment that removes the hostilities between God and his creatures, introducing them into a new relationship with him. The meaning of the sacrifice will be interpreted in legal terms.[7]

Sacrifice, however, can also look towards the effects it has on man, which is often the way it is seen today. There are generally two ways of presenting this, but the end product is more or less the same. Sacrifices, including the sacrifice of the cross, have an exemplary value. They are thought to be a gift offered in a free but costly way to God as an expression of devotion and obedience. The sacrifice of the cross is said to be an act of supreme love for God on the part of Christ and human beings can identify with this sort of love.[8] Such thinking plays down the horror of the cross by sublimating it in a demonstration of love. The second way of presenting the cross seeks to take its violent character more seriously. The message of the cross is that Jesus continues to love in the face of rejection and replies to violence with the almighty powerlessness of love. So animosity, injustice, and wickedness are countered by love, underlined by the innocence of the victim.[9] The collective forces of human evil are unmasked by Jesus' non-retaliatory stance.

If it remains possible from these two points of view to speak of Christ dying for us as God's gift of love—'God did not spare his own Son, but gave him up for us all' (Rom. 8: 31)—it is obvious that the 'for us' has little to do with Christ dying in the place of sinners to take away their sin. These perspectives want to establish as much distance as possible from the idea that Christ died for and because of sin. They consider that Christianity has too long indulged in this unhealthy scenario.

The problem with these propositions does not lie in their exemplary emphasis. The cross *is* God's supreme demonstration of love. It lies in their reduction of the meaning of the cross to one of its aspects and in the distance they take from the biblical teaching about sacrifice as a whole.

A BIBLICAL DEFINITION

Recent studies have tended to indicate the universality of sacrificial practice in religion.[10] The problem of beginning a study with general notions about sacrifice is that these notions are used to classify the biblical materials and the heart of the matter is obscured.

In biblical studies it has become current to indicate the variety of sacrifices particularly in the Old Testament in such a way that their essential unity of meaning is not always obvious.[11] Sacrifice is presented as a way of giving a gift, of finding cleansing and restoration, of establishing a contact between the world and the realm of the holy, or of dealing with violence.[12] The approach to the question is disjunctive and the dynamic behind various sacrificial practices too often fails to come to light.[13] Rather than starting with general ideas, even those that can be drawn from the biblical revelation, a more specific and less descriptive approach is more fruitful.

In a Christian context, the nature of sacrifice has rarely been better defined than by Augustine: 'Four things are to be considered in every sacrifice: to whom it is offered, by whom it is offered, what is offered, and for whom it is offered.' He is obviously echoing Hebrews 5: 1: 'Every priest is selected from among men and is appointed to represent them in matters related to God, to offer gifts and sacrifices for sin'. Priests who are called to sacrifice do so as representatives of others because of their solidarity with them. Their function is not to demonstrate something to those they are representing, be it forgiveness or reconciliation with God. Sacrifice is primarily an act that is related to God, a 'gift and sacrifice' presented to him. The offerings are specifically made for sin and do not in the first instance concern love for God, homage offered to him, or communion with him in the eating of a sacrificial meal. It is because of sin that sacrifices are necessary and their efficacy deals with the problem of sin.

The point of sacrifices is indicated in Hebrews 5: 3. The limitations of human priests, looking back to the Old Testament, is not forgotten: they 'have to offer sacrifices for their own sins, as well as the sins of the people.' Jesus fulfilled what former priests represented in an imperfect way. He did not take the function upon himself, but God appointed him as representative. He was 'designated by God to be high priest after the order of Melchizedek', and 'became the source of eternal salvation for all who obey him' (Heb. 5: 4, 8–10). Augustine commented: 'the one and true Mediator himself, reconciling us to God by the sacrifice of peace, remains one with him to whom he offered, makes those one in himself for whom he offered and is both the offerer and the offering.'[14] The dynamics of the sacrificial system become clear. The various types and figures contained in the Old Testament sacrificial system find their complete expression in Christ, the source of eternal, therefore perfect, salvation (Heb. 8: 5; 10: 1).

To these considerations must be added an element sometimes overlooked, perhaps because of the human cultic aspects of sacrifices. The rationale of sacrifice offered by men does not lie in human acts or needs, but in God himself. God it was who instituted the sacrificial system for his people. Jesus was 'faithful to the one who appointed him...as a son over God's house' (Heb. 3: 2, 6). The in-house rules for approaching God were established by him and Jesus followed them to the letter. If many sacrifices were legitimate because prescribed by God, their viability depended ultimately on the obedience of the incarnate Son himself, prefigured as he was by the high priests and their ritual acts. God instituted sacrifice and he alone could accomplish sacrificial obedience perfectly.

MANY SACRIFICES

Two fundamental differences exist between the Old Testament sacrifices and the sacrifice of Christ presented in the New Testament. Firstly, there was a multitude of sacrificial acts to be observed under the old covenant. This is related to their limited efficacy and their lack of finality. Secondly, in and of themselves, these sacrifices could never remove sin. Their function was to point to the one and only real sacrifice that would take away sin. If the Old Testament sacrificial system is established in the form of a legal code, this code could not have had an inner dynamic without the promise of God to care for the needs of his people.

These two differences focus on the major reason for the imperfection of the Old Testament system. They highlight that only God in person can forgive the sins of his people and save them. What is lacking in the Old Testament is Christ himself. The old covenant sacrifices are symbols, because their exterior form contains an inner spiritual meaning. They are also types, as their future reference is to the one anti-type, the person of the Saviour himself. The types of Judaism are substitutes for the final reality that has not yet appeared. Together the types and symbols set the tune for what the promised Saviour will be like, but in another key. The outward observance had an inner spiritual meaning and was not just an empty ceremony.

Two things are striking about the Old Testament sacrificial legislation, which is called 'Levitical' because the tribe of Levi were the priests, and the laws about sacrifice are found in the book of Leviticus. The sheer number of sacrifices offered is staggering. The Jewish historian Josephus records a census taken at the time of Nero. For the Passover feast in AD 65 nearly three million people were present at Jerusalem and the number of lambs slain could be estimated at over 250,000. The temple enclosure itself was large enough to hold twice the number of a very large football stadium.[15] Imagine the quantity of blood shed, the amount of oil used, the smell of blood and incense on this festive occasion! Only prime animals could be offered and, in modern parlance, the sacrificial system was a considerable drain on the economy. Such excess demonstrated the total demand of God for holiness and the greatness of the need for purification. It is a stark contrast with the 'one sacrifice' of Christ and its effectiveness for covering all sin.

The second aspect of the Levitical legislation is the variety of sacrifices and offerings, which were offered on all sorts of occasions.[16] Repentance for sin and purification, commemorative feasts, national crises, personal consecration, family feasts, the covenant renewal, the great day of atonement for the purification of the people—rare were the aspects of personal or public life in Israel that went unmarked by some sort of offering. The regular sacrifices included the offering of cereals, the meal offering, the drink offering, and various animal offerings. The latter were most important and included the burnt offering, the peace offering, the sin offering, and the guilt or trespass offering.

Precise procedures were laid down to regulate the way sacrifices were to be made. The offerer 'drew near'—a word that became a synonym for sacrifice—having selected an animal to bring to the altar. Then came the laying on of hands by applying pressure on the head of the animal, representing substitution.[17] After the offerer had slain the animal, the priest collected its blood, which was sprinkled and put on the horns of the altar of incense, the rest being poured at the altar. Finally, parts of the animal were burned on the altar, or the whole animal in the case of burnt offering, and parts of the remainder were given to the priest or eaten by the worshippers in a fellowship meal. Sacrifice implied substitution, and was accompanied by confession and prayer. 'What distinguishes sacrifice from all other things, however sacred these may be, is that part or the whole of its substance comes upon the altar. Without the altar there would be no sacrifice…for Jehovah dwells in the altar.'[18] The significance of sacrificial acts is a subject of discussion, although the sin and trespass offerings made *for* communion with God had precedence over those made *in* communion with God, such as the burnt and the peace offerings.

The central text on this subject is Leviticus 17: 11, which expresses a general principle, even if it is in incidental fashion: 'The life of a creature is in the blood, and I have given it to you to make atonement for yourselves on the altar; the blood that makes atonement for one's life.' Three important truths about sacrifice are present here.[19] Blood is a symbol of life (Dt: 12: 23) because life flows out when blood is shed. The life of the sacrificed animal is given for the life of the one who sacrifices. This means that blood is shed for a condemned life. Life is offered for life by way of substitution, the innocent for the guilty. The offerer is to 'lay his hand on the head of the burnt offering and it will be accepted on his behalf to make atonement for him' (Lev 1: 4). Finally, God has instituted sacrifice on the altar to make atonement for sin and guilt. The life of an animal is in no way equivalent to the life of a man, but the procedure serves to underline the seriousness of sin and the need for sacrifice to deal with it. It emphasises God's freedom to forgive those who draw near to him for sin to be removed and fellowship to be restored.

LOOKING BACKWARDS AT SACRIFICE

From an historical perspective it is natural to consider the Old Testament sacrifices as scrolling forward to Christ and fulfilment. The epistle to the Hebrews, however, looks at it from the angle of the finality, perfection, and effectiveness of Christ's sacrifice.

The Levitical system is a copy of the final reality: 'the copies of the heavenly things were purified with these sacrifices, but the heavenly things themselves with better sacrifices than these' (Heb. 9: 23). The blood of Christ was necessary for heavenly purification and the Old Testament sacrifices were but earthly shadows of this final reality. This means that 'Christ's own sacrifice was the great exemplar after which the levitical sacrifices were patterned.'[20] The new order established by Christ was not an earthly one (v. 10). He 'went through a greater and more perfect tabernacle that is not man-made...not with the blood of goats and calves...he entered the most holy place once for all by his own blood, having obtained eternal redemption' (v. 11–14). Christ did 'not enter a man-made sanctuary that was only a copy of the true one; he entered heaven itself, now to appear in God's presence...once at the end of the ages to do away with sin by the sacrifice of himself...Christ was sacrificed once to take away the sins of many people' (v. 24–8).

In other words, we do not understand the sacrifice of the cross through the Old Testament economy, but vice versa. The Jewish pre-figurations were just copies and modelled along similar lines to the great and final reality. 'The necessity of the blood offerings of the Levitical economy arose from the fact that the exemplar after which they were fashioned was a blood offering, the transcendent blood offering by which the heavenly things were purified.'[21] In a sense, to look at things from the angle of historical development is to interpret them back to front. The unique person of Christ and the nature of his work are the key to understanding the Old Testament types. Christ's purpose in coming into the world was to live a holy life and die on behalf of others for their sin. The main purpose of the old covenant legislation was to present purity in the service of God and to cover sins by sacrifice.

In Christ the two elements of sacrificial worship, *in and for* communion with God were coordinates. This was uniquely so in his person, because he was without sin and perfectly obedient, the *sine qua non* of communion with God. Because of this he could offer himself as sacrifice for others and for their reconciliation with God. In sinful men the sacrifice for communion must precede worship and service in communion with God. Both are founded on the completed work of Christ, promised and represented in an earthly way in the Old Testament and fulfilled in their spiritual 'heavenly' meaning in the New Testament.

From this perspective, the Levitical practices take on their full meaning. The foundation of Israel's life was the Passover and their liberation from Egypt, celebrated each year. It represented the birth of Israel at the beginning of the year (Exod. 12: 2). God is present as Judge in the Passover, bringing death, but he is also the Saviour who protects his people through the sign of blood (Exod. 12: 11–13). God calls them into the desert and consecrates them by a unique fellowship offering that establishes his covenant with them (Exod. 24; Ps. 50: 5). The covenant is sealed by sacrifice and the sprinkling of blood on the people (Exod. 24: 5–8). But Jesus is the ultimate Passover lamb, the one who died on the cross at the time the Passover lambs were being sacrificed in the temple.[22] He is presented as 'the lamb of God who takes away the sin of the world' (John 1: 29, 36).[23] He lays down his life for his friends and sets himself apart for them (John 15: 13, 17: 19). He is adored as the one who has paid the price in blood for the redeemed. (Rev. 5: 6–12; 12: 11) The sacrifice marks the birth of the new people of God, whose consciences are made pure by the sprinkling of blood (Heb. 9: 19; 10: 22; 12: 24; 1 Pet. 1: 2).

The other great moment in Israel's cultic year was the Day of Atonement (Lev. 16). It spoke of a universal need for the removal of sin from the people, the priests, and even the sanctuary itself. Hebrews 9–10 is a commentary on how this day prefigured the work of Christ. In the ritual, one male goat was sacrificed and another, the scapegoat, bore the confession of the sins of the people. Together these two animals symbolised sacrifice for the expiation of sin and its removal from among the people. The high point of the ceremony was the entry of the high priest into the holy of holies with the blood of the sacrifice and the sprinkling of the mercy seat. His emergence from within the veil signified the collective pardon of the people. Then the priest 'laid both hands on the head of the live goat and confessed over it all the wickedness and rebellion of the Israelites, all their sins, and put them on the goat's head.' After this the scapegoat was sent away into the wilderness— 'the goat will carry on itself all their sins to a solitary place' (Lev. 16: 21–2).

What can this mean? It has been said that this is not a sacrificial act or a sin offering as the goat goes free.[24] An older explanation perhaps hits the mark: 'The live goat "let go" was every year a remover of the sins which yet were never really removed in the sense of being blotted out—only deposited and reserved until he came "whom God presented as a sacrifice of atonement...

because in his forbearance he had left the sins committed beforehand unpunished" (Rom. 3: 25).'[25] Considered in this light, the scapegoat was a most explicit sin offering, as part of the global symbolism of atonement. The sin, however, was only removed from view, not blotted out or purged: this could only be accomplished by Christ. Perhaps the later rabbinic practice of pushing the goat over a rocky cliff to kill it betrayed a desire to complete the symbolism, although this was impossible other than by divine action.

The cross of Christ fulfilled the Day of Atonement in its reference to God's people: 'Jesus Christ the righteous one is the atoning sacrifice not only for our sins, but also for the sins of the whole world' (1 John 2: 2). The actual atonement for sins, those committed before and after Christ's death, was only accomplished at the cross. 'The Lord has laid on him the iniquity of us all' (Isa. 53: 6). The scapegoat's 'removal' was an imperfect picture of the expiation of sin, as was the entry of the high priest into the holy place: 'The Holy Spirit was showing by this that the way into the Most Holy Place had not yet been disclosed as long as the first tabernacle was still standing' (Heb. 9: 8). Christ entered heaven once for all to obtain forgiveness for his people.

Looking backwards at the sacrificial system, the author of Hebrews says: 'the law was only a shadow of the good things that are coming, not the realities themselves. For this reason it can never, by the same sacrifices repeated endlessly year after year, make perfect those who draw near to worship' (Heb. 10: 1, 4, 11, 26). They could never take away sins. Only the divine scapegoat could.

THE ACCOMPLISHED SACRIFICE

'One could hardly have thought it possible that anyone who had read the Gospels with their best interpreters, the authors of the Epistles, should ever have entertained a doubt whether the death of Christ was a real sacrifice.'[26] One might think that was written yesterday, but no, it dates from 250 years ago.

That the death of Christ was not a real sacrifice is current fare. The cross, so it is said, was not an altar, Christ was not a victim, and sacrifices do not rise from the dead. These three statements are contrary to Hebrews 13: 9–16. The cross is the altar from which the body and blood of Christ are distributed as nourishment (v. 10; cf. John 6), Christ was a sacrificial victim outside the city gate (v. 12) and he became the king of an enduring city (v. 14).

In the New Testament, sacrificial language is applied unremittingly to Christ and his work, by himself and his witnesses. The Scriptures constantly represent Christ's dying as the means for the salvation of his people, and thus dying as a sacrifice. Christ dealt with sin in the same way as the Jewish sacrifices did.[27] He came into the world as the heavenly template of salvation by sacrifice and, having opened the way to God by the anticipated sacrifice, returned to heaven with the result of his completed work (1 Pet. 1: 21). But the template had to leave its impression on history and to do this Christ had to learn obedience (Heb. 5: 8), be made perfect through suffering (Heb. 9: 26), and offer himself 'without blemish' to God (Heb. 9: 14). The types and the symbols had to become realities.

Nowhere is this more true than when we read of Christ shedding his blood for the remission of sin. This means Christ *died* for sinners because of sin. 'Blood in its normal state…does not expiate. It expiates as blood that has passed through the crisis of death and is therefore fit to be the exponent of death.'[28] Not all references to blood in the New Testament concern sacrifice,[29] but several definitely do:

- 'God presented him as a sacrifice of atonement through faith in his blood' (Rom. 3: 25), which explains that 'we have been justified by his blood…reconciled through the death of his son' (Rom. 5: 9–10).
- 'Christ our Passover lamb has been sacrificed…' (1 Cor. 5: 7).[30]
- 'You were redeemed…with the precious blood of Christ, a lamb without blemish' (1 Pet. 1: 19, cf. 1: 2).
- '…the blood of Jesus his Son purifies us from all sin.' (1 John 1: 7).
- 'You have come to Jesus the mediator of the new covenant, and to the sprinkling of blood that speaks a better word than the blood of Abel' (Heb. 12: 24).[31]

The concept of the sacrificial death of Christ is an unavoidable and central part of the apostle Paul's gospel message. It lies behind the instances where he affirms that Christ 'died for us' or 'gave himself up for our sins': 'God made him who knew no sin to be sin for us' (2 Cor. 5: 21).[32] This should come as no surprise. Paul's gospel tallies with Jesus' own witness to his sacrificial ministry: 'The Son of Man came to serve and to give his life as a ransom for many' (Mark 10: 45; Matt. 20: 28). The Father loved him because he laid down his life (John 10: 11–18). His blood is the 'blood of the covenant, poured out for many' (Mark 14: 24; Matt. 26: 28).

CONCLUSION

It is true that the biblical language of sacrifice is light years away from modern world-views. The problem is not one of the biblical evidence for the cross as sacrificial, which is clear enough, it is an apologetic one. In an age that admires total self-sacrifice with no strings attached as an expression of hospitality, is it possible to see the cross of Christ other than as a divine transaction?

The cross is not, in the first instance, the personal victory of Christ or an example of great love, even if it is both of these. It is primarily *God's* way of salvation and *his* self-giving in the interest of sinful human beings. 'Sin is condemned by God in sending Christ in our nature and as a sacrifice for sin.'[33] In a real sense it is *God alone* who makes the sacrifice, who provides for sin, who comes in the person of the Son, who covers guilt as if it had never been. The cross is the *self substitution* of God for sin.[34] God is not a bloodthirsty, revengeful, angry deity. On the contrary:

> In the New Testament the cross of Christ is conceived as the self-offering of God. It is God who does it, it is God himself who suffers, it is God who takes the burden on himself…Hence the real revelation and the real atonement are closely connected with each other; indeed rightly understood, they are one. The God of love, the One who loves us despite everything, can only be known as he really is in this aspect of his love. Apart from this fact of atonement, he is not the loving God at all.[35]

No love is greater than the self-giving love of God revealed in Christ: 'greater love has no one than this, that he lay down his life for his friends' (John 15: 13). That wonderful demonstration of love was unfolded as God's gift to sinners in the life and death of Christ: 'He did not spare his own Son, but gave him up for us all' (Rom. 8: 32).

What had God to gain by it?—nothing. What had we to gain by it?—everything. That is the sign of ultimate love.

ENDNOTES

[1] Sacrifices (the word *zebach* refers to the slaughtered animal) belong to the general category of offerings (*qorban*—that which is brought near) or 'gifts of holiness' (*mattenoth qodesh*). An offering can also have the sense of present (*minchah*).

[2] 'Every sacrifice is a holy gift, but not every holy gift is a sacrifice'; 'there is worship in sacrifice, but worship by no means constitutes the whole of sacrifice.' G. Vos, *Biblical Theology*, 157 f.

[3] E. Brunner, *The Mediator*, 484f, says that rationalism is the reason why sacrifice has disappeared completely from the modern world-view.

[4] K. J. Vanhoozer, 'The Atonement in Postmodernity', in *The Glory of the Atonement*, eds. C. E. Hill, F. A. James, 382 ff.

[5] A. von Harnack, *What is Christianity* (1901) 157 ff, quoted by B. B. Warfield, 'Christ our Sacrifice', *Works* II, 435.

[6] J. Denney, *The Christian Doctrine of Reconciliation*, 29 f.

[7] As developed in the following chapter.

[8] Cf. P. S. Fiddes, *The Christian Idea of Atonement* (London: Darton, Longman, Todd, 1989), ch. 4. The author calls this a slippage from what the New Testament writers mean by 'sin offering'.

[9] This is often related to the scapegoat theme. *Cf.* M. Winter, *The Atonement*, 80–6, K.J. Vanhoozer, art. cit, 383–90.

[10] Including the study edited by M. Neusch, *Le sacrifice dans les religions* (Paris: Beauchesne, 1994).

[11] Cf. The influential work of R. de Vaux, *Ancient Israel*, II, (New York: McGraw-Hill, 1965), ch. 10.

[12] J. Goldingay, 'Old Testament Sacrifice and the Death of Christ' in *Atonement Today*, ch. 1, M. Winter, *op. cit.*, 12ff.

[13] As has been pointed out by H. Blocher in his remarks about *Atonement Today* in 'The sacrifice of Jesus Christ: the Current Theological Situation', *European Journal of Theology* 8:1 (1999).

[14] Augustine, *On the Trinity*, IV.14.19.

[15] Josephus, *Wars*, VI, quoted by A. Edersheim in *The Temple. Its Ministry and Services at the Time of Christ*, 183.

[16] Space forbids a detailed description, but the reader can refer to the description given by J. Stott, *The Cross of Christ* (Leicester: IVP, 1986), ch. 6.

[17] The question of vicarious substitution will be discussed in the next chapter.

[18] G. Vos, *op. cit.*, 157.

[19] Cf. J. Stott, *op. cit.*, and E. Nicole, 'Atonement in the Pentateuch' in *The Glory of the Atonement*, 35–50.

[20] J. Murray, *Redemption Accomplished and Applied*, 14 ff.

[21] Ibid., 15.

[22] Cf. J. Jeremias, *The Eucharistic Words of Jesus* (London: SCM, 1966), 41–61.

[23] Cf. 1 John 3: 5. L. Morris, *The Cross in the New Testament* (Grand Rapids: Eerdmans, 1965), 175, suggests that this is a reference to the sacrificial system as a whole and its general purpose, not to any particular ceremony. J.R. Michaels, 'Atonement in John's Gospels and Epistles' in *The Glory of the Atonement*, eds. C.E. Hill, F.A. James, 107 f. takes 'lamb' to be a symbol of purity and the taking away of sin to refer to the victory of Christ.

[24] P. S. Fiddes, *op. cit.*, 74.

[25] A. Edersheim, *op. cit.*, 282.

[26] W. Warburton, *The Divine Legislation of Moses*, IX. Ch.2, quoted by Warfield, art. cit, 402.

[27] A. A. Hodge, *The Atonement*, ch. VIII.

[28] G. Vos, *op. cit.*, 164.

[29] For example, Romans 5: 9, Colossians 1: 20, Ephesians 2: 13, 16. *Cf.* on this subject L. Morris, *The Apostolic Preaching of the Cross* (London: Tyndale Press, 1965), 121 ff.

[30] In this context the Lord's supper as sacrificial meal of the new covenant in 1 Corinthains 11: 17–34 can also be referred to. *Cf.* H. Ridderbos, *Paul. An Outline of His Theology* (Grand Rapids: Eerdmans, 1975), 216–18.

[31] Cf. also Hebrews 9: 12, 14, 26; 10: 12, 19; 11: 4; 13: 11 f. In particular Hebrews links the priest and the sacrifice in the same person, as in Ephesians 5: 2 and 1: 7.

[32] 1 Corinthians 15: 3; 2 Corinthians 14: 15; Romans 5: 6, 8; 14: 15; 1 Thessalonians 5: 10; Galatians 1: 4; 2: 20 etc. The idea of substitution is present in all these cases.

[33] J. Denney, *op. cit.*, 249.

[34] J. Stott, *op. cit.*, ch. 6.

[35] E. Brunner, *op. cit.*, 482, 488.

11

Penalty

A player commits a foul in the box and the referee points to the spot. He awards a penalty according to the laws of the game; his decision is fair because a player has committed an offence. The penalty given to the other team pays for the foul. This illustrates how rights are wronged in any situation where the law is upheld. When wrong is done, the law is applied, the penalty is paid, and the situation is righted.

This is the way God deals with sin against his law. For him to overlook sin would be a denial of his righteousness. Wrong would go unpunished and the situation would never be righted. God sets things straight as far as man's sin and its consequences are concerned by the sacrifice of the cross. Christ died to pay the penalty for sin according to God's standards of justice. The outcome reconciles God and man.

The sacrifice of the cross is penal, substitutionary, and vicarious. It is penal because Christ suffers the punishment of death according to the requirement of God's law; substitutionary in that Christ, who has no call to suffer, dies in the place of sinners; and it is vicarious in that he dies on their behalf. Putting these elements together, it can be said that through the cross God makes atonement by a penal substitutionary sacrifice. In fact the language of sacrifice nearly always carries with it the idea of substitution and the reason for substitution is the punishment of sin.[1]

The point of contention lies in the *penal* aspect of the sacrifice. The idea that Jesus might die for sinners out of perfect love is not too hard to swallow, but that he should have to die as a punishment for sins committed by others and on their behalf seems to be the height of arbitrariness and injustice—a total contradiction of God's moral nature. It is accused of being 'the religious absurdity of a moral law which God can and must satisfy by punishing the innocent in the place of the guilty.'[2]

Despite the abuse to which it is subjected, the penal substitutionary theory of the cross as atonement for sin remains the only one that offers anything like a coherent explanation of why the death of Christ was necessary to satisfy the demands of divine love and justice, to meet the precise needs of sinful human beings, and to procure a sure and certain salvation on their behalf. Nor is it an invention of the legalistic rationalism of scholastic protestantism—its pedigree can be traced to the likes of Tertullian, Athanasius, and Augustine, who also spoke of the penal aspect of the atonement.[3]

The question of what it means to say that Christ paid the penalty for sin and whether the New Testament teaches penal substitution is therefore unavoidable.

PENAL SUBSTITUTION, A DOCTRINAL MODEL

Luther and Calvin adopted Anselm's idea that the sacrifice of the cross satisfied the demands of God in dealing with the offence of sin. They redefined it in relation to God's law, holiness, and judgment against sin. Punitive justice requires sacrifice and makes the office of a mediator necessary. These concepts, which have been termed narrow, can only be properly understood in the light of the covenantal relationship between God and man.

The Biblical language concerning sacrifice is often metaphorical and symbolic, but this does not mean it is mythical.[4] Nor is the language of penal substitution parabolic, using natural language to describe spiritual realities, with only a loose connection to the reality it describes. The language of penal substitution is used as a theological model to present a downscaled picture of what the cross really meant. It describes the cross in a way that is detailed, true to type, and useful, just like the Airbus in the travel agent's window gives an idea of the plane you might travel in. However, the model remains a model. Just as looking at a model Airbus is not the same as the experience of flying, the doctrine falls short of the awful reality experienced in the enactment of penal substitution by God the Father and his Son. Despite this fact, the model serves its purpose. A model Airbus shows that you will not be flying in a Boeing or a Fokker and in the same way, the reality of the cross cannot be properly represented by other models such as the exemplary model.

The doctrine of penal substitution is therefore called an *analogical model* in which the picture presented corresponds in objective but limited fashion to the given reality.[5] The doctrine of penal vicarious substitution, like any other doctrine, is an approximate model that must be verified by lining it up with Scripture. The paradoxical nature of penal substitution is that it joins, in one divine act, expressions of justice and love, wrath and approbation, judgment and grace, and death and life. Because God is at work in these various respects, the mechanics of his acts escape even the most detailed explanations. Penal substitution does not pretend to explain the *how,* but only the *fact* of atonement. Mystery surrounds atonement, as all the works of God.

Substitution is the basic model for the atonement presented by sacrifice. It is the act of taking the place of, acting for, and fulfilling the duties of another, as happens in a football game when one player comes on and plays in another's place. In the act of sacrifice, the victim takes the place of the ones who present the offering and their liabilities are transferred to it. When the word *penal* is added to *substitute* the nature of the substitution is made more precise. The model of one who takes the place of another is qualified by indicating that the replacement has the negative legal connotations of judgment undergone.

Penal substitution means that divine justice punishes sin in the substitute, which is the object of judgment. It means that Christ acted for others in the sense of their liability to judgment, punishment, and retribution. Penal substitution wipes away sin, removes God's reason for anger against it, and lays the basis for a new relationship beyond condemnation and death. The result is reconciliation, which works both ways. We are reconciled to God and God to us.[6] It takes two parties to have a disagreement and two parties to make peace!

'The vicarious penal suffering, which is rightly described as the vicarious suffering of the wrath of God at sin, rests on the fellowship that Jesus Christ accepted with us sinners and with our fate as such. This link is the basis on which the death of Jesus can count as expiation for us.'[7]

SUBSTITUTION BUT NO PENALTY?

Attempts have been made to present the death of Christ as substitution or representation, but without legal or penal connotations. Substitution, it is true, can have a variety of meanings other than the legal one, because a substitute can act in various ways and for different reasons. Is the biblical sense of substitution a legal and penal one? Did Jesus die in a legal way and was his death a punishment?

The vicarious principle of sacrifice described as one life covering another in Leviticus 17: 11 could have three possible meanings when it is applied to the death of the cross.[8] Firstly, Christ could be thought to substitute his perfect life of service for ours as a gift offered to God, but his sacrifice has nothing to do with suffering and punishment for sin.[9] Secondly, the cross indicates how God reckons with sin, but does not punish it. He accepts the death of Christ as a positive offering in recognition of wrong done. The cross is a confession of sin that expresses repentance for humanity and new life in relation to God.[10] Thirdly, the sacrifice of the cross is presented as death for death and forfeit for forfeit. It pays the debt for sin contracted by man because Christ accepted to be punished in the place of sinners. The debt was fully paid by his death.

There are splinters of truth in the first two positions. The first, however, bypasses the question of the wrath and judgment of God. It makes Christ into an 'alongside Saviour' who experiences suffering with men and brings a holy presence into human experience. This does not save from death as the result of sin. The second proposition supposes that confession of sin and repentance is what is needed for forgiveness, which is not the case. Can recognition of wrong done change the situation by doing away with it? Furthermore, can repentance be effective for others' sins? The answer is negative in both cases. Only the third position does justice to substitution in the fullest sense.

In the 19th century the second theory, that of 'vicarious repentance', became influential as a third way between the alternatives of saying Jesus substituted either his perfect life or his sinless death in the interest of sinners. Jesus made a confession for humanity and by 'coming clean' obtained forgiveness without a transfer of sin.[11] Variations on the theme of sacrifice without penalty continue to have a pulling power, including for theologians in the neo-evangelical camp, who are some of the most vocal opponents of penal substitution. There is a serious attempt to find a basis for this view in Scripture, to redefine the sacrifice of Christ as a demonstration of love in sharing human misery and as a vicarious turning from the way of sin by confession to God. From this point of view, the cross involves incarnational identification and not penal substitution. While it is recognised that sacrifice includes legal and cultic aspects, the legal is invariably played down in favour of the cultic.

Because of the new-found popularity of this idea, it is not superfluous to look at some of its basic lines of thought.

ATONEMENT TODAY?

Recent criticisms of penal substitutionary sacrifice, even among those who call themselves evangelicals, tend to echo traditional objections, which can be reduced to a short-list of five or six.[12] The model of penal substitution is deemed unacceptable by its detractors because it is said to be:

- *objective*, and not subjective in a way that involves us directly and personally;
- *unethical*, as sin and guilt are personal and non transferable;
- *un-trinitarian*, as it sets the Father against the Son and implies tri-theistic divisions in God;
- *self-contradictory*, since God the Father cannot act for and against Christ at the same time;
- *a wrong interpretation of the biblical texts* that distorts their meaning by imposing foreign legal ideas on them.

Although nearly all these criticisms of penal substitution are still current, the final one is of prime importance. Its various aspects are presented in *Atonement Today* (1995), a challenging book, as it comes from what is thought to be an 'evangelical' stable. It shows how modern academic evangelicalism is evolving and how it shies away from the doctrine of penal substitution.[13]

The first criticism of penal substitution is that the penal view of the cross is not adequate as it is not intelligible any more. People today, it is claimed, are not worried about sin, but about suffering. It is not feasible in the present climate to speak of suffering in relation to sin because human suffering comes from twists of fate. Human experience is not related in any meaningful way to sin and righteousness. The problem for people is alienation and meaninglessness. Our contemporaries are not interested in the solution of penal substitution, because they are not even aware of the problem.[14] Furthermore, the wrath of God and punishment are offensive to the modern mind.

It is hard to disagree with this analysis. Christian preaching finds itself in difficulty when God's holiness and law, judgment against sin, and eternal punishment must be mentioned. Modern individualism has led to a break down of the belief in universal moral law, and when moral law goes down in the cosmic computer, judicial law inevitably follows suit. When the link between moral right and wrong, and judicial consequences, is weakened on the social level, it is difficult to speak about judgment for moral wrongs. It is even more impossible to understand how any man could undergo penal consequences for the moral wrongs of others. The problem appears to be correctly stated, but is the right answer to jettison penal substitutionary atonement, particularly if that is the teaching of Scripture?

Concerning the interpretation of the biblical texts about sacrifice and the atonement, the argument in *Atonement Today* is clear. The New Testament language is metaphorical, which implies a great diversity of ways of speaking of Christ's death and a comparable diversity in understanding it. The legal metaphor, which is one among many for describing the death of Jesus, is not necessarily the central one in Scripture and should not be separated from others in such a way that it exercises control over the whole. The biblical metaphors for the death of Christ do not come together in one precise theory of the atonement.[15] If Jesus' death was punitive, it is argued, it was not to satisfy divine justice, but human justice. Moreover, if Jesus died a cursed death, his death was not a sacrifice because he was killed by an act of violence, by the shedding of blood. Sacrifice does not require cruelty or violence. It was the way in which Jesus 'absorbed' the power of evil to bring peace into the world.[16] So if Jesus' death can be called sacrificial, it has little to do with divine retributive justice. On the exegetical level, penal substitution is not adequate to explain what happened at Golgotha—it is only one of many dimensions involved in the cross.

What is the meaning of substitution, sin, and guilt from this point of view? Paul, it is stated, is taken with the results of Christ's work, and like the rest of the New Testament is more concerned with the outcome of salvation than with its cause.[17] The traditional doctrine of atonement by penal substitution, on the other hand, implies two ideas—punishment inflicted from the outside and a form of logic in which punishment corresponds to sin. In the New Testament some texts superficially seem to support this point of view.[18] But penal retribution, we are told, is an unlikely interpretation for them. If God does take sin seriously and if Christ experienced divine judgment on our behalf, to speak of Christ suffering vicariously or undergoing the penalty for sins is to go further than Scripture allows. Paul has more than one framework for speaking about the death of Christ. The symbolism of sacrifice does not fit in with retribution.

According to *Atonement Today* it is questionable whether Scripture presents sacrifice as propitiating God's wrath.[19] The language of atonement, propitiation, and expiation does not come together in the New Testament in such a way as to give a unified picture of the meaning of the cross. Sin pollutes and stains; sacrifice deals with stain and repulsiveness. The sinner can identify with the sacrificial victim as sin is transferred to the animal and destroyed through death. God has made it possible for our stain to be dealt with. Sacrifice is not something humans do for God, but something God does for humans in removing the stain of sin. The basic language of sacrifice is not that of retribution but of *participation*. Paul does not imply that Christ bore the penalty of divine justice for our sins, an interpretation that presses the legal metaphor too far. Rather, Christ experienced the destructive consequences of sin, which is different from undergoing punishment.

Sin is not judged from outside. When Paul speaks of condemnation and salvation he is speaking about relationships. Christ bore and destroyed the effects of man's separated relation with God by absorbing and exhausting sin. The cross is not primarily a case of legal dealings, but one of relation, and Christ in his death absorbs the mass of human condemnation.

Guilt and debt are not like fines incurred by one person and paid by another.[20] The cross is not the story of legal imputation, but of Christ's identification with us. Christ did not remove sin as punishment through payment, but when he died he removed *sinful humanity* and replaced it with new humanity. The 'for us' of the cross does not mean Christ was a substitute dying instead of us, although it can include this. What Christ did for us and without us concerns the goal of his suffering, which includes union with Christ and the restoration of true human identity.

To summarize: in *Atonement Today*, as in much current theology, the joining together of the past perspectives of the biblical texts and those of the present is achieved via the claim that there is no unified biblical teaching about sin, its punishment, and the cross. This permits a selection of what seems adequate in the text in the light of present needs. Sin is seen in a personalistic way and sacrifice is not related to penal guilt, but as the dissolution of alienation and meaninglessness. The sacrifice of Christ removes the barrier separating us from a restored humanity.

A PRECISE SUBSTITUTION

Was the specific purpose of the substitution of Christ for sinners a penal one? Did Christ bear the anger of God against sin and die because of divine judgment? This is the heart of the matter. 'The penal substitution of Christ is the vital centre of the atonement, the linchpin without which everything else loses its foundation and flies off the handle, so to speak.'[21]

A text often referred to in discussions about penal substitution is 1 Peter 2: 24, where we read that Christ 'bore our sins in his body on the tree'. How was this 'bearing' of sin accomplished? It can hardly be claimed that Christ absorbed sins, and died with them, like a sponge sucks up water and makes it disappear. Sin is spiritual not material. The only way he could have borne sins in a plain sense, was by accepting the judgment against sin and assuming its consequence—death.

This is more evident when it is considered that the apostle is referring here to the suffering servant of Isaiah 53: 4–5:

> Surely he has borne our infirmities
> and carried our sorrows,
> yet we considered him stricken by God,
> smitten by him and afflicted.
> But he was pierced for our transgressions,
> he was bruised for our iniquities;
> The punishment that brought us peace
> was on him,
> and by his wounds we are healed.

The following points need to be underlined to do justice to the text:

- the bearing of sin indicates figuratively that sins are taken away and pardoned;
- the way sins were borne was by the servant being bruised, smitten, and afflicted;
- the nature of sin bearing was a punishment;
- the punishment was of divine origin;
- it was accomplished for others;
- the suffering of the victim resulted in healing.

In the subsequent verses of Isaiah 53, we also read that suffering was accepted by the Servant in a voluntary way (v. 6), that it was sacrificial suffering (v. 7), and that it made full atonement for sin according to the will of God (v. 10–11). In all, this passage 'makes twelve distinct and explicit statements that the Servant suffers the penalty of other men's sins: not only vicarious suffering, but penal substitution, is the plain meaning of its fourth, fifth and sixth verses.'[22]

Prick the skin of the New Testament writers and the blood of Isaiah 53 comes out. The penal nature of the substitution can be considered from two angles—either that of the penalty laid on the redeemer or of the acquittal that secures the prisoner's release. Some examples serve to illustrate the point.

God made Christ 'who had no sin, to be sin for us', indicating that the judgment was laid on him; the result was that sins are no longer 'counted against' men (2 Cor. 5: 21, 19). How can sins be 'counted' as the reason for accusation other than in the legal sense?

To be 'reconciled to God through the death of the Son' is to be 'saved from God's wrath through him' (Rom. 5: 9–10). This is so because the Son has borne the wrath of God in his death in such as a way that it can no longer reach those for whom Christ died.

Being redeemed from 'the curse of the law' is not only a possibility but a reality, because Christ has been cursed by hanging on the tree (Gal. 3: 13). The death of Christ was the legal consequence of his standing in the place of sinners to redeem them.

The believer is alive to Christ, because his sins have been forgiven and cancelled out by being nailed to the cross (Col. 2: 13–15). The death of Christ is the cause of forgiveness, because the accusation of the law has been abolished.

As a substitute for sinners, Christ is more than just a representative, he is the mediator between God and man, who gave himself as a ransom, who paid the legal debt for others (1 Tim. 2: 5).

In Romans 8: 32 Paul says 'God did not *spare* his own Son but *gave him up* for us all.' The terms 'sparing' and 'giving up' have a technical sense in Scripture. The first is sacrificial and the second is legal. The expression 'not sparing' is used in the Old Testament to describe the sacrifice of Isaac (Gen. 22: 12). In Acts 2: 23 we read that Christ was 'given over' to condemnation and death by God's decision and foreknowledge. Romans 8: 32 tells us that God sent his own Son to be a sin offering. It is not forcing the text to see that Christ's death as a sacrifice was also a legal act, divinely ordained, and that Christ was a substitute for others. Legal and sacrificial language do come together to describe the cross as a penal substitution.[23]

In Romans 3: 24–6 penal and sacrificial expressions are also used in a complementary way. Christ is 'presented as a sacrifice of atonement' and he is also said to be a demonstration of divine justice in God's dealing with sin through the cross. God shows that he is 'just and the one who justifies those who have faith in Jesus'. God is 'just', because his justice against sin has been executed in a righteous sentence. He is 'justifier' because there can no longer be any condemnation against those who believe, because their sins have died the death in the death of Christ.

Consideration of these passages alone is sufficient to show that the death Christ died was of a penal nature, under the conditions of God's law. It was also death in the sense of substitution, as Christ died 'for' sinners, being condemned in their place. It was a sacrificial act in which sin was taken away, once and for all. The language of sacrifice and of the law court come together in the New Testament in a precise way to show what was necessary for salvation.

PAYING THE PRICE OF SIN

How was it possible for Christ to bear the sins of others? Was God the Father ever angry against Christ? These questions have long been a stumbling block as far as the doctrine of penal substitution is concerned.

How would it be possible for God to transfer sin, which is rebellion and hatred against God, from sinners to Christ and for him to die with this sin on the cross? The transfer itself seems to be highly unlikely because sin is a spiritual quality and not like money that can be shifted from one account to another. Can a person's sins be counted up, so that Christ bears every one?

Sin can be spoken of in three different respects, and it is important to know exactly which is involved when it is said that Christ 'bore our sins in his body on the tree.' Sin can be considered in a formal way as a transgression of the law. (1 John 3: 4). It can also be taken in a personal and subjective sense as something that pollutes and stains the moral character of the one who sins (Rom. 6: 11–13). Or thirdly, it can refer to sin as guilt and liability to punishment in the juridical sense. 'The soul that sins is the one that dies' (Ezek. 18: 4, 20). Sin as guilt is the ground of punishment. In this sense it is almost a synonym of the condemnation involved in the judgment declared against sin.

When the crude non-biblical metaphor of 'Christ absorbing sin' is used it seems to refer to the sinner's moral stain. There is, however, absolutely no imaginable way in which personal and subjective blemishes belonging to one person could be taken on by another person. Subjective guilt is inalienable; our sins remain ours and will do so until the final redemption of the body, when we are freed from them altogether. Subjective sin can never be dissolved or transferred to another. What was done yesterday belongs to the sinner until the final resurrection and judgment. Past memories, past sins and dreams can't be offloaded.

It is sin understood in the third sense that explains coherently how Christ bore sins. Dual triads serve to contrast the condition of sinners and that of believers:

- sin, condemnation and death,
- righteousness, justification and life.

They are theologically intelligible in legal terms, not in subjective and personal ones. There is an essential distinction between subjective sinfulness and objective guilt, which corresponds to Scripture's doctrine. Sinfulness is not removed subjectively during this life. But the cross removes guilt as condemnation, judgment, and death. Is not this the meaning of Luther's *simul justus et peccator*?

Although sin is progressively limited in believers by mortification and sanctification through the Spirit (Rom 8:12 ff.), Christ, by his sacrifice as penal substitute, does not remove the personal responsibility and temporal consequences of our sin, which will only die with the body. The mediator removes liability to penal judgment and guilt in the sense of condemnation leading to death. That Christ 'bore our sins' means he took on himself their fatal consequences and died the death we ought to have died.

But how is it possible that the life Christ yielded up on the cross could be sufficient in lieu of the lives of all who have sinned against God, and who merit judgment and death? Christ does not simply obtain the favour of God on our behalf; he pays the full price for the acquittal of sinners. The equivalence is not like that of a sum of money, such as 1 euro = 6. 7 francs, it is an appropriate penal equivalent. In the unique person of Christ, his humanity bore away sins through his suffering in the body and death, which was an appropriate sentence for human sin. His divinity constitutes the assurance of its unlimited value and sufficiency for those for whom Christ died. None can really know what the eternal Son suffered in a single moment or time, what the possible extent of such suffering might be, and to what length its effects might reach. 'One died for all, and therefore all died. And he died for all, that those who live should no longer live for themselves but for him who died for them and was raised again' (2 Cor. 5: 14–15). No doubt can be entertained as to the appropriateness of this one act and its effectiveness for all it concerns. God's justice was satisfied. The forgiveness of sin is the result of 'redemption through blood', that is the death of Christ as the legal price paid to obtain forgiveness (Eph. 1: 7). Christ 'made peace through his blood, shed on the cross' (Col. 1: 20), which means that his death obtained peace with God for sinners.

Surely God could never be angry with his own Son? That is wholly the case. God was never for an instant angry against the beloved Son. God was not at odds with Christ, he was at odds with sin. His anger was not pointed at the person of Christ like the anger of one person can be directed at another or at an object.[24] In the particular function of mediator he accepted for others, Christ acted together with and for God and took the anger of God on himself. Forgiveness is not wrung from a violent and a grudging God. Christ is the subject and the object of his own acts. By taking the anger of God against sin to himself, and dying for it, he obtained forgiveness.

'The one who will himself be the acting subject in the last judgment became its object in the place of sinners. But as he stood in their place he exhausted the punishment due to them, and the presence of God to Jesus turned from curse to blessing.'[25]

In Christ, God took the penalty of sin on his own self to abolish the cause of enmity existing between himself and sinners. Nothing unethical or unjust is implied, as Christ freely accepted this role as mediator. Consent and free choice characterise his actions for sinners (John 10: 18; Heb 10: 14). Penal substitution through sacrifice implies that he accepted to stand as the innocent one in the place of the guilty, accepts the judgment for their guilt, and assumes and abolishes it by his vicarious death. This is condescension to the highest degree imaginable and grace to the fullest extent possible.

Thanks be to God that Jesus abolished the objective liability of sinners! This allows the Christian to get up tomorrow a justified sinner knowing that the sacrifice of Christ covers all sins, past, present, and future.

CONCLUSION

The great motivating cause of the atonement is God's love for sinners. God does not just show us love—'here it is, this is what it's like, take a look and show some yourself!' At the cross God enacts his own love in a stupendous demonstration of the height, depth, and breadth of love. He commends *this* love to us as the only love that is worthy of the name: 'God demonstrates his love for us in *this*: While we were still sinners, Christ died for us...while we were God's enemies...' (Rom. 5: 8–9). The amazing thing is that this love does not have any quibbles with God's holiness and justice. It reaches its full expression when the holiness and justice of God in his judgement against sin reach their height:

'A properly formulated view of penal substitution will speak of retribution being experienced by Christ because that is our due. Moreover, the penalty inflicted by God's justice and holiness is also a penalty inflicted by God's love and mercy, for salvation and new life.'[26]

To demonstrate this love, God's Christ accepted the role of mediator, condescended to take on sinful human flesh, to enter into a world of misery, to drag his way along the road of anguish to the place of the skull, and there to take sin on himself, not sin in the abstract, but sin as judgment and death.

'Substitution under the curse we had deserved, so that divine justice is satisfied and we go free, marks the culmination of God's love for us, the ultimate point on the road to self-denial and self-giving, farther than which none can be conceived.'[27]

The ultimate point on that road was God's abandonment of his Son to the curse of sin, and now to this we must turn, so our understanding of the strictures of substitution can be complete.

ENDNOTES

[1] Cf. B. B. Warfield, 'Christ our Sacrifice, *Works*, II, 424 ff.

[2] J. Hick, *The Metaphor of God Incarnate*, 119.

[3] See the documentation on this subject in H. Boersma, *Violence, Hospitality and the Cross*, 160ff; H. Blocher, 'Agnus Victor' in J. G. Stackhouse, ed., *What does it mean to be Saved?*, 74ff.

[4] C. Gunton, *The Actuality of the Atonement*, ch. 2.

[5] Cf. J. I. Packer's fundamental article on the subject, 'What did the Cross achieve? The logic of penal substitution', *Tyndale Bulletin* (1974), 1ff;

D. Kidner, 'Sacrifice, metaphors and meaning', *Tyndale Bulletin* (1982), 119–36.

[6] Cf. J. Murray, *Redemption Accomplished and Applied*, 33 ff.

[7] W. Pannenberg, *Systematic Theology*, II, (Grand Rapids: Eerdmans, 1994), 427.

[8] G. Vos, *Biblical Theology*, 165 f.

[9] Cf. J. B. Green, M. D. Baker, *Rediscovering the Scandal of the Cross*, 63: 'The sacrifice offered by Jesus is understood by Paul to entail the final solution to the problem of the human bias towards sin. This does not mean that Paul thinks of Christ's having been punished by execution on the cross so as to satisfy the rancour of God. What is at stake is the mediation of restored relationships, the mediation of God's holy presence among those whose holiness is lacking.'

[10] C. Gunton, op. cit., 138: 'the death of Jesus under the law reveals the way in which God puts right the lawlessness of the universe, not punitively but transformatively, by sheer grace.'

[11] J. McLeod Campbell, *The Nature of the Atonement*, 1856, (Grand Rapids: Eerdmans, 1996). Cf. J. Denney's comments in *The Christian Doctrine of Reconciliation*, 117–20: 'the vocabulary of imputation, if not replaced by that of identification, is interpreted through it.'

[12] R. L. Dabney, in his book published in the last century, *Christ our Penal Substitute*, 20 ff, lists six. *Atonement Today*, ed. J. Goldingay, presents five, 68 ff.

[13] G. Williams gives a noteworthy critique in 'The Cross and the Punishment of Sin', D. Petersen, ed., *Where Wrath and Mercy Meet*, (Carlisle: Paternoster, 2001). See also P. Wells, 'A Free Lunch at the End of the Universe?' in *Themelios* 29 (2003:1), 38–52, some of which is used here.

[14] T. Smail, 'Can one Man die for the People?' in *Atonement Today*, 76.

[15] A similar approach is found in J. B. Green, M. D. Baker, op. cit., 97ff, which says there are two different story lines about Golgotha in the New Testament, 'one with God as subject the other with Christ as subject', 113. Cf. 146f. for their criticism of penal substitution.

[16] The word 'absorb'was used earlier by P. T. Forsyth and C. F. D. Moule to describe how the cross relates to sin. Cf. F. M. Young, *Sacrifice and the Death of Christ* (London: SPCK, 1975), 94, P. S. Fiddes, *Past Event and Present Salvation*, 105 ff.

[17] S. H. Travis, 'Christ as Bearer of Divine Judgment in Paul's Thought about the Atonement', *Atonement Today*, 21–38.

[18] Namely Galatians 3: 3; 2 Corinthians 5: 21; Romans 3: 24–6; 5: 9–10.

[19] The article by Christina Baxter excepted, 'The Cursed Beloved', 54–72.

[20] T. Smail, 'Can one Man die for the People?'p. 73–92.

[21] R. Nicole, 'Postscript on Penal Substititution' in *The Glory of the Atonement*, 451.

[22] J. S. Whale, *Victor and Victim* (Cambridge: CUP, 1960), 69f. quoted in J. I. Packer, 'What did the Cross Achieve?' 34 n.36. Cf. J. A. Groves, 'Atonement in Isaiah 53', in *The Glory of the Atonement*, 61–89, on the relation of 'bearing guilt' and making atonement.

[23] H. Blocher, art. cit., 'The legal and sacrificial metaphors in Scripture have such frequency and regularity, they constitute such a stable network, with predictable usages, they are so consistent, that they cannot be dealt with as 'mere' metaphors... there are concepts attached to linguistic signs.'

[24] Cf. J. I. Packer, art. cit., 25ff.

[25] G. Williams, art. cit., 98.

[26] D. Petersen, 'Atonement in the New Testament' in D. Petersen, ed., *Where Wrath and Mercy Meet*, 38.

[27] H. Blocher, 'The Atonement in John Calvin's Theology' in eds. C. E. Hill, F. A. James, *The Glory of the Atonement*, 286.

12

Abandonment

During the six terrible hours of crucifixion, Jesus uttered seven clipped sentences. Even though they are recorded in different gospels, there is general agreement as to their order. The first three 'words' from the cross concern the end of Jesus' life and ministry and sever his links with the world.

'Father forgive them for they know not what they do' (Luke 23: 34), is a prayer for the forgiveness of those instrumental in his death—immediately and more generally since its ultimate reason is the sinfulness of humanity. This request procures the common grace which allows history to go on, as it is inconceivable that man should lay hands on God's own Son without immediate consequences.

Jesus answers the brigand's plea, 'Remember me when you come into your kingdom' with 'Truly today you will be with me in paradise' (Luke 23: 42–3). This is special grace and salvation. Even while dying, Christ is capable of saving a sinner. This reveals that the effectiveness of the cross lies in the death of Christ itself.

John and Mary are at the foot of the cross. Seeing them there Jesus says, 'Woman, here is your son', and to the disciple, 'Here is your mother' (John 19: 26–7). Quite apart from the human drama of these words, they convey that from the cross Jesus acts as Lord over his people. He heals and reorders their lives.

As the mediator for men, Jesus acts as their Lord, even during moments of intense suffering. He holds the future history of humanity in his hands; he has the power to save; his church will be a community organised under his lordship in a way different from worldly standards. The final three words that end Jesus' hours of suffering were pronounced in rather quick succession. Jesus now offers himself as the mediator to God the Father, the perfect offering, and for this reason, he is certain of being accepted.

'I thirst' (John 19: 28) can be taken in its primary physical reference as Jesus' desire to present himself to the Father in full consciousness. It can also be understood as longing for renewal of spiritual communion, 'eating and drinking anew' with his own in the kingdom (Luke 22: 16, 18).

'When he had received the vinegar, Jesus cried out, "It is finished."' (John 19: 30). The end of the line has been reached, but more than that. The purposes of divine redemption have reached their true end.[1] The whole of God's history with his people from creation onward has now reached its conclusion. There is nothing more to be added to what Christ has done.

Finally, Jesus cried with a loud voice, 'Father, into your hands I commit my spirit' (Luke 23: 46). He breathed his last not with a sense of failure, but with the certainty of victory. Jesus died with the knowledge that since his work was perfectly complete, there was no doubt that his Father would welcome him into glory. As he has glorified the Father in every way on the earth, now he has a rightful claim to glory in heaven, the same glory he had 'before the world began' (John 17: 5).

The six words portray the relationship Jesus bears to men, time and created reality, and to his Father, eternity and divine reality. Between earth and heaven stands the cross; there hangs Jesus—alone, in isolation and abandonment. He is not an intermediary but the mediator. Isolation is the essence of this office. This stark contrast is reflected in the fourth saying: 'Eloi, Eloi, lama sabachthani?—my God, my God, why have you forsaken me?' (Mark 15: 34; Matt. 27: 46).

This word is the only one reported by two of the evangelists. Its position in the seven makes it central in Jesus' words from the cross. The door of redemption swings on this hinge, in time and eternity. Jesus knew abandonment not in death, but before death, and this amazing fact is a clue to his understanding of the transaction being made at Golgotha. When he died, Jesus knew that abandonment was over and death was already defeated. His dying was the end of sin and a return to the Father's presence.

What is the meaning of this anguished cry?

DARKNESS AT NOON

It was toward three in the afternoon, following three hours of apocalyptic darkness that Jesus uttered these words.[2] They lack the dignity in suffering and Lordship expressed in the previous words, in which Jesus relates to the humans around. All through the hours of his passion he had not replied to the insults of the crowd, but remained silent as he had done before Pilate and Herod. He seems impervious to the mockery of his persecutors, accomplishing the prophecy of Isaiah 53: 7, 'he was mistreated and humiliated but did not open his mouth.' When he does intervene, it is not to defend himself, but to exercise grace in sovereign fashion. Although racked by physical pain, Jesus shows mental serenity. Not even the vilest abuse shakes his confidence.

At midday, an abnormal obscurity falls on the land. Bystanders shiver with fear. A kind of oppressive darkness makes it hard to breathe. The moment has arrived when a veil is drawn over the suffering of Jesus. Human activity ceases. Insults dry up. The soldiers' dice stop rolling. Silence falls. Jesus is given over to isolation in this moment in which the power of darkness does its terrible work (Luke 22: 53). During this time when activity ceases around the cross, Jesus is supremely active—an adequate picture of how God accomplishes salvation without human means. The cry of dereliction, 'Why have you abandoned me?' expresses the travail of soul Jesus undergoes in the dark heat.

IMPOSSIBLE ABANDONMENT

When human activity ceases, salvation is accomplished in a way that mutually implicates the Father and the Son. Christ has already been through assaults from the outside, the satanic temptation in the desert, the derision of his fellows, and mental anguish in Gethsemane as he anticipates his arrest, trial, and exclusion from the city of David (Matt. 26: 36–46).

But now his cry is not an expression of moral or physical suffering, nor does it express the fear of death. Something much more terrible is in view. What seems impossible happens. The

Son experiences, to the depth of his being, in his understanding of his plight, the heartbreak and distress because the Father is no longer at hand. However can this be, for the one who is the beloved Son?

'My God, my God'—these two *Eli* stand in stark contrast to the normal interaction between the Son and the Father. No longer do we hear 'My Father', as almost everywhere else in the gospels. The Father has become God for Jesus, like he might be for any other stranger. What can have happened? This simple substitution of a word reflects a change of situation. It can only be understood by a return to origins and the tension created by man's rebellion and sin.

Between Jesus and God, there is a contract to be honoured: the covenant broken by Adam at the start of human history, as by each of his descendants after him. Jesus as true man in the image of God, must obey this contract through perfect obedience.[3] Only total compliance with the will of God can merit blessing. As one who has been totally just, Christ has met the divine requirement. But now he finds himself alone, the lines between him and the Father have been cut. This is incomprehensible, and the Son feels the paradox to his very bones. His 'Why' has a profoundly pathetic ring to it. Three considerations can serve to draw this out.

Firstly, Jesus is the righteous Son of the covenant. At the outset of his public ministry, he received the seal of divine approval: 'This is my beloved Son, on whom I have set all my affection' (Matt. 3: 17). Throughout all his human suffering, he demonstrated his justice before the Father. Even when he anticipated that his disciples would abandon him he was able to say, 'You will leave me all alone. But I am not alone, for my Father is with me' (John 16: 32). Jesus' belief that the Lord will be with him is rooted in the promise found in Isaiah's first 'servant song':

> Here is my servant whom I uphold,
>   my chosen one in whom I delight;
> I will put my spirit in him
>   and he will bring justice to the nations.
> He will not shout or cry out,
>   or raise his voice in the streets.

> Isa. 42: 1–4

The abandonment of the Son cannot be considered as a withdrawal of divine approval, nor of the particular love of the Father for the Son. The Son has not abandoned the Father, so why now the distress of desertion, this desperate cry?[4]

Secondly, Jesus knows that God the Father is present at Golgotha. The whole tenor of Jesus' ministry has been the proximity of God and his kingdom. No prophet in Scripture, no mystic outside of biblical revelation, has ever spoken of the presence of God as he has. For him it has been the reason for his life and mission. 'The one who has sent me is with me; he has not left me alone' (John 8: 29, cf. 11: 42).

The presence of God, the coming of the kingdom is bound up with the person of Jesus. He it is who is anointed with the spirit of the Lord to bring in the year of the Lord's favour (Isa. 61; Luke 4: 18). This makes it difficult to imagine that the abandonment of the cross is a withdrawal of the unction of spirit that sanctifies the person and work of the Lord. The experience of the cross does not lessen the holiness of the Son. On the contrary, it is in a spirit of holiness that the presence of God is revealed among men, as the Son obeys and suffers: 'through the eternal spirit Christ offered himself unblemished to God' (Heb. 9: 14).

It must also be said that there was never, in the person of Christ, not even in the abandonment of the cross, an opposition between the divine and human natures, nor was his humanity separated from his divinity because of his trials. The ordeal that the suffering Christ experiences is that the Father abandons the Son, and not that the divine nature is dissociated from the human. Any speculation along these lines misses the point. That the Son never lost the divine unction, nor his sense of the presence and the blessing of the Father, only serves to heighten the tension expressed by the fourth word. Why then this inexplicable separation?

Thirdly, Jesus is certain that he is doing the divine will. Never for an instant has he doubted that the way to blessing is along the road of obedience, strewn as it might be with interrogations and anguish. Jesus has striven with all the will-power of a human being to overcome the inner temptations of the broad way that discards the desire to please God. Golgotha completes the trial of Gethsemane. In agony of mind and sorrow to the point of death he prayed, 'my Father, if it is at all possible, may this cup be taken away from me...' and received the cup of suffering. In the triumph of complete submission and acquiescence to the will of God, he sets his course: 'yet not as I will, but as you will' (Matt. 26: 39).

Throughout his life, Jesus predicted his own death. Now he fully embraces the dreadful fate he had come to realise was his.[5] Where does this terrible assurance that this is the will of God spring from? Surely from no human source; could a human being obtain the knowledge that God desired his death? Only Psalm 22, which provides the background for 'why have you abandoned me?', can be of any help.[6] The texts of Matthew and Mark transcribe the Greek of Psalm 22: 2 and we can presume that Jesus was conscious of the whole context of the words in the psalm when he uttered them. The author of the psalms is following his own script. Psalm 22 is a prayer of supplication which runs from anguish to assurance, from conflict to confidence. The righteous son of God is humiliated, mistreated by men, and put to death.[7] Yet, he reminds God that he is the Saviour of his people, their creator and a God who is present in deliverance. Finally, he states that the rulers of the nations will recognise the Lord.[8]

Despite the appearance of desertion and the goading of his enemies precisely on this score—'he saved others but he can't save himself!...He trusts in God. Let God rescue him if he wants him'—Jesus' assurance is unshaken.[9] What David wrote in a hyperbolic way is true of the scene enacted at Calvary. The prophetic word is fulfilled in a wonderful way. But God will deliver the faithful child of the covenant. In the most extreme anguish of soul, Jesus is nourished by his own word and the truth that God will not fail those who trust in him, since he is faithful to his promise. Stripped of every human comfort, he found inner resources in the word of God as the only glimmer of light in the dark.

The fourth word conveys the mysterious fact that Jesus is torn between the knowledge of his faithfulness with the blessing it must bring and the silence of God, between the 'my God' and the experience of rejection. Jesus, having perfectly obeyed the Father's will and saved the dying thief, finds himself in supreme isolation. Abandonment of the Son by the Father, even in a temporary sense, is unthinkable. No explanation for it can be found either in the humanity of the Son or in the way his mission has been carried through. Yet he hangs with the condemned and the accused, contrary to his just deserts.

THE REALITY OF ABANDONMENT

There is no doubting the grim reality: it is the Father who abandons his own Son. Nothing can be said to diminish it. The Son is isolated in darkness and his words are a poignant lament reflecting this incredible fact.

In a real sense, it is impossible to get to the bottom of it, and no explanations can do so; only the Son has been along the path to the supreme point of human anguish. He alone through this experience can feel the horror and the misery of being deserted by God. Even the dying thief experienced divine comfort, a comfort Jesus was deprived of during the three hours of darkness. The fourth word from the cross is the most mysterious enigma of biblical revelation and it is not surprising that interpretations as to its meaning abound. No psychologising can approach the catastrophe experienced by Jesus as he is forsaken by the Father. Depression, mental anguish, despair, or revolt against physical suffering all fall short of the apocalyptic tenor of these words. Nor is it ultimately more satisfying to speak about the 'passion of God' as a suffering assumed by God when the Father is deprived of the Son and vice versa.[10] Talk about death in God or death of God strays beyond the bounds of the covenant relationships between God and humanity into the nether lands of murky metaphysics. Literary attempts that see the story as a mythical artifice lending rhetorical weight to the event serve to bring us no nearer to the terrible reality.

The exclusion of Jesus by the Father is impossible because Jesus is the true covenant Son. Yet it happens, and in such a way that the Son can only be considered as suffering like any other human being might expect to suffer. He knows divine absence and rejection by God that any sinner might legitimately fear. The Son's situation is paradoxical. Despite his righteousness, his fate is that of fallen men. '*My God, my God, why…*' distils the concentrated anguish of the world.[11]

THE HEART OF DARKNESS

'From the sixth hour to the ninth hour darkness came over all the land' (Matt. 27: 45). Was it an eclipse, a black sirocco, a thick fog, or supernatural night? It hardly matters, because this is no accident, but an act of God's doing. Jesus finds himself at the antipodes of his transfiguration, when the Father had declared him to be the beloved Son in the presence of his people. God is the author of the darkness that now shrouds the Son. But what is the reason for it?

One lead is found in Jesus' words in John's gospel, where the word 'darkness' is given a spiritual connotation, as elsewhere in Scripture. When he healed the man born blind, Jesus said: 'As long as it is day, we must do the work of him who sent me. Night is coming, when no one can work. While I am in the world, I am the light of the world' (John 9: 4–5; cf. 5: 17). Later, when Jesus predicts his death, he says: 'You are going to have the light just a little while longer. Walk while you have the light, before darkness overtakes you. The one who walks in the dark does not know where he is going' (John 12: 35–6; cf. 12: 46; 8: 12).

When Golgotha is plunged into darkness, God demonstrates that the work of his Son among men as the 'light of the world' is over (John 1: 1–14). For this reason, Jesus has not replied to his persecutors and now the darkness cuts him off from other forms of created life. He stands alone. No longer does he know 'where he is going', no longer can he 'work' in the light of life. His work with men is finished, but there remains a strange and mysterious task to accomplish. Jesus in his suffering is neither a martyr who welcomes death, nor a stoic of Socratic equanimity, nor a mystic who embraces the journey into the unknown with serenity. God *abandons* his son. If Christ was in the darkness, it was to keep his mediatorial work on course and to prove it fully.[12] This explains the reason for the '*Why*'—the Father abandons his Son and leaves him to complete his work.

The reality of the divine desertion is all the more real when we see that God's first act of ordering creation was to give light. Deprived of light Jesus plunges below the conditions which govern creation. He loses even the common grace by which God sends his light on the just and unjust (Matt. 5: 45). At Golgotha he no longer benefits from it, as the conditions that uphold creation are suspended and the conditions of future judgment are injected into history.[13]

In his abandonment, Jesus experiences judgment before the end of the world, as if he were a sinner in the hands of an angry

God. He knows exclusion not only from light, but also from creation, nature, and time. 'The day of the Lord is coming, it is close at hand—a day of darkness and gloom, a day of clouds and blackness...such as never was before nor ever will be in the ages to come' (Joel 2: 1–2).[14] There is no doubt a parallel between the three days which precede the Easter morning and the three days of darkness in Egypt preceding the death of the firstborn, but this darkness is exceptional.[15] God does not come to the aid of the suffering Son.

Everything is in suspense and during these vital moments the future of creation hangs on the success of the Son's mission.

WAS IT HELL?

The abandonment is not just a sign of a judgment typical of the day of the Lord, it also shows that the Son tastes the reality of the judgment of hell. In the Old Testament, the absence of God is experienced as a descent into the gulf of separation where there is no communion with God. No praise can rise from this place; the faithful earnestly desire deliverance from it and restoration to the land of the living.

> 'Therefore my heart is glad
>   and my tongue rejoices;
> my body will also rest secure,
>   because you will not abandon me
>   to the grave,
>   nor will you let your Holy One see decay.
> You have made known to me
>   the path of life;
> you will fill me with joy in your presence,
>   with eternal pleasures at your right hand.
>
> Ps. 16: 10[16]

The abandonment of Christ bears the mark of hell in three ways: in physical suffering, in spiritual affliction, and in divine judgment.

First of all, Jesus experiences judgment in his human nature. The 'rights of man' have no place at the cross. All possibility of physical movement has been taken away from Jesus, neither is anything more to be said—the Word incarnate is silent before his mockers. His lips are closed (Isa. 53: 7). The most terrible of all, however, might well be that Christ has also been deprived of freedom of thought, being mentally bound and oppressed by the curse and torment he endures. The incoherence of his suffering in the light of his spotless humanity is a great contradiction to bear. Such judgment cannot be right and this thought must prey constantly on his mind. No aspect of his human constitution can escape that God has left him to unjust deserts.

Secondly, there is the spiritual suffering implied in exclusion from the presence of God. The law of hell is the opposite of the law of God—the hatred of others (Isa. 14: 9–15). Jesus has already tasted it to the full and he will do so briefly once again even as he laments his desertion. They will also mock his being cursed in his God-forsakenness. 'So he is calling Elijah now is he? Lets see if Elijah comes to get him down' (Mark 15: 35–36).[17] Concretely, on the cross Jesus is cut off from any communication with other humans or with God and the consolation and support it could bring. It was spiritual quarantine. The Son is truly 'despised and rejected by men, a man of sorrows...cut off from the land of the living' (Isa. 53: 3, 8).

Finally, 'heaven hides, only hell remains'.[18] The extremity of the suffering of Christ arises neither from human opposition, nor from physical pain.

> The punishment of desertion, suffered by Christ was not a bodily but a spiritual and internal suffering. It arose not from any torment he could feel in his body, but from a most oppressive sense of God's wrath resting on him on account of our sins.... God suspending for a little while the favourable presence of grace and the influx of consolation and happiness that he might be able to suffer all the punishment due to us.[19]

How agonising it must have been for the Son of God to feel the pain of divine rejection because of his identity with sinners in judgment! The abandonment of Christ corresponds to a descent into hell, as Christ knows full well that the Father only rejects the wicked. 'He was suffering the pains of hell. What the Father wanted to say to the Son was this: Have you desired to suffer the passion of hell? Then you must do so fully aware that you are doing so.'[20] He tastes the bitterest anguish as looking to God in faith, love, and trust, he finds that he is not saved from the ordeal. His heart yearns for the communion and glory he shared with the Father before the world was (John 17: 5) and all the time he has ringing in his ears 'Esau have I hated'! (Rom. 9: 13).

For three terrible hours Christ knew the pangs of hell as if he were a sinner under the lash of divine judgment. 'This cry is like the lamentation of those who are abandoned for ever.'[21] Tormented by the astonishment of finding himself in hell without belonging there, Christ strains for heaven but is transfixed by the divine condemnation he undergoes. Only he could have stood up to this soul-destroying paradox without losing confidence in the Father. He descended into our hell to break its power. 'Dying on the cross, forsaken by his Father…it was damnation—and damnation taken lovingly.'[22]

A TERRIFYING DESCENT

It has been suggested that the fourth word—'My God, my God, why have you forsaken me?'—is less of a reality than a profound feeling in a situation of extreme distress. It certainly was deeply and bitterly felt, but the root of the experience lay in objective reality beyond feeling or imagination.

The question of the exact nature of Christ's abandonment is unavoidable and it only serves to highlight our ignorance. Since it concerns the relationship between the Father and the Son it is as mysterious as all the Trinitarian dealings—perhaps the reason for the discretion of the New Testament writers. The only way to avoid undue speculation is by way of reference to the place and the function Jesus occupies in the covenant. His desertion was surely catastrophic and apocalyptic, corresponding to the curse of the covenant. Rejected by the Father, hanging on the cross, Christ's word expresses the knowledge of profound absence, along with loss of favour and communion with God. The intimacy of the covenant relation between God and the righteous Son, characterised by blessing, approbation, deep communion in spirit and in truth, mutual joy and peace in love, sink from the horizon when the darkness falls. Even God's covenant faithfulness, experienced by his sinful people in the Old Testament, seems to have evaporated.

It cannot be thought that the Son was personally the object of divine desertion. The Father could have only satisfaction with regard to his person. The abandonment he so cruelly feels is no personal rupture provoked by him or by the Father. His acceptance of the work of mediation according to covenant conditions means Christ has accepted the office with all it implied. At the height of his passion, standing as the just in the place of the unjust (1 Pet. 3: 18), he experiences the consequences of judgment in dereliction of life and hope. The sudden and unanticipated emptiness as the Father turns away, and as the tide of communion ebbs away, is a world of bitterness for Jesus. In the fragility of his human person, he knows desertion by the Father, who was for him the source of life. In the valley of the shadow of death, Christ fears evil, as the rod and staff of God's presence are removed (Ps. 23: 4).

God's law cannot condemn Jesus. Sinners, on the other hand, deserve desertion and judgment according to the requirement of divine law. Christ has no personal de-merit with regard to the law. He occupies the place of sinners in his office as representative. He is the victim, the injured party, the substitute whose abandonment to death is the Holy God's way of salvation for his executioners. No natural way exists for man into God's presence. The Father's supernatural abandonment of the Son to infernal judgment opens the way once again. 'And the curtain of the temple was torn in two from top to bottom' (Mark 15: 38) as God accepts the sacrifice for sin offered by the Son.

CONCLUSION

Christ renounces his own personal rights and privileges to be the mediator between God and sinful man. The abandonment of the cross is the terminus of the incarnation and the completion of human humiliation (Phil. 2: 8). Yet, Christ's faith in the divine promise remains firm. 'Eli, Eli', my powerful God, he shouts, even if the 'why' receives no answer as yet. 'In his extreme torment his faith remains firm, so that even while he was lamenting the divine abandonment, he never lost assurance of the help and favour of God.'[23] As he hung among mockers and evil doers Christ maintains the will to obey the Father to the end. 'The Saviour continued to believe even when there was no deliverance, in spite of the fact that he was momentarily abandoned.'[24]

'My God, why have you forsaken me': this is the gash cut in a holy and righteous conscience by the silence of God. The beloved Son in this position![25] Only the Son of God had the right to pronounce these words. He bears the full weight of the position he has accepted for sinful man and enters into intimate knowledge of the consequences of sin in the dark inferno of divine rejection. 'My God, to what end have you forsaken me?'[26]

ENDNOTES

[1] Cf. chapter 7.

[2] Luke says the sun became darkened (ekleipein, Luke 22:45).

[3] As in chapter 2.

[4] Only those who abandon God are foresaken by him. See 2 Chronicles 12: 5; 15: 2; 24: 20.

[5] See Matthew 16: 21–8; 17: 22–3; 20: 17–20; 28.

[6] It is not necessary to imagine, as some have done, that Jesus prayed this psalm while hanging on the cross. However, Jesus would have sung the psalms during the Passover meal.

[7] Psalm 22: 7–9, 12–19, 16 c.

[8] 22: 4–6, 10–12; 20 and 29–32.

[9] Matthew 27: 42–3 echoes Psalm 22: 9.

[10] Cf. J. Moltmann, *The Crucified God* (London: SCM, 1974), ch. VI and *The Trinity and the Kingdom of God*, 83.

[11] C. H. Spurgeon, uses this expression in his sermon on John 19: 30 in *The Treasury of the New Testament*, II, (London: Marshall, Morgan & Scott, n.d.), 671.

[12] K. Schilder, *Christ Crucified* (Grand Rapids: Eerdmans, 1940), 373 ff.

[13] See Psalm 22: 7, 15–16.

[14] See Joel 1: 15; 2: 11, Amos 5: 18, 20; 8: 9; Isaiah 13: 9, 13; Zephaniah 1: 15.

[15] Exodus 10: 22, 11.

[16] See Psalm 86: 13; 103: 2–4; 116: 1 ff.

[17] Several explanations have been suggested as to the change of Jesus' Eloï into Elijah. Perhaps we need look no further than the crowd's collective delirium aggravated by fear.

[18] R. Stier, *The Words of the Lord Jesus*, VII, (Edinburgh: T. & T. Clark, 1873), 484.

[19] Turretin, *Institutes of Elenctic Theology*, II, 354.

[20] Schilder, op. cit, 373.

[21] J. Flavel, *Works*, II, (Edinburgh: Banner of Truth, 1968), 409.

[22] Quoted in A. Moody Stuart, *The Life of John Duncan* (Edinburgh: Banner of Truth Trust, 1991), 105.

[23] J. Calvin, *Commentaires sur l'Harmonie Evangélique*, I, (Toulouse: Société des livres religieux, 1892), 569a.

[24] A. W. Pink, *The Seven Sayings of the Saviour on the Cross* (Grand Rapids: Baker, 1958), 76

[25] R. Stier, *The Words of the Lord Jesus*, 478.

[26] So E.W. Hengstenberg, *Commentary on the Psalms*, I, (Cherry Hill, NJ: Mack, nd.), 369.

13

Mediator

A person who feels no call for a mediator to be able to approach God is a person who has no understanding of the need of divine mercy and forgiveness. Many people are in that unenviable position and they try to find their own way to God, through a variety of beliefs and experiences.

There is, however, no direct contact between God and man in a natural sense. The relationship between God and the world is not an immediate one. It is mediated, and that mediation is accomplished in a unique way through the person of Jesus Christ. 'We have no capacity for God, so God capacitates himself to us. God in Christ brings Godself down to our level so that God might communicate God's will and grace to us. God in Christ condescends.'[1]

Christ is the mediator in two specific respects. Firstly, he stands between two alienated parties to remove the cause of contention and restore friendship. In this sense, the mediator steps in between God as the offended party and men as guilty sinners to restore men to favour. As the mediator of men needing to be saved, Jesus 'is not a mere teacher, not a moral reformer, not a mediator of intercession, but of reconciliation, who removes the cause of quarrel by making reparation for the wrong.'[2]

Secondly, Christ is more than just a go-between, a third person standing between God and man, like a conciliator called in to negotiate a settlement between two estranged parties. He is mediator in a special sense, in that he has a part in God and man because of the divine plan of salvation and the incarnation. The God-man is what Christ is in himself as a person. For this reason, it can be said that he is what he does and he does what he is.[3] If the atonement has a transactional aspect in the perspective of penal substitution, it can never be forgotten that the cross as Christ's work is his free and personal choice.

The person of Christ as mediator coincides with his vicarious action and in this action he is a substitute standing in the place of others, acting on their behalf. As the mediator between God and man, Christ is also more than a representative, he is a real substitute, bearing the sins of his people in a sacrificial way. 'Sacrifice points to substitution and substitution in turn points to the person and work of the Messiah.'[4]

It is natural that because of these considerations the office of Jesus Christ as mediator has been considered primarily in the context of salvation. The two natures of Christ, divine and human, have framed discussion about the mediatorial work of the Messiah, in relation to its progress from suffering to glory and to Christ acting as prophet, priest, and king. He deals with God for men, and with men for God. In his saving work, he represents man to God by coping with the problem of sin; he represents God to men in revealing the wonder of God's love in the salvation of sinners.

A broader perspective on Christ's work as mediator is legitimate, however, in the light of the biblical witness. Not only is Christ active in accomplishing salvation for his people, he is also the mediator between God and creation as a whole. Furthermore, he stands in a central position between God and history in such a way that God's purposes for the whole of created reality depend on who he is and what he does.

In this chapter, we reflect briefly on the three aspects in which Christ is mediator: in relation to creation, to salvation, and to the fulfilment of God's purposes in history.

CHRIST AND CREATION

John Calvin is undoubtedly the great theologian of mediation through Christ. He spoke about it in a variety of ways, the most striking of which is seen in the following quotation:

> Our most merciful Father decreed what was best for us. Since our iniquities, like a cloud cast between us and him,

had completely estranged us from the Kingdom of Heaven, no man, unless he belonged to God, could serve as the intermediary and restore peace. But who might reach to him? Any of Adam's children? No, like their father, they were terrified at the sight of God. An angel? They also had need of a head, through whose bond they might cleave firmly and undividedly to their God. What then? The situation would have surely been hopeless had the majesty of God not descended to us, since it was not in our power to ascend to him. Hence, it was necessary to the Son of God to become for us 'Emmanuel, that is, God with us', and in such a way that his divinity and our human nature might by mutual connection grow together.[5]

Calvin's view of mediation is, however, much broader than what is revealed above, as already indicated in his reference to the angel's need of a head to concretize their relationship with God. For the Genevan reformer, mediation is headship and the headship of Christ is his lordship over all creation. Calvin argues that 'even before the issue of the incarnation as a response to our fall arises, Christ was the mediator in relation to creation as God's eternal Word.'[6]

This perspective is important as it not only delivers us from a narrow view of Christ's mediation that can be reduced to its operation in an individualistic salvation, but it also indicates that all creation and new creation, in a personal and an impersonal sense, are placed under the headship of Christ. All God's relations with created reality past, present, and future are grounded in Christ, the eternal word and wisdom of God. God has no relations with reality outside himself other than those that pass through the mediation of Christ. Because of this, Christ is the head over all creation, over humanity, and is the Lord of the new creation already present and yet to appear fully. Appeal can be made in this respect to two passages in Paul's epistles referring to the creation and the resurrection:

'He is the image of the invisible God, the firstborn over all creation. For by him all things were created…he is before all things and in him all things hold together. And he is the head of the body, the church; the beginning and the firstborn from the dead, so that in everything he might have the supremacy' (Col. 1: 15–18).

'And God placed all things under his feet and appointed him to be head over everything for the church, which is his body, the fullness of him who fills everything in every way' (Eph. 1: 22–3).

All things were created through Christ and for him. He is the alpha at the beginning of creation and the omega at its ending.[7] The whole 'alphabet' of created reality is under his control. All things achieve their ultimate destiny in Christ. The eternal Son of God who 'is before all things' is now also the risen Lord, 'the firstborn from the dead'. If, as eternal Lord, the Son had a right to exercise authority over creation, he now exercises that prerogative as the risen Lord. His rule extends not only in the realm of creation, but also in that of salvation. The claims of Christ are threefold as they are eternal, creational, and redemptive; in this respect he 'holds all things together'. As the one who has supremacy in all things, appointed by God the Father to this function, Christ is also given to the church as its head. The origin of all things in creation and new creation, headship over them, bringing his work to its final goal, and appointment to fulfilling this task are aspects of the position and work of Christ as the mediator.

From a biblical perspective, Christ is mediator of the divine covenant. God's covenant is made with the whole of creation and with man as the image of God, created according to the likeness of the one mediator, the divine Son.[8] When man sinned in Eden, the entire cosmos was plunged into a situation marked by alienation and corruption. Through sin, creation as a whole loses its order, its harmony and holiness in communion with God. For the apostle Paul, 'sin is not in the first place an individual act or condition to be considered by itself, but rather the supra-individual mode of existence in which one shares through the single fact that one shares in the human life context.'[9] Christ the mediator, the last and true Adam, comes as saviour of the world to restore it, so that it lines up once again with God's intention for blessing. The covenant is restored and made new by the death and resurrection of Christ, who dies to redeem the sins of the old humanity and bring to light a new humanity through his victory over death. He has 'destroyed death and brought life and immortality to light though the gospel' to fulfil 'the grace given us in Christ before the beginning of time' (2 Tim. 1: 9–10).

Christ remains head over the old world of sin to bring out of it a new creation with a new humanity. In his resurrection he is the first to enter the new realm over which he is appointed to rule as its righteous head. As mediator he introduces the many who are in Christ into the new creation, a realm in which, under his lordship, old things have passed away and all things have become new (2 Cor. 5: 17). Christ's headship makes him saviour of the world and of humanity. 'What is involved in the demonstration of God's righteousness through the atoning death of Christ and his resurrection for the justification of many and in his ongoing activity as Lord, advocate, saviour and judge of the world is nothing less than the establishment of the right of God over the whole cosmos.'[10]

Far from limiting their importance, these broad perspectives about Christ's mediation underscore his work as mediator in the second and more specific sense of his standing between God and man to accomplish salvation. The two are complementary and, from a biblical perspective, one cannot stand without the other. If Christ were not Lord over all, his lordship in salvation would lack effectiveness, and if he were not the Lord in salvation then his rule over the cosmos would be without purpose and finality. The two stand or fall together.

CHRIST THE MEDIATOR AND REDEMPTION

Several aspects of the specific work of redemption and the renewing of the fallen creation accomplished by Christ as mediator are important: that his divine and human natures are involved in his work, the different ways in which Christ acted, the functions he fulfilled, and finally his condescension in accepting appointment to this office.

It is sometimes incorrectly thought that Christ became mediator between God and man when he rose from the dead and ascended into heaven, but before being a heavenly office, the mediation of Christ in salvation is first of all an earthly one, through the incarnation. Nor was Christ mediator simply as a man, but he stood between God and man in his divine and human natures.[11] Both natures are certainly involved in Christ's work as mediator in salvation, but it is almost impossible to designate them to Christ's individual actions. To say that Christ was mediator as the God-man in his unique person is more biblical.

The all-embracing scope of the mediation of Christ is nowhere more prominent, even if the word 'mediator' is not used, than in the Christological hymn of Philippians 2, with its four steps:

> Christ Jesus, being in very nature God did not consider equality with God something to be grasped, but he made himself nothing, taking the very nature of a servant, being made in human likeness. And being found in the appearance of a man humbled himself and became obedient to death, even death on a cross! Therefore God exalted him to the highest place...Christ is Lord.
>
> Phil. 2: 6–11

Here, as elsewhere in Scripture, the mediation of Christ refers to his person and not to either of his natures. It begins with the eternal aspect of equality with God the Father, descends to the earthly appearance of the man Jesus, dips lower to the point of death on the cross, having as final counterpoint the exaltation and lordship of Christ. The subject of the descent, incarnation, and ascent is the same person—the God-man. Two non-temporal frames enclose the temporal 'sandwich' of servanthood and death. In eternity, Christ is equal with God before his incarnation and he occupies the highest place as Lord in his exaltation. The eternity–time–eternity historical frame gives a temporal picture of the movement corresponding to the equality–suffering–glory status of Christ. The continuity of the movement means that eternity and time find expression in the unity of the person of Christ. The divine and human coexist in one unique person. Scripture presents the mediation of Christ, between God and man, from three complementary perspectives: temporal movement; the situation of Christ in glory, or in suffering; the two natures united in one person.

If Paul's approach in Philippians 2 is theological, John in his gospel (20: 10–18), brings out the sense of Jesus' mediation at the heart of his historical presentation of the resurrection. It is striking that in his first resurrection appearance in the garden, Christ spoke of his work of mediation to Mary Magdalene and made it the content of the message she was to bear to the disciples. She is ordered not to try to hang onto the Jesus she had known in his earthly ministry (v: 17), as he no longer belongs to that reality. The empty tomb and his personal appearance is the first stage of a dynamic process spanning the forty days and culminating in his ascension to the glory of heaven and the Father's presence.[12] Through the resurrection, Jesus already belongs to another form of reality and it forms a watershed between his suffering on earth and his glory in heaven. That Jesus chose a woman and not a disciple to be the first witness of his resurrection is itself surprising, but the message he gives her to transmit is theologically laden: 'Go instead to my brothers and tell them, "I am returning to my Father and your Father, to my God and your God." ' (John 20: 17).

As in Philippians 2, the ascension is a return to base, a homecoming. There is, however, a difference. Because of the finished work of redemption from sin, Christ becomes the mediator of Fatherhood with regard to his brethren in a new and complete way. The first use of 'Father' in Jesus' order given to Mary has a natural sense, that of the Pauline equality with God; the 'your Father' is not natural, but adoptive, a result of Christ's work of grace. It is only on the basis of Jesus as go-between that the One who is his Father can be our Father. Christ speaks with the authority that can only be his as the divine mediator. Why then should it be necessary for Christ to add 'and to my God and your God'? Far from being superfluous, Christ presents himself in these words as the human mediator. 'My God'! The last time Jesus had used this expression was the fourth word on the cross, in which he addresses God from the perspective of abandoned sinners.[13] In his human nature he knew judgment for sin and forsakenness; as mediator for sinful men, he encountered God. Jesus represents man to God and God to man as the author of salvation. The God he encountered on the cross is God in the judgment of sin, our sin; his Father is our Father, by grace and adoption. In this remarkable way salvation is accomplished by the divine and human mediation of Christ, interposing his unique person and making a new relation with God possible for sinners such as Mary Magdalene, Peter, and the rest.

There is no natural bridge for sinners across the gulf separating 'God' and 'Father'. But the two sides meet and are joined in the person of Christ, human and divine. Personally and concretely he is the mediator between two estranged parties.

MEDIATION AND THE THREE OFFICES

The divinity of Christ as mediator was necessary not as an enabling factor in Christ's work of redemption, but because of the nature of that work itself.[14] Salvation is something that no man could accomplish, and Christ's divinity was involved in the task in a variety of ways. It was Calvin who developed the threefold office of Christ as prophet, priest, and king as a way of presenting the different facets of the accomplishment of salvation.[15]

As we have seen, in the Old Testament the three mediatorial offices were present in anticipation.[16] Moses was the Old Testament mediator par excellence as he pleaded with God for Israel and spoke the divine word to God's people.[17] 'Though the word is not used, mediatorship is at the heart of Old Testament religion. The theologically significant point is that God cannot be approached at our pleasure, but only when he offers himself for fellowship.'[18] All the older covenant mediators lacked in finality, because if they were mediators in their offices and functions, they were not in their persons. By contrast, Jesus was the mediator in person. 'The mediator concept is Christianised (in the New Testament). The new thing as compared with all previous conceptions is that the function of the mediator is related exclusively to Christ.'[19]

In his divine and human person Christ is prophet and Word incarnate, priest and sacrifice, king of Israel and Son of God:

> Nothing, in fact, is more constantly emphasised than that the mediator is of God's appointment—in his coming into the world (1 John 4: 9), in his priestly act at Calvary (Heb. 5: 4–6) and in his continuing priesthood in heaven. (Heb. 7: 20–22)...All that he does as man had the value of God's doing: his righteousness is the righteousness of God for us (Rom. 1: 17), his atonement is the achievement of God for us (Rom. 8: 3, 2 Cor 5: 21), and his victory is the triumph of God for us (Rom. 8: 31–39).[20]

Christ mediates for a holy God and for a sinful people. Because of this, the priestly office of Christ has central importance. God may speak to sinful man in a prophetic way, or as judge, without salvation ensuing from his word. He rules over men as the Lord who disposes of nations and individuals without being recognised as king. As the true prophet Christ bore witness to himself through his word, but his truth was not received or obeyed; as king he was rejected despite demonstrations of miraculous power and justice. The efficacy of Christ's mediation depends on the priestly office of Christ, which is central in reconciling God and sinners. The primary decisive work of Christ in establishing the new covenant lies in his death and God's acceptance of it as a satisfaction for sin.

> Christ's work of reconciliation must be seen as the basis for his prophetic proclamation and the royal gifts of eternal life and protection he bestows on the church. Christ as prophet functions as inner teacher to actualise the priestly work of reconciliation and thereby usher sinners in to the kingdom of God. Christ the king protects those who were purchased by Christ the priest and called by Christ the prophet. It is in terms of kingship that the eschatological consummation of the other two offices will occur.[21]

Jesus is first of all the true mediator between God and man in his priestly office. If he died a human death that death was not effective as a sacrifice for sin without the involvement of his divinity. As the divine-human priest, Jesus overcame death and rose in the Spirit, receiving life from his own eternal power and becoming the giver of life as the divine Lord. His priestly function was not only that of approaching God with the acceptable sacrifice for the expiation of sin to obtain reconciliation. It is also appearing in heaven as the one who intercedes for others as their advocate and defender. The ascension of Christ is a priestly act and the continuation of the work of the cross for his people. Christ 'lives to intercede' (Heb. 7: 25; Psalm 110: 4).

In his prophetic office, Christ is true mediator as the one anointed and confirmed by God, who not only brings God's word, but is that Word incarnate. Christ's word and miracles are prophetic acts, but far more amazing is the messianic person who does them:

> Don't you believe that I am in the Father and the Father is in me? The words I say to you are not just my own. Rather it is the Father living in me, who is doing his work. Believe me when I say that I am in the Father and the Father is

in me; or at least believe on the evidence of the miracles themselves.

John 14: 10–11

Christ's mediation could not be exercised without the kingly office: 'Christ was called Messiah especially with respect of and by virtue of his kingship.'[22] If this kingship was only fully inaugurated with his ascension into heaven, Christ began his kingly ministry in the days of his suffering by acts of sympathy and identification with his people. Christ's anointing with the Spirit at his baptism, the preaching of the gospel to the poor, and the liberation of captives are all aspects of his kingly rule. Identification with the needy, protection of the helpless, compassion for the suffering, healing of the sick, comforting the bereft, all these depend on the proximity of Christ to fallen human beings, but also on his kingly power to reply effectively to human needs. Christ's mediatorial kingship in heaven is a reality in Christ's life-giving rule over his people. He builds his church, protects and nurtures his people, and leads them in victory to glory (Eph. 4: 8–9). Once Christ was exalted in glory, his mediatorial office operated fully (Matt. 28: 18). 'The head that once was crowned with thorns, is crowned with glory now'[23]—a reason for worship (Matt. 28: 17), joy (John 20: 20), and wonder, 'It is the Lord!' (John 21: 7).

> The kingship of Christ is of a kind that could never be rightly claimed or really exercised except by one who was both God and man, divine and human. It stretches through the entire cosmos and it reaches into the hearts and minds of men. Where God alone rules there Christ the Lord is king. In perfect knowledge of the thoughts and hearts, the feelings and fears of millions of souls, Christ presides over his church, knowing every one of his subjects as only God could do, but knowing them too as only a fellow human could do; that is, knowing them not only from within the divine omniscience, but also from within the human condition.[24]

STOOPING TO CONQUER

The divine human constitution of Jesus implies that in the person of mediator, God comes down to our level and, accommodating himself to our condition, condescends to our

weakness and needs as sinners. Although one with the Father in
being, glory, and power, the eternal Son becomes subordinate
to the Father; he accepts the lowliness and humiliation that
are a necessary part of the work of salvation. God's divinity
is too much for us. It must be veiled under the appearance of
humanity for Christ to act as mediator in salvation.[25]

The text that jumps to mind in this respect is Paul's, 'For
there is one God and one mediator between God and men,
the man Christ Jesus, who gave himself as a ransom for all'
(1 Tim. 2: 5–6). It is clear from the final clause that Christ was
a mediator when he gave himself as a ransom, which indicates
the sacrifice of the cross and the payment made to satisfy divine
justice. The apostle emphasises the human aspect of Christ's
work with the words 'the man Christ Jesus'. He was acting as
a man for other men, representing them and fulfilling their
obligations in suffering and death. It is through the humanity
of Christ that men find a concrete link with God. 'The Son
of God offers us his hand like a brother and being one with
us in nature, he raises us to heaven from out of our miserable
condition.'[26] The emphasis on Christ the man highlights the
attitude of condescension that was the mainspring of the
actions undertaken by the mediator. He descended to our
level to raise us to his. The name 'Christ Jesus' indicates that
he was the Christ, the unique man, without any equal or
parallel, 'one' just as God is 'one'[27] because he was the anointed
Son. Taken together the combination 'the man Christ Jesus' is
a concrete way of indicating the unity of the divine and human
natures in the person of the mediator.[28] His act of self-giving
is a sign of his love for lost sinners and an act of obedience
to God accomplished in a totally spontaneous fashion. Paul
echoes the words of Jesus himself—'the Son of man came not
to be served, but to serve, and to give his life as a ransom for
many' (Matt. 20: 28). A real ransom is paid, his own self, as the
offering is a priestly gesture, and the redeemer is the mediator
who makes the payment.

> When we put these elements together,—the captive, the
> redeemer, the ransom, the party who held the sinner till he
> received the necessary equivalent to the claims of His law
> and who then takes them into a new endearing relation as
> His purchased property,—we have all the elements of a real
> transaction. It was not metaphorical, but real.[29]

A transaction there is, one that involves a mediator standing between both parties, and yet it is made within God, not outside him, in the person of the mediator. Such a delicate operation could not have taken place without the self-humbling of Christ in the service of sinners. It was for us, not just for our good, but in our place, as a real vicarious act of atonement.[30]

THE MEDIATOR, SALVATION AND HISTORY

The work of Christ as mediator runs along historical tracks from suffering and self-oblation to glory and exaltation. The period of suffering in Christ's personal experience ends with the resurrection and the ascension. Christ reigns now in glory. Even though as mediator he is still touched with the infirmities and sorrows of his people, and he assumes them as advocate and intercessor, suffering is no longer his own personal situation.

From the standpoint of salvation as God's gift, however, another perspective opens up. We can talk about what Christ did, what he is doing, and what he will do as the mediator of the covenant of grace, which he arbitrates between God and man. The incarnation, the earthly ministry of Christ, his death, resurrection, and ascension constitute what Christ has done in the accomplishment of salvation. Now, the risen and glorified Christ applies his work of redemption in his mediatorial reign as prophet, priest, and king. He applies the salvation accomplished for his people as he calls them to himself, gives them life through new birth, access to God through justification, and spiritual life manifested in sanctification. The future holds the prospect of Christ's return in glory and what he will do together with us as transformed human beings in the new creation. Christ accomplishes his mediatorial work for us in salvation mainly during his life and ministry on earth. Following the resurrection, the present work of the Holy Spirit, who unites us to the living Saviour, applies salvation to us and in us. Christ will be with us as Lord when, after his coming in glory to make all things new, we will be transformed into his glorious image.[31]

The following diagram illustrates the three 'stages' of Christ's mediatorial work, past, present, and future and the three levels of salvation: in its accomplishment (the triangle under the person of Christ), in its application (the three subsidiary triangles) and in the three living principles of its appropriation (faith, love, and hope—1 Corinthians 13).

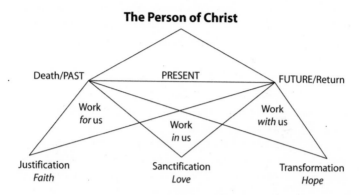

The Person of Christ

As the divine-human mediator between God and his people, Jesus is the substance of the covenant. The one covenant of grace is unfolded in three stages of salvation with an organic unity in a temporal and a logical sense, just as the bulb, the stem, and the flower of a tulip are three stages of development of the same plant. The eschaton, the final time of salvation accomplished by God in Christ, has three moments of development: salvation accomplished by one alone, by Christ the only mediator; salvation applied to many through the gospel; final salvation in the eternal kingdom. At the heart of the whole historical process of salvation stands the person of Jesus Christ as the mediator through whom God reveals himself in a definitive fashion and who is appointed 'heir to all things' (Heb. 1: 1–4).

Why, it may be asked, are there three successive stages in the historical mediation of Christ? The answer lies in the nature of the salvation accomplished, which must spread and eventually take possession of all the creation. If Adam had not sinned under the first covenant, fulfilment would have been immediate following his period of probation. Because of sin, however, creation as a whole has been 'subjected to vanity' (Rom. 8: 20). The covenant must firstly be renewed without us, from above, because of the heritage and reign of sin in creation. The covenant is re-established in Christ from outside, by a mediator. Salvation comes in the death and resurrection of Christ a first time, it comes to us through renewal by the work of the Holy Spirit because of the fulfilment in Christ, and finally it will come to the whole of creation in a final mediatorial act of Christ. 'Creation itself will be liberated from its bondage to decay and brought into the glorious freedom of the children of God' (Rom. 8: 21).

CONCLUSION

On Christ the 'one mediator' between the 'one God' and men hangs the whole of Christianity. Without a mediator, God can never be known and there is no salvation, no future. With many mediators there is no way to God either, only a multitude of dead-end streets going nowhere. With human mediators of all shades—priests, mediums, gurus, or witch doctors—there is nothing but the slavery of human formalism or worse, satanic oppression.

With Christ, because he is God and man, we can know what God is like. He is like Jesus and he welcomes us with good news of love and salvation. God loves lost sinners to the uttermost because he became man in the incarnation and made an unbreakable bond between himself and his creation. The whole of salvation is suspended on the person and work of Jesus. His death for sins means that we are freely accepted, justified by his grace through faith; his risen life and communion with us confers true humanity and progress in love and holiness; the promise of a transformed heaven and earth in the future gives us real hope.

> The face of Jesus is identical with the face of God, his forgiveness of sin is forgiveness indeed for its promise is made good through the atoning sacrifice of God in Jesus Christ, and the perfect love of God embodied in him casts out all fear. But all that depends on the identity between Christ's mediation of divine revelation and reconciliation in his own personal being as mediator.[32]

To depart from Christ-centredness is to lose everything.

ENDNOTES

[1] S. Edmondson, *Calvin's Christology* (Cambridge: Cambridge University Press, 2004), 38.

[2] G. Smeaton, *The Apostles' Doctrine of the Atonement* (Edinburgh: Banner of Truth, 1991), 318.

[3] E. Brunner, *The Mediator*, ch. XV. Cf. R. A. Peterson, *Calvin and the Atonement*, 42: 'Calvin's favourite way of saying 'the person and work of Christ' is simply to speak of the mediator'.

[4] A. Edersheim, *The Temple, its Ministry and Services at the Time of Christ*, 99.

[5] J. Calvin, *Institutes of the Christian Religion*, II.xii.1.

[6] S. Edmondson, op. cit., 29.

[7] Revelation 1: 8; 21: 6; 22: 13; Isaiah 41: 4, 6.

[8] On man as 'the image of the true image' see P. E. Hughes, *The True Image* (Grand Rapids: Eerdmans, 1989).

[9] H. Ridderbos, *Paul*, 92 f.

[10] P. Stuhlmacher, *Revisiting Paul's Doctrine of Justification* (Downers Grove: IVP, 2001), 27.

[11] Calvin debated this point with the Lutheran Osiander, who claimed that mediation concerned only the divine nature and Stancaro who affirmed that Christ acted as mediator only in his human nature and not in his person as the God-man.

[12] H. Ridderbos, *The Gospel of John* (Grand Rapids: Eerdmans, 1997), 638.

[13] As in the preceding chapter.

[14] S. Edmondson, op. cit., 32.

[15] R. A. Peterson, op. cit., ch. 3. Also J. F. Jansen, *Calvin's Doctrine of the Work of Christ* (London: James Clarke, 1956).

[16] See chapter 7.

[17] See Exodus 24: 4–8; 32: 31–2; 33: 7–11; Numbers 12: 6–8 and Galatians 3: 19; Hebrews 3: 2–5.

[18] A. Oepke, 'mesistes', ed. G. Kittel, *Theological Dictionary of the New Testament*, IV, 614. In the New Testament 'mediator' is used in Galatians 3: 19, 20, 1 Timothy 2: 5 and Hebrews 8: 6; 9: 15; 12: 24.

[19] Ibid., 619.

[20] P. Lewis, *The Glory of Christ* (Carlisle: Paternoster, 1992), 220. All chapter 15 is most useful.

[21] R. A. Peterson, op. cit., 59. As Martin Luther said, Christ 'reached his priesthood through his death and his kingdom through his priesthood.' Quoted by H. Blocher, '*Agnus Victor*. The Atonement as Victory and Vicarious Punishment', 89.

[22] J. Calvin, *Institutes of the Christian Religion*, II.xv.2.

[23] Thomas Kelly's hymn, 1820.

[24] P. Lewis, op. cit., 226.

[25] Subordination is not ontological, but a loving decision shared by the Father and the Son. Cf. S. Edmondson, op. cit., 38.

[26] J. Calvin on 1 Timothy 2: 5–6 in *Commentaires sur le Nouveau Testament*, VII, (Aix-en-Provence: Kerygma, 1991), 119.

[27] The Old Testament confession of faith, Deuteronomy 6: 4.

[28] As in 1 Corinthians 15: 21 ff; 45–9, Romans 5: 15–21 and Philippians 2: 7–8, this passage speaks of Christ's humanity in a context 'where his divinity is either implied, alluded to or stated.' G. W. Knight, *Commentary on the Pastoral Epistles* (Grand Rapids: Eerdmans, 1992), 121.

29 G. Smeaton, op. cit., 321.

30 Ibid., 322. Cf. 1 John 2: 2.

31 This structure is proposed by A. König, *The Eclipse of Christ in Eschatology. Toward a Christ-centered Approach* (Grand Rapids: Eerdmans, 1989).

32 T. F. Torrance, *The Mediation of Christ* (Exeter: Paternoster, 1983), 70 quoted by Lewis, op. cit., 227.

14

Peacemaker

In the preceding chapters we considered what the passion of Christ entails and how he is the mediator between God and man in his life and death. Jesus died on the cross as a sacrifice for sin. He suffered the penalty of death for others, physically and spiritually. He was given up to judgment, and won the victory over Satan and the powers of evil.

Now it is time to consider how the work of Christ opens the way from sin and death to freedom and new life in communion with God. Christ lives and reigns as Lord. His work of salvation is completed as an earthly mission, but as mediator, Christ is now the enthroned Saviour who applies its benefits to his people. Thus the plan of God to 'bring many sons to glory' (Heb. 2: 10) follows its course until his return at the end of the age.

Christ's present work is one of intercession in which he acts as advocate for those for whom he died. His intercession secures the remission of sin on the merits of his work on the cross. Through his mediation God is rendered favourable to sinners. This is expressed by the word propitiation: sin that arouses God's anger is covered through Christ's death on the cross. Sin is removed through expiation: the vicarious blood of Christ removes sin. Therefore those who were lost are redeemed.[1]

Sinners have a new-found freedom because Christ's work is effective. They stand in a new relation to God as they are no longer in a situation of alienation, but are reconciled with him.

These are the practical results of the death of Christ and its benefits for those who need salvation. Together they can be summed up by the word 'satisfaction': God welcomes sinners because he is satisfied with what Christ has achieved as a sure basis for forgetting the past, for giving new life in the present, and for the promise of future salvation.

Thus the effects of the work of Christ 'are set forth in three capital relations: as these effects concern God, they are termed propitiation, and hence reconciliation; as they respect sin, expiation; and as they respect the sinner himself, redemption.'[2] In this chapter we will consider the result of Christ's work of propitiation and expiation, that he lives to represent others to God, and that he obtains the remission of their sin through his intercession. The way this change of relationship happens is important and can be summed up like this:

> It is one thing to say that the wrathful God is made loving. That would be entirely false. It is another thing to say the wrathful God is loving. That is profoundly true. But it is also true that the wrath by which he is wrathful is propitiated through the cross. This propitiation is the fruit of the divine love that provided it. 'Herein is love, not that we loved God, but that he loved us and sent his Son to be the propitiation for our sins' (1 John 4: 10). Propitiation is the ground upon which the divine love operates and the channel through which it flows in achieving its end.[3]

How does this renewal of relationships with God become a reality? Through the intercession of Christ, the remission of sins, and by his mediatorial work of propitiation and expiation. God is no longer estranged, but welcoming to sinners in Christ.

ATONEMENT AND INTERCESSION

Atonement and intercession are intertwined because both are aspects of the office of Jesus as priest. The priestly activity of Jesus began while he was on the earth and continues in heaven.

Christ's intercession for his people permeated his suffering, as illustrated in the 'high priestly prayer' of John 17. Jesus prays not only for himself but also for his followers, those alive then and those in generations to come. He intercedes precisely because he will no longer be with them in the world, and so that in his absence, they might be protected from the evil one (v. 15). He prays they might be truly sanctified in the truth, recognising that the Father sent him into the world (v. 17) and being of one mind in making this known (v. 23). He asks that his disciples might know and confess that he alone is the mediator, the one who makes the Father's glory known (v. 1–5).

In the final words of this prayer, the most remarkable one that ever ascended from earth to heaven, Jesus vows to continue to intercede for his people: 'I have made you known to them, and I will continue to make you known in order that the love you have for me may be in them and that I myself may be in them' (17: 26). This 'continuing' might refer to the cross, or to the coming of the Comforter according to Jesus' promise (John 16: 7). It seems wise, however, not to adopt a restrictive interpretation. This promise corresponds to the final words of Jesus' discourses to his disciples recorded in the previous chapter: 'I have told you these things so that in me you may have peace. In this world you will have trouble. But take heart! I have overcome the world' (16: 33). Jesus as the source of victory and life will continue his work in favour of his people for ever.

As the great high priest who passes through the heavens and enters the presence of God at the ascension he continues to offer intercession to the Father for his own (Heb. 4: 14, 8: 1, 9: 11). He 'ever lives to make intercession' and is able to save 'to the uttermost' (Heb. 7: 25) because what he presents to the Father is himself, the ultimate 'gift and sacrifice for sin' (Heb. 5: 1). As the one who offered the atoning sacrifice for sin, Christ is the advocate who 'speaks to the Father in our defence' (1 John 2: 1–2). The atonement is actively continued in heaven, but without suffering. It passes over from a ministry of humiliation to one of glorious and effective intercession (Rom. 8: 34). 'Every active principle that was in operation in Emmanuel's soul on the cross passes over without a break, and blends into the permanent function of intercession.'[4] The love of Jesus for his Father, the desire to do his will, his self-giving in the interest of others and his love for them, his respect of the divine covenant and desire to bring it to fulfilment, the intimacy of communion with the Holy Spirit—all that characterised his earthly activity in obtaining salvation is present in his continuing activity.

Christ cannot fail in his intercession, no more than his self-offering to fulfil the conditions required for atonement could have failed. In both aspects of his work the Messiah will see success and be satisfied (Isa. 53: 11). The present intercession of Christ has two distinct aspects. It is firstly the defence of the cause of accused sinners: 'he bore the sin of many and made intercession for the transgressors' (Isa. 53: 12). This is a legal defence relating to accusations that might be brought against those he represents. An illustration is found in the prophecy of Zechariah. The high priest, Joshua, comes before the angel of the Lord to seek protection and the Lord replies by defending his own: 'The Lord rebuke you Satan! The Lord who has chosen Jerusalem rebuke you! Is not this man a brand snatched from the burning?' (Zech. 3: 1–2). In the case of this Old Testament Joshua, the priestly office is incomplete, because the priest is dressed in 'filthy clothes' (Zech. 3: 3–5) and needs new clothing. Jesus' defence of his people, by contrast, is a perfect one, as its pleading is made on the basis of his own 'blood and righteousness' and the removal of sin, which according to Zechariah's prophecy will be accomplished in a single day (Zech. 3: 4, 9).[5]

Secondly, the intercession of Christ is characterised by profound sympathy and loving care, as he is touched by the dangers, needs, and sufferings of his people. It is real affinity because in the days of his own suffering, Christ went through everything his people experience and even more. This is the foundation on which they may themselves receive 'mercy and grace' in time of need (Heb. 4: 15–16). Its efficiency lies not only in that Christ was 'without sin', 'made like his brothers… to make atonement for the sins of the people' (Heb. 2: 17–18), but also because he is the divine mediator and intercessor, 'now crowned with glory and honour' (Heb. 2: 7). Because of this, Christ speaks 'good and comforting words' to his people (Zech. 1: 13).

How does the intercession of Christ work in practice? By his promises not to leave his people and to come to them through the presence of the Holy Spirit. Being sent in the name of the Father and the Son, he witnesses to believers of the reality of Christ's heavenly work because he is sent to bear witness to the reality of Christ's intercession (Rom. 8: 26–7).

INTERCESSION AND THE REMISSION OF SIN

As Mediator, Christ stands between God and sinners. He interposes himself as the intercessor. If we cannot approach God other than through Christ, so also God does not come to his children other than through Christ. The light of God's holiness, which would only serve to reveal and condemn our sin, comes to us through Christ as light through a prism. The purity of God's light is diffused through his person with the many colours of God's grace for us.

This is possible because our sin is already atoned for by the cross of Christ. Texts such as Hebrews 2: 17; 7: 25, and 1 John 2: 2 establish a direct connection between Christ's intercession and the remission of sins. As high priest Jesus is 'holy, blameless, pure, set apart from sinners...he sacrificed for sins once and for all when he offered himself' (Heb. 7: 26–7). The intercession of Christ has its justification in that in his sacrifice there is remission of sin. In his death guilt is cancelled and with it the liability to punishment.[6]

So there is an objective foundation for the pleading of Christ for his people as their advocate. He can hold up the evidence of his righteousness and his undergoing judgment for sin before the divine tribunal. The appeal Christ makes is to the justice of God and to his law, which has no longer any power of accusation. Christ is 'the end of the law for righteousness' (Rom. 10: 4) as the one who stands between divine judgment and his people. The ground of the appeal is the work of atonement he has accomplished. Christ himself was 'made sin for us', that is, he presented himself as an offering for sin, in order that we might become 'the righteousness of God' (2 Cor. 5: 21). Paul expands on this in Romans 8: 3–4: 'God sent his own Son in the likeness of sinful man to be a sin offering. And so he condemned sin in sinful man, in order that the righteous requirements of the law might be fully met in us.' The result of Christ's appeal is the recognition by God that our sins have been remitted.

Where the divine judgment would find us in our sin and condemn us, it finds Christ and his righteousness; where it finds the holy and pure Christ it also finds us in love. Such is the evidence Christ brings forward as the fruit of his saving work. Upon those grounds he pleads for the remission of our sin. If there is no remission of sins apart from the atonement of

Christ, there is no atonement in a practical sense apart from the remission of sins the risen Christ pleads for in God's presence. This dual consideration is the motivation of the intercession of Christ.[7]

Atonement, remission of sin, and the intercession of Christ all spring from the same deep and inexplicable love of God for sinners, despite their sin. By nature men are 'objects of wrath'. But because of his 'great love for us, God, who is rich in mercy, made us alive with Christ even when we were dead in transgressions—it is by grace you have been saved' (Eph. 2: 4–5).

TURNING AWAY GOD'S ANGER

Propitiation relates to the anger of God brought about by sin. It concerns a change in the relation between God and sinners, although it does not imply a change in God himself. Such a change takes place when the wrath of God is turned away because of an offering presented to God.

Sin excites the anger of God, which once inflamed is difficult to extinguish. There is nothing unholy or incompatible with God about such a belief. If human beings recognise that it is not wrong to be shocked when one is the object of offensive behaviour, why should it be wrong for God to be angry at sin that is odious and hateful to his moral character? The judgment of God does not spring from impure motives, but from his holiness itself. It is not out of joint with God's other dispositions, such as his goodness and love. It is the love of God that is rejected by sin. As a result, the judgment of God against unrighteousness in all its forms is unavoidable.[8]

Propitiation is presented in the Old Testament by the verb *kāpar*[9] and in the New by the words *hilaskomai* (Heb. 2: 17), *hilasmos* (1 John 2: 2; 4: 10), and *hilasterion* (Rom. 3: 24).[10] The words in this group have the precise sense of covering or overlaying sin indicating that the anger of God is appeased and that God is well disposed.[11] The Old Testament provides the background for the concept of propitiation. In the temple's Holy of holies, where the presence and glory of God were found, stood the mercy seat, the throne of God, a slab of pure gold covering the ark of the covenant, which contained the tables of the law. On the great Day of Atonement, the high priest entered the holy place, sprinkling the blood of the sacrificed goat over the mercy seat and seven times before it (Lev. 16: 14–15). Thus when God, in his glory, looked down toward the ark containing the law, the condition of the covenant, his eye met the blood-sprinkled mercy seat. The blood of the sacrifice covered sin and thus the anger of God was turned away from the people. Sin was purged away, atonement was made and God was reconciled to his people. The slab of gold, called the propitiatory, was the most important place in the temple, and the sprinkling of blood upon it was the culmination of the sacrifice for sin. The Holy of holies itself was sometimes called 'the house of the covering' (1 Chron 28: 11). The removal of sin is founded on that God is merciful, his anger is turned away from the wrongdoer, and therefore forgiveness is possible. That the fate of non-reconciled man is to be subjected to the anger of God is recognised as being inevitable:

> We have sinned and rebelled and you have not forgiven. You have covered yourself with anger and pursued us; you have slain without pity. You have covered yourself with a cloud so that no prayer can get through.
>
> Lam. 3: 42–4

Terrible words indeed! Yet, God can react mercifully in relation to sin:

> Their hearts were not loyal to him, they were not faithful to his covenant. Yet he was merciful: he forgave their iniquities and did not destroy them. Time after time he restrained his anger and did not stir up his full wrath.
>
> Ps. 78: 38, cf. Ex 34: 6–7

Forgiveness intervenes thanks to sacrifice. God is reconciled only by the covering of sin and this can only be accomplished by sacrifice. The act of propitiation has its origin in God who provides the way for reconciliation by substitution, and through sacrifice he establishes a new relationship with the sinner:

> The life of the creature is in the blood, and I have given it to you as an atonement (propitiation) for yourselves on the altar; it is the blood that makes atonement (propitiation) for one's life.
>
> Lev. 17: 11[12]

Things are formally no different in the New Testament. The following are the relevant examples to the question of propitiation:

> God presented Christ Jesus as a sacrifice of atonement, through faith in his blood.
>
> Rom. 3: 25 (*hilasterion*)

> Jesus Christ, the righteous one is the atoning sacrifice for our sins...
> God loved us and sent his Son as an atoning sacrifice for our sins.
>
> 1 John 2: 2, 4: 10 (*hilasmos*)

> A high priest in service to God that he might make atonement for the sins of his people.
>
> Heb. 2: 17 (*hilaskesthai*)

The most discussed text in the New Testament series is that of Romans 3: 25. The context in which God is said to present Christ as a propitiatory sacrifice is important. It is the universal fact of sin that all have fallen short of 'the glory of God', cannot stand in his presence, and are condemned by his law (Rom. 3: 21, 23). But because of the 'righteousness of God that comes through faith in Jesus Christ to those who believe', as sinners they are 'justified freely by his grace through the redemption that came by Jesus Christ' (Rom. 3: 24). Faith in Christ is the answer to the problem of sin for those who believe. This is explained in three different ways in verse 24, all of which have relation to sin. In the language of the law courts, sin is forgiven because they are justified. The language of slavery presents sinners as having been redeemed from sin, its accusation and power, with the payment of a price by Christ. In commercial language this is done freely, as the ransom has been paid.[13]

Justification, redemption, and freedom are results of the way salvation is accomplished in Christ. This is explained in cultic language in Romans 3: 25. What was hidden behind the veil of the temple, what was done every year by the high priest, has now been made public and done once by Jesus Christ. 'Jesus is the ultimate "mercy seat" the ultimate place of atonement, and, derivatively, the ultimate sacrifice...a human sacrifice, in public, once for all—and placarded by God himself.'[14] The way the atonement is achieved is by the death of Christ 'presented as a sacrifice'. Salvation is secured by propitiation, the covering of sins through blood. God is the subject of the act of propitiation, as he 'presents' Christ. He is also the object of the act. God, not sin, is propitiated. He takes the necessary action to turn away his wrath from judging sin by the sacrifice offered.

Many objections are raised with regard to this, mainly the accusation that the idea of placating or pacifying God is more pagan than biblical. It is also claimed that propitiation is incoherent because God does something to himself that changes his relation to sinners. Retribution is vindictive, barbaric, and savage. Why should he not just change his mind and decide on forgiveness? Such objections fail to appreciate what the atonement really is.[15] Sin has created a situation in relation to the Lord, and in particular to his holiness, justice, and love that make propitiation necessary. Would God multiply sufferings unnecessarily if simple relaxation were possible?[16] Romans 3 affirms precisely that God's way of replying to sin, far from being arbitrary or incoherent, is a demonstration of his righteousness (v. 5, 21).

How then is the righteousness of God demonstrated? We often think that right and wrong, virtue and sin, justice and injustice, approval of one and disapproval of the other are two principles that stand in antithesis. But it is not the case, as there is only one principle in question. One law, one form of rule or principle provides the criteria for distinguishing between what is acceptable and what is not. 'No litter' means that it is right to use the bin and wrong to use the pavement for disposing of one's wrappings. There are two possible acts but one principle at stake.[17] Likewise with God. The principle of right and wrong is his law. The law itself is simply an expression of what God requires because of what he is. Love and judgment of sin, holiness and condemnation, justice and vengeance, righteousness and rejection are not two principles for God, but the expression of one acceptable standard. His own perfectly pure and spotless person is the criteria for approval of the right expressed in love, holiness, justice, and righteousness; and also for disapproval of the wrong expressed by judgment, condemnation, vengeance, and rejection of sin. So according to the same standard God must love the one and hate the other.

Propitiation and the 'mechanics' of the atonement in Romans 3: 24–6 tell us something deep about God 'that demonstrates his justice'. 'It explains the need for Christ's propitiating sacrifice in terms of the just requirements of God's holy character.'[18] Love and holiness are not opposed to justice and judgment in God, but are two sides of the same coin. A God without indignation for sin would also be a God lacking in love for righteousness. Retribution for sin is not an impetuous vendetta on God's part, but a love for what is holy and good. Justice is necessary to God being a God of love. Sin is unpardonable unless satisfaction is made for it, which implies substitution—Christ in the sinner's place and sacrifice for forgiveness.

As far as God is the subject and object of propitiation, the sacrifice does not cause God to demonstrate a love for sinners he did not have; it is a demonstration of love in the act of propitiation and justice with regard to sin. The sacrifice of Christ does not turn the anger of God into love, it is a vindication of all he is as a righteous and a loving God. That the sacrifice of Christ is necessary to God as the subject and object of the atonement does not diminish God's love, but enhances it, because God does what is needful for himself and for the salvation of sinners.[19]

> Far from finding any kind of contrast between love and propitiation, the apostle can convey no idea of love to anyone except by pointing to the propitiation—love is what is manifested there; and he can give no account of the propitiation but by saying, 'Behold what manner of love'. For him, to say 'God is love' is exactly the same as to say 'God has in his Son made atonement for the sin of the world.'[20]

The initiative comes from God. Propitiation is real. God turns away from his anger; his righteousness and love are demonstrated in one act. God is vindicated as he is true to himself and his moral order, and sinners are justified. This is the last chance for sinners. Not that the love of God touches them and inspires them to turn over a new leaf, but that Christ in the love of God has borne our sins.[21]

PROPITIATION OR EXPIATION?

Nothing causes modern people to react negatively more than the idea of God's anger and displeasure at sin. But should you propose a benevolent God, people despise softness and laxity. Underneath they know that God's love is not marshmallow sentimentality and that God is not a great romantic expecting the best from sinners.

The rejection of an angry God and of the benevolent God puts Christian theology and preaching into a double bind. The anger of God in the Old Testament, it is claimed, refers to particular wrongdoings, such as disloyalty, and is not a characteristic attribute of God. Furthermore the language of atonement, propitiation, and anger do not come together there.[22] Recent objections along these lines owe a good deal to the influence of C. H. Dodd who claimed, with regard to Romans 3: 25, that it is not about propitiation, but about the expiation of sin.[23] The atonement in question is therefore not a pacifying of the wrath of God against sin, but the deliverance of the sinner, which wipes out sin and avoids disaster. On the cross Jesus made expiation for sin, but he did not appease the anger of God. In other words he made an expiatory sacrifice and not a propitiatory one.[24]

This discussion may seem like splitting hairs, but it is important. If it is simply a question of expiation and not propitiation in these texts, then man becomes the object of the act of the cancellation of sin through the cross. The removing of sin is something that concerns man. This implies that sin does not affect God in a direct way. If dirty windows are cleaned and the grime removed, then so much the better, as it is easier to see through them than when they are dirty. To say that expiation concerns the removal of sin from man, means that it makes things better for him. In Scripture, however, sin is not just a question of impurity or uncleanness in man that needs removing.

Ask the question: Why must sin be removed if God is not angry? Surely the answer is not that it is just better for man for it to be so. It must be removed because of God and what God thinks of it. Ask a further question: If a man's sin is not cleaned up and he dies with it, what happens to him? Biblically the answer must be that he undergoes the judgment of God because of his sin. Why?—because God is bound to judge sin according to retributive justice. These answers show that sin is not simply something unacceptable in man as a form of subjective wrong that can be wiped away. It is also hostility in relation to God and the removal of this hostility cannot be other than two-sided. This is just another way of saying that God is angry at sin. The expiation of man's sin is half the story and propitiation is the other half. Expiation without propitiation is like mending a punctured tire without blowing it up again.

Put another way, sin and guilt are not things that can be wiped away, like dirt from the window. They are serious because they block communion with God in the personal realm. They come between man and God because they are offensive to God. Sin alters relations between God and man, so the problem must be tackled in such a way as to restore the relationship. The offence of sin must be dealt with by removing the reasons for anger in God. Expiation must have a godward perspective for God to treat the sinner differently. It must be brought back to propitiation to express the meaning of grace in the restoration of a personal relation between God and the sinner.[25]

It is in this sphere that the whole of Christ's work as advocate and intercessor takes on its importance. Expiation is not a removal of sin announced to man in a prophetic declaration on the part of God. It has its meaning as an aspect of propitiation related to the priestly office of Christ who enters into God's presence pleading the merits of his own death for sin. God in Christ fulfils the meaning of the Old Testament sacrificial system in that he himself provides the means for removing his own wrath.

'TOUGH' LOVE AND AN ANGRY GOD

The anger or wrath of God is an anthropomorphism, a way of speaking of God's dispositions as though he were a human being, in the interest of making things about God clear to us in human terms.[26] It has the disadvantage of unfavourable comparisons being drawn with the more insalubrious aspects of human anger: selfish passion, involving irrationality or vindictive spite, together with lack of self-control. Even in the case of human anger, however, we can recognise situations where injustice has been so flagrant that righteous indignation or anger is a justifiable response.[27]

The anger of God is stubbornly rooted in the Old Testament, despite what some modern theologians might try to argue.[28] If the Bible never says that 'God is angry' in the way it says that 'God is love', God's anger is an aspect of his holiness, and strangely of his love as he reacts to the breaking of his covenant and to sin.[29] God can say to Israel, 'You only have I chosen of all the families of the earth, therefore I will punish you for all your sins' (Amos 3: 2). 'God's holy anger does not cast shadows over his love, but is the other side of it.'[30] It is 'tough' realistic love, not sentimentalism.

If the affective and punitive aspects of the anger of God cannot be denied, it is not a passion or an emotion in God as with human beings, subject as they are to emotional instability. It is tied to God's holiness, righteousness, and love, which are eminently 'stable' attributes of his nature. The following consideration serves to underline and explain this:

> The relationship between God's love and his wrath can best be seen by considering two intermediate concepts, God's righteousness and his jealousy. God's love always observes the boundaries of his righteousness...The sacrifice of Christ insures that God's redemption is loving and righteous, so that Scripture can even appeal to God's righteousness as a ground for the forgiveness of sins and thus God's righteousness becomes a form of his love. But it is also God's righteousness that insures the final punishment of those who reject his love—that is, his wrath against them. Without the wrath of God against those who finally disbelieve, God's love is no longer righteous. So God's righteousness binds together his love and his wrath...God's love is covenantal. It creates a special relationship between God and his creatures— a marriage, in effect. So when people reject him, he is filled with holy jealousy, and the result is wrath...it is a jealous love that leads to wrath when it is abused.[31]

Wrath and anger are not fitful in God. Because God's love 'passes through' his righteousness and his jealousy in relation to his creatures, when God expresses love toward them it is righteous and jealous love. If man, as a sinner, is found in the state of alienation from God and rejection of him, God's holiness and jealousy rise to the surface of his love and find their normal expression in his anger and wrath. That a wrathful God is a loving God is profoundly true.[32] The anger with which God is angry is propitiated by the cross of Christ, at great price, and by the initiative of his loving kindness and mercy.

CONCLUSION

The expiation of sin is achieved because sin is removed by a forfeit that is equivalent to the wrong perpetrated. It has a legal and impersonal flavour. Propitiation, on the other hand, is relational and personal. It corresponds to the appeasement of God's anger against some person or persons. Propitiation is closely linked to the holiness and righteousness of God by the judgment of sin in the person and sacrifice of Christ. It expresses the love of the Father in giving the Son and the love of the Son in bearing the weight.

This replies precisely to the needs of sinners. The forgiveness of sins allays our natural fear of judgment; remorse and guilt that assail us as sinners require expiation and the removal of sin; our war with God ends in armistice because the anger of God is neutralised, just as Jesus calmed the wind and the waves of Galilee and said, 'Peace, be still'.

ENDNOTES

1   I have slightly modified the definitions given by S. Kistemaker in 'Atonement in Hebrews', in C. E. Hill, F. E. James, eds., *The Glory of the Atonement*, 163–4.

2   A. A. Hodge, *The Atonement*, ch. XII.

3   J. Murray, *Redemption Accomplished and Applied*, 31–2.

4   H. Martin, *The Atonement*, 61.

5   H. Blocher, '*Agnus Victor*. The Atonement as Victory and Vicarious Punishment', in ed. J.G. Stackhouse, *What does it mean to be Saved?*, 88.

6   B. B. Warfield, 'Christ our Sacrifice' in *Works*, II, 430.

7   See H. Martin, op. cit., ch VII, who provides a full development of the concept of intercession.

8   See J. Stott, *The Cross of Christ*, ch. 5, on satisfaction for sin.

9   Leviticus 16: 6–34 in the Greek Old Testament uses *exilaskomai*, 'to make antonement'.

10   In classical Greek this word group also has the sense of the turning away of anger, which is the meaning retained by Josephus and by Philo and also in the writings of the apostolic fathers such as 1 Clement or the Shepherd of Hermas. Cf. F. Büchsel, J. Hermann, 'hilaskomai', in ed. G. Kittel, *TDNT*, III, (Grand Rapids: Eerdmans, 1965), 300–23.

11   Older translations of the Bible used the word 'propitiation', but modern versions often replace this word with 'expiation', 'atoning sacrifice' or some form of dynamic equivalence.

12   See chapter 9.

[13] D. A. Carson, 'Atonement in Romans 3.21–26' in *The Glory of the Atonement*, 128.

[14] Ibid, 129–30.

[15] Cf. J. Murray, op. cit., 32, 30.

[16] F. Turretin, *The Atonement of Christ*, 27. 'His goodness and wisdom do not permit us to harbour the idea that the Father could expose his most innocent and beloved Son to an excruciating and ignominious death, without a necessity which admits of no relaxation.'

[17] Cf., R. L. Dabney, *Christ our Penal Substitute*, 48 ff.

[18] D. A. Carson, art. cit., 138.

[19] J. Murray, op. cit., 33–4

[20] J. Denney, *The Death of Christ* (Carlise: Paternoster, 1977, 1951), 152. Here Denney is speaking about 1 John 4: 10 and says 'John rises above all comparisons to an absolute point of view at which propitiation and love become ideas which explain each other.', 151.

[21] Cf., J. Denney, *The Christian Doctrine of Reconciliation*, 161–62

[22] J. Goldingay, *Atonement Today*, 51–2.

[23] C. H. Dodd, *The Epistle to the Romans*, 1932 and *The Bible and the Greeks*, (London: Hodder & Stoughton, 1935). Dodd refers to the Old Testament Greek translations of *kāpar* which render it as 'expiation' (*hilaskomai*) in the sense of purifying, removing impurity or cancelling sin. See L. Morris, *The Cross in the New Testament*, 347–50.

[24] J. Stott, *The Cross of Christ*, ch. 7, for a discussion of the whole question and the influence of Dodd, particularly in the translation of The New English Bible. On propitiation see the two chapters in L. Morris, *The Apostolic Preaching of the Cross*, 144–213 and also the detailed studies by R. Nicole, in *Standing Forth. The Collected Writings of R. Nicole* (Fearn: Christian Focus, 2002).

[25] Cf. L. Morris, op. cit., 203–13.

[26] J. Frame, *The Doctrine of God*, 366–8.

[27] L. Morris, ibid, 208–9. J. Frame, ibid, 464, points out that if human anger is named in New Testament lists of sins, 'anger, like hatred, is appropriate when directed against God's enemies.'

[28] See J. B. Green, M. D. Baker, *Recovering the Scandal of the Cross*, 53ff. Cf. L. Morris, *The Apostolic Preaching of the Cross*, 149, who indicates that words about the wrath of God in the Old Testament occur over 580 times, 'a formidable body of evidence.'

[29] If texts such as Psalm 7: 11 and Nahum 1: 2 say that 'God expresses his anger every day' and 'the Lord takes vengeance and is filled with wrath' these texts are speaking of God in a human way in relation to specific historic situations. By his anger God expresses holiness in judging man's sinfulness. The anger of God is not an essential divine attribute comparable to, for example, his love. It is an aspect of his righteousness and appears in situations that present God's attitude toward sin, described by anthropomorphic language. In God himself, considered eternally and essentially, there would be no anger at all.

[30] See E. Peels, *Shadow Sides. God in the Old Testament*, 113. Peels says that God's vengeance has a positive meaning as well for restoring justice and

redressing wrong. It is linked to the anger of God and calls God's people to return to the covenant, 81 ff. It is a function of kingship and judgeship.

31 J. Frame, op. cit., 476.

32 It will not do to say, as do J. B. Green and M. D. Baker, op cit., 52, that 'God's graciousness is foundational to his character; hence, it outlasts his wrath and spills over in abundance in activity that saves and sustains life.' How can something 'disappear' from God, unless of course, the factor that mars the relation between God and the sinner is removed? Green and Baker's attenuation of God's anger corresponds to their low view of sacrifice as not the 'exclusive way to deal with sin', 48.

15

The 'Three Rs'

To be saved is to be translated from one state to another, from death to life, captivity to freedom, sin to righteousness, despair to hope, from a lost past to a hopeful present. It is the reason for thankfulness, praise, and love for God, which burst out like a butterfly from a chrysalis in a new way of life. The dynamic is centred on the saviour, God who intervenes to deliver his people in the Old Testament, and on the person of Jesus, the God-man in the New.

The 'negative' side of salvation, as we have seen, eliminates that which kept man captive. Remission of sin, expiation and propitiation are the result of Christ's intervention as mediator. This aspect of his work is God-wards. In perfect obedience Christ offered himself to God as a sacrifice for sin, suffering death, judgment, and the bitterness of separation from the Father. In doing so, he dealt with God on our behalf.

As risen Lord, he deals with us on behalf of the Father. The 'positive' application of salvation is man-wards. The results of salvation can be described in a precise way by the 'three Rs': redemption, righteousness, and reconciliation.[1] In the New Testament these words indicate the outcome of salvation, focussed on the person of Christ:

- the redeemer who provides freedom;
- the holy one who establishes rightness before God;
- and the author of reconciliation between God and sinners.

The following schema illustrates the movement involved in salvation by grace:

Salvation

	sacrifice and death of Christ	
Sin		Righteousness
Guilt		Forgiveness
Condemnation		Justification
Death → propitiation	redemption	expiation ← Life

God and man—alienation　　　　　**God and man—reconciliation**

Two little words, 'in Christ', sum up the new relationship. In his resurrection life, Christ unites himself to his people and makes them participate in the benefits he won for them. Having acted as their substitute, he now stands as the one who guarantees their salvation.[2] 'We in Christ' is the outcome of this double action for those who inherit the 'three Rs'. The salvation 'which was first announced by the Lord, was confirmed to us by those who had heard him.' Christ lives and reigns to bring 'many sons to glory' (Heb. 2: 4, 9).

A change of heart is not what saves, nor does faith in and of itself obtain salvation and peace with God. Christ himself is the author of salvation. He saves as the Lord and covenant head, working salvation in the lives of his people. His covenantal position relates all he is and has done to the life of believers (Heb. 5: 9, 12: 2).

REDEMPTION FROM SIN

> Ransom presupposes some kind of bondage or captivity, and redemption, therefore, implies that from which the ransom secures us. Just as sacrifice is directed to the need created by our guilt, propitiation to the need that arises from the wrath of God, and reconciliation to the need arising from our alienation from God, so redemption is directed to the bondage to which our sin has consigned us.[3]

The meaning of redemption is close to that of salvation.[4] It indicates a past, a present, and the intervention of one who saves or redeems. But it is more than deliverance, as it points to the means by which salvation is achieved, through the payment of a ransom or a fee. In the ancient world it was an easily understood metaphor of freedom from slavery and the new social status which followed. Until the advent of instant credit the three brass balls of the pawn shop in British towns presented a vivid symbol (apparently borrowed from the Medici merchant bankers) of debt and release on payment to redeem articles.

Sinners are in pawn to Satan and need to have their lives repossessed at a price for them to be freed from sin and death. 'Guilt is too great to be removed by forgiveness pure and simple. Before this can take place something else must happen, upon the basis of which forgiveness can become possible.'[5] The something that must happen is redemption.

Christ actually purchased and procured redemption. He effectively redeemed his people to God by his blood (Rev. 5: 9). 'Our great God and Saviour, Jesus Christ gave himself for us to redeem us from all wickedness and to purify for himself a people that are his very own' (Tit. 2: 14; cf. 1 Tim. 2: 6). This is an inspired definition of redemption. Its price is the self-giving of Christ, who really redeemed us, rather than just making it possible.[6] Redemption is freedom from sin and iniquity and involves the purification of his people, who become his property. More than being freed, it is belonging to Christ.

In the Old Testament legislation, life and property could be redeemed (Exod. 21: 30). The model for redemption was provided by the exodus of Israel from Egypt, the house of bondage that became a picture of the slavery of sin. Since the first-born sons were spared when God passed over the land, thanks to the protecting blood on the lintels of the dwellings, thereafter all the firstborn livestock in Israel were to be offered to the Lord as belonging to him. Firstborn sons were also to be redeemed (Exod. 13: 11–15). This was a memorial to the fact that 'with a mighty hand the Lord brought us out of Egypt, out of the land of slavery.' God's deliverance is redemption and he is the redeemer of Israel (Exod. 6: 6; Ps. 78: 35). In the same way, liberation from the exile in Babylon was pictured as a redemptive release. The Lord will 'ransom' and 'redeem' his people: 'their redeemer is strong, Almighty is his name' (Jer. 31: 11; 50: 34).

It is often pointed out that in the Old Testament redemption is generally not from sin and iniquity, but from captivity, which is not an individual experience of salvation, but the liberation of a community. If, however, sin was the cause of exile, deliverance from captivity could scarcely be construed other than as redemption from what had led to it. The release of Israel and their return to the promised land displays the glory of the Lord who redeems his people because he says: 'I have swept away your offenses like a cloud, your sins like morning mist. Return to me for I have redeemed you' (Isa. 44: 22–3). If sin separates Israel from God, causing him to hide his face and not hear, 'the redeemer will come to Zion, to those who repent of their sins (and) the days of sorrow will end' (Isa. 59: 2, 20; 60: 16, 20). God's day of vengeance and redemption will come again, as in the time of Moses: 'You O Lord, are our Father, our redeemer of old is your name' (63: 16).

Nor was the individual aspect of redemption lacking in the Old Testament. Did not Job know that his redeemer was living and that he would plead his cause? (Job 19: 25). The Psalms bear witness to God's benefits in healing power, sins that are forgiven, and lives that are 'redeemed from the pit' (Ps. 103: 3–4).[7] If no man can 'redeem the life of another or give God a ransom for him' (49: 7), it is surely because God alone is the redeemer. He has provided the means for redemption through the offerings of the ever-present sacrificial system, by which the sin offering made atonement for the person of the offender, and the trespass-offering provided a ransom for specific wrongs. When David prays to be washed of his iniquity and cleansed from his sin, he is requesting nothing less than redemption (Ps. 51: 2).

In the light of the call of Abraham (Isa. 29: 22), the exodus, and the deliverance from the exile in Babylon, it is only natural that in the Old Testament the power of God as the redeemer should stand in the foreground, overshadowing the ransom itself.[8] God redeems by mighty power (Deut. 9: 26), against all human odds, in a display of free and unmerited love toward a people who have little to recommend them (Deut. 9: 4–6). In power and grace God delivers his people, and because of this, redemption 'enters its religious use…in that it describes the loving reacquisition of something formerly possessed' (Deut. 7: 6–7; 14: 2).[9]

THE REDEEMER'S RANSOM

What the Old and the New testaments have in common is the 'realism of redemption'.[10] God is the redeemer and his redemption is accomplished according to the conditions of his own character, demonstrating his sovereignty, grace, and truth. Just as the person of the saviour comes into focus in Jesus in the revelation of salvation, so also do the ransom paid for redemption and the personal nature of deliverance from sin and death. The new covenant with God's people will be different from the former liberation from Egypt, because God will inscribe his law on the hearts of his people, he 'will forgive their wickedness and remember their sins no more' (Jer. 31: 33–4). This salvation is not of a temporary nature; it has finality.

In Mark 10:45 Jesus explained what drove him. It is amazing to think that unlike us, Jesus had no human goals of self-realisation and ambition: 'The Son of Man did not come to be served, but to serve, and to give his life as a ransom for many.' Jesus' purpose is service in the particular sense of self-giving. He states his position to be that of a representative acting 'for many'. The result is an effective ransom for others. What is in view here is not primarily the liberation of those in slavery, but that Jesus is personally a ransom for those condemned to death. His self-giving saves their lives. The death of Jesus provides the conditions necessary for redemption through ransom.

Paul also speaks of salvation as liberation through ransom: 'in Christ we have redemption though his blood, the forgiveness of sins, in accordance with the riches of God's grace' (Eph. 1: 7). Redemption and forgiveness are virtually synonymous: 'in the Son we have redemption, the forgiveness of sins' (Col. 1: 17). Considered in relation to Romans 3: 24, it is clear that the price of the ransom is the blood of Jesus, the giving of his life. Sinners who fall short of the glory of God 'are justified freely by his grace through the redemption that came by Christ Jesus. God presented him as a sacrifice of atonement through faith in his blood.' In this case the setting at liberty 'is most closely connected with the reconciliation God has given through the blood of Christ.'[11]

That the death of Christ is the cost of man's redemption is also indicated when the apostle says 'you were bought at a price' (1 Cor. 6: 20; 7: 23). The ransom paid by him is the price needed to purchase those who were captive to sin and it is the occasion of an exhortation for Christians to free themselves from a slave-mentality: 'Do not become slaves of men'. Death is condemnation according to the conditions of God's law; Christ redeemed us by accepting that curse. He was 'born under the law to redeem those under the law' and 'became a curse for us' by hanging on the tree (Gal. 4: 4–5; 3: 13).[12] Christ's death as a curse is the way in which he has ransomed and purchased us, which can barely be put in a more precise way than in 1 Peter 1: 19: 'You were redeemed from the empty way of life…with the precious blood of Christ, a lamb without blemish or defect.'[13]

Christ pays the price for others and redeems them, but this is not just like a formal business transaction between two people who fix a price in the best interests of both. The interests are ours. The love is God's. The price is the self-sacrifice of Christ. When Christ pays the price he does so out of love for the Father and in harmony with his divine purpose to save the world from sin and the wrath of God. That Christ is substitute, representative, and mediator lies at the heart of redemption, just as much as it does in atonement. The curse of the law from which Christ redeems is not an 'independent blind force detached from God, but the fulfilment of the divine threat against sin.'[14] Christ takes the burden of the curse on himself; in dying on the cross in the place of men, he pays the price for their redemption.

For believers who are in Christ by faith, Christ has 'become redemption' (1 Cor. 1: 30), and not only do they look back on redemption, but also forward to it. Sealed by the Holy Spirit, they have the 'firstfruits', which bring the coming 'day of redemption' into view (Rom. 8: 23; Eph. 4: 30). Their liberation, secured by the ransom of Christ, is a present experience through the forgiveness of sin. It is also a future hope of the resurrection of the body and deliverance from death. 'In this hope we are saved…as we await eagerly for our adoption as sons, the redemption of our bodies' (Rom. 8: 24). This will happen within the context of the cosmic dimension of the appearing of the new creation: 'the creation itself will be liberated from its bondage to decay and brought into the glorious freedom of the children of God' (8: 21).

Redemption has three concentric circles in the New Testament: the inner circle is made up of individual believers united to Christ; next, the people of God as the body of the redeemed; lastly, the whole creation delivered from the curse of sin.[15] The ransom paid on the cross as the price of redemption has universal consequences. Believers, the human race, and the creation will all be saved because of Christ's redeeming work. The new creation and all it contains grows from the cross planted at Calvary.

REDEMPTION FROM AND REDEMPTION FOR

Sin is slavery to evil and loss of life in a spiritual and a physical sense. Redemption is liberation from bondage and the title deed to a renewed life. The final goal is eternal redemption and life, obtained by Christ and into which he has already entered (Heb. 9: 12). The power of sin is the law because of its accusing and condemning force; to be redeemed is to be liberated from the oppression of condemnation, either in the sense of the recognition of objective wrong, or in that of subjective guilt.

Christ, however, does not only redeem from the law, but also from the sin that makes the law's accusations effective. Redemption liberates from the guilt of sin because Christ's people are 'bought with his own blood' (Acts. 20: 28) and translated from the kingdom of darkness to the kingdom of life (Col. 1: 13). Redemption liberates from the power of sin, because sin no longer rules in their lives as they are 'dead to sin and alive to God in Jesus Christ' (Rom. 6: 11, 14). So when Paul speaks about redemption from sin, he also refers to newness of life and sonship: 'You are no longer a slave but a son; and since you are a son, God has also made you an heir' (Gal. 4: 7). To receive redemption is to enter into 'the blessing given to Abraham' and to 'receive the promise of the Spirit' (3: 14).

The blessing of redemption is being made one with Jesus Christ, not only purchased by him through the ransom paid for freedom, but also united with him in his life. The realities of the curse and blessing of the covenant are joined in Christ, who has dealt with judgment and brought life to light in his resurrection from the dead. Redemption completed in this way includes both of these factors, sin and death defeated and salvation bought through his life (Rom. 5: 10).

Redemption accomplished by the mediatorial work and sufferings of Christ has a concrete outworking in the lives of believers. Not only did Christ obtain their release from sin and its condemnation, but as the living redeemer he works sanctification in those he has delivered from sin by the gift of his Holy Spirit. 'Redemption from guilt and the penal consequences of sin was intended to be the means to an ulterior end—that end being our personal sanctification.'[16] The scope of redemption as holiness of life in those who have been delivered from sin is the basis for many exhortations to live a different life: 'You were bought with a price, therefore honour God in your body' (1 Cor. 6: 19–20).

THE RIGHTEOUSNESS OF GOD

Union with Christ, the mediator and head of the covenant, is the fruit of redemption. It also embraces in its scope the righteousness in Christ in which the believer participates. Through union with Christ, the righteousness of Christ is the righteousness of the believer.

This righteousness is wrought in a concrete way by the mediator in all his work, in his life and death. In the light of this astounding fact, discussions about whether or not righteousness is infused or whether being righteous concerns the believer's status as 'a member of the covenant' pale into insignificance.[17] If the righteousness of God in Christ is the determinative factor, then the important issue is how it is received. We believe that it is by imputation, God counting what belongs to Christ alone as being ours because of our oneness with him.[18] How does this come about?

What is the ground for the pardon and acceptance of sinners? There is only one answer in Scripture to that question—the righteousness of God himself. Ultimately there is only one kind of righteousness, and it belongs to God. It is unique and can be claimed by no one else. It stands over against any other form of rightness claimed by man either because of obedience to the divine law, or good works, or even because of belonging to God's people.

The gospel reveals the righteousness of God (Rom. 1: 17; 3: 20–1) and it is revealed in the justification of sinners. 'It is a God-righteousness, not simply because it is provided by God, nor simply because it is approved by God, nor simply because it is bestowed by God, but chiefly because it is a righteousness with divine quality or property…a righteousness with divine attributes.'[19] The righteousness of God, or the righteousness of Christ in God, always belongs to God, even when it is imputed to us and he becomes 'the Lord our righteousness' (Jer. 23: 6).[20]

REVEALED RIGHTEOUSNESS

What is this 'God-righteousness'? Certainly it is not an abstract quality in the eyes of Paul or other New Testament writers. It is most concrete because it is revealed from heaven, revealed in the gospel. As divine righteousness, it stands over against man's ideas about it or any acts of justice and goodness by which man might attempt to establish his own rightness. The revelation of the righteousness of God has as its content Jesus Christ himself and what has taken place in him, in the events of the cross and resurrection.

In a key text, Romans 3: 21–6, the apostle speaks about redemption and propitiation as being demonstrations of the righteousness of God:

> But now the righteousness of God, apart from the law, is revealed…even the righteousness of God through faith in Jesus Christ to all and on all who believe…(who are) justified freely by his grace through the redemption that is in Christ Jesus whom God set forth as a propitiation by his blood, through faith, to demonstrate his righteousness… that he might be just and the justifier of the one who has faith in Jesus. (NKJV)

The righteousness of God is set forth in the death of Christ, in a demonstration of divine justice.[21] In this text the righteousness of God has two aspects. In the first two references it concerns something that God reveals and gives to man through Christ. It is conferred upon man and replies to his needs because it is 'apart from the law' and any human efforts to obey it. The second aspect, found in the third use of 'righteousness' in the above text, is the action of God as the righteous one in his way of handling sin. He 'sets forth' Jesus as the atoning sacrifice for sin. To be justified by 'blood' is to be 'saved from the wrath of God' through Christ (Rom. 5: 9). God is 'just' because he has dealt with the problem of sin in the death of the Lord Jesus and he is therefore the 'justifier' of those who believe in Christ.

God-righteousness is 'double righteousness' in the way it is revealed. It also has a twofold foundation, concerning the Father and the Son—the Father in his justice in judging sin, and the Son in his perfect obedience, which is a counter-demonstration of righteousness, replying to the judgment of God. The two aspects cannot be separated or pitted one against the other because they are the one righteousness of God revealed in the whole work of salvation. Firstly, the righteousness of God the Father requires satisfaction so justice may be established. It also inflicts punishment for sin on his Son, who stands in the place of sinners.[22] Secondly, in his life and death the Son acts out righteousness by becoming 'obedient to death, even the death of the cross' (Phil. 2: 8). Christ, through his mediatorial work, accomplishes the righteousness required of sinners, who have none in themselves (Rom. 5: 6). It is enacted before God as voluntary and perfect obedience, in their place and on their behalf. So Paul can say in Romans 5: 18–19 that 'the result of one act of righteousness was justification that brings life... (and) through the obedience of one man, the many will be made righteous.' This was the purpose of Christ's death, that the 'gift of righteousness reigns in life through one man, Jesus Christ' (Rom. 5: 17; Gal. 2: 21).

SIN AND RIGHTEOUSNESS

This is spelled out in 2 Corinthians 5: 21: 'God made him who had no sin to be sin for us, so that in him we might become the righteousness of God.' It was for sinners that Christ was 'made to be sin' and on their behalf he enacted all the righteousness required for their acquittal. Christ 'being made sin' cannot be considered personal to him, as this would contradict that he had 'no sin'.[23] It could be taken in the sense that Christ was made a sin-offering for us, but the expression 'made sin' seems to imply more than this.[24] If there was no sin in Christ, it can only be that he was made as one with sin by standing in our place to undergo the judgment of sin for us. 'God made him sin: that is to say that God the Father made his innocent incarnate Son the object of his wrath and judgment for our sakes, with the result that in Christ on the cross the sin of the world is judged and taken away.'[25]

What was already enacted in Christ at the cross was God's final judgment against sinners, the sentence of death against them. The outcome of the cross was acquittal because of his righteousness and obedience, and consequently his resurrection and life:

> In Christ's death God has sat in judgment, has judged sin, and in this way he has caused his eschatological judgment to be revealed in the present time. But for those who are

in Christ, he has therefore become righteousness, and the
content of the gospel of the death and resurrection of
Christ can be defined as the revelation of the righteousness
of God for everyone who believes.[26]

The righteousness of God revealed in the present is the
mystery of salvation—what God has done in Christ. Sin has
been judged in a way that vindicates the righteousness of God
the Father and is acceptable to him. It has been dealt with in
the righteousness of the Son, through his pure holiness and
obedience in being 'made sin' and suffering in the place of
sinners. This is the whole and complete 'God-righteousness'
imparted to sinners who can thereby stand justified before
God: there is 'no condemnation' for those who are in Christ
Jesus (Rom. 8: 1).

But how is this righteousness imparted? The answer is
not by it being instilled in believers as a moral quality. The
perfections of Christ cannot be transferred from him to others
like a serum can be injected into a body. Only by imputation
can we be made beneficiaries of Christ' work. Christ stood
'for us' that we might stand 'in him'. This is because God
counts his righteousness to us. This makes the righteousness
of God received in the gospel so different from the Jewish
'works righteousness' opposed by the apostle in Romans.
Righteousness cannot be acquired by the law or by obedience
to its commandments. It is revealed without the law because by
works none can be justified (Rom. 3: 21, 28).

Abraham is the great model of righteousness apart from the
law. 'He believed God and it was credited to him as righteousness'
(Rom. 4: 3, 22, cf. Gen. 15: 6).[27] What did Abraham do?
Nothing. He trusted the promise of God. His righteousness
and acceptance lay in God; it came from God and his promise.
If a man works, says Romans 4: 4, recognition of his work is
not a 'gift', but a salary due to him. Abraham did not work,
but rested in God's word: 'to the man who does not work but
trusts God who justifies the wicked, his faith is credited as
righteousness' (Rom. 4: 4–5). Abraham was 'fully persuaded
that God had power to do what he had promised. That is
why it was credited to him as righteousness' (Rom. 4: 21–2).
Righteousness was not in Abraham but in God. This fact, says
Paul, was not recorded for him alone. The words 'credited
to him', adds Paul, were written for believers to whom God

will impute righteousness because they 'believe in him who raised Jesus our Lord from the dead. He was delivered over to death for our sins and was raised to life for our justification' (Rom. 4: 23–4).

The apostle underlines this by referring to David who says in Psalm 32: 1–2: 'Blessed are they whose transgressions are forgiven, whose sins are covered. Blessed is the man whose sin the Lord will never count against him.' Precisely, this is the blessedness of one 'to whom the Lord credits righteousness apart from works' (Rom. 4: 6). And it is to the 'ungodly' that this happens! It happens because 'Christ died for the ungodly' while they were still powerless and while they were sinners (Rom. 5: 6–8).[28]

'Justification finds its necessary presupposition in the imputation of righteousness.'[29] In other words, if a person is justified, it is by a declaration made possible by the imputed righteousness of God. What is imputed is a reality because it is constituted on the basis of Christ's work, as he died for sins and was raised for the purpose of justification.[30]

FEATURES OF BIBLICAL IMPUTATION

The imputation of God's righteousness described above has four specific features that describe its unique character.

Firstly, it is a double imputation, with two directions and two sides—from God with righteousness and from us with sin. 2 Corinthians 5: 21 says Christ was made sin and we are made righteousness. God justifies the ungodly (Rom. 4: 5). What belongs to God alone becomes the sinner's and what is the sinner's becomes Christ's. Because the Lord's righteousness is eternal it is for ever effective for the salvation of sinners, but because Christ died 'once for sin' (Heb. 9: 26–8), the sin of the ungodly has been judged and abolished in him. A glorious transfer indeed, that bears witness to amazing grace!

Secondly, imputation is real and not legal fiction. Sinners really become the righteousness of God when the merit of Christ is counted to them, and God considers them accepted and righteous because of Christ. In like manner, Christ was really made sin on their behalf and died condemned, to do away with sin.

Thirdly, imputation is direct, or immediate, as the older theologies put it. As a picture projected on a screen appears in full technicolour, so it is with the double imputation of righteousness and sin. Nothing in the screen itself can produce the picture shown on it. The spectators watching the film are not watching the screen but the light and colour projected on to it. So also when God beholds sinners, he does not look at their condition, but at the righteousness of Christ they have received. When God beholds Christ as their mediator, acting in their place, he sees sin condemned in his suffering and death. 'We ourselves have done nothing of what is imputed unto us, nor Christ anything of what was imputed unto him.'[31]

Finally, righteousness is counted to sinners in the light of faith in Christ. Faith in Christ is like the whiteness of the screen that receives the projected pictures. Just as a black screen would not reflect light and colour, imputation does not exist where faith is not present. But Scripture does not say that the sinner is justified because of faith or on the consideration of faith. 'It speaks always of our being justified by faith, or through faith, or upon faith, but never speaks of our being justified on account of faith or because of faith.'[32] That would make faith into the reason for our being justified and, to use the illustration again, would be akin to pretending that the screen creates the picture. Faith would become a meritorious work and a ground for justification. However, the reason or the ground for the justification of the ungodly is only ever the righteousness of God in Christ and its imputation to sinners.

By way of conclusion: sinners are justified only because of the righteousness of Christ imputed to the ungodly. The following texts resume and illustrate the argument in this section:

- Justification is free (Rom. 3: 24; Eph. 2: 5; Titus 3: 7);
- Christ is our guarantee. His righteousness is counted to us and our sins are counted to him (Heb. 7: 22; Isa. 53: 6, 11; 2 Cor. 5: 21; 1 Pet. 2: 24);
- He is our propitiation (Rom. 3: 25; 1 John 2: 2);
- We are justified through Christ, or for his name, or his sake, or by his blood (Acts 10: 43; 13: 38–9; Eph. 1: 7; 4: 32; Rom. 5: 9; 1 John 2: 12);
- Christ is called 'our righteousness' (Jer. 33: 6; 1 Cor. 1: 30; Rom. 10: 4);

- Sinners are justified by his obedience, or righteousness (Rom. 5: 18–19);
- The righteousness that justifies is God's and Christ's, not our own (Rom. 1: 17; 3: 22; Phil. 3: 9).[33]

THE RECONCILIATION OF GOD

Biblical revelation is a tale of two cities: Athens and Jerusalem, contrasting two different claims to truth—human wisdom or revelation; the city of man and the city of God described by Augustine, with two different projects and constructions— one for this world and one for eternity; and the city of enmity or the city of reconciliation with God—indicating man's situation in a state of opposition to God as opposed to life in harmony with him. Peace with God is made a reality through the propitiation and expiation of sin and reconciliation is the state resulting from the finished work of Christ.

It is sometimes stated without more ado that reconciliation between God and man does not require any repairing of broken relationships other than simple forgiveness on the part of God. Jesus was the authentic spokesperson for the human race and he made peace overtures on our behalf. We in turn must ask for forgiveness to be accepted. When God grants amnesty because of Christ, and man asks to be forgiven, the result is the rebuilding of a relationship of love and confidence between man and God.[34]

This man-centred view of reconciliation seems the opposite of what the New Testament actually says. Reconciliation has three complementary aspects: it comes from God, it is a reality in Christ, and it applies to men's needs as they become reconciled sinners, saved by grace.[35] The three aspects are present in the classic passage in 2 Corinthians 5: 17–21.

First of all, reconciliation is the goal of the atonement, and comes from God: the 'new creation' has appeared in Christ and 'is from God who reconciles himself to us through Christ' because 'God was in Christ reconciling the world to himself' (2 Cor. 5: 18–19).[36] Colossians 1: 19–22 presents the same truth with equal clarity and refers to the universal perspectives of reconciliation: 'God was pleased to have all his fullness dwell in Christ, and through him to reconcile to himself all things...Once you were alienated from God and were enemies in your minds because of your evil behaviour. But now he has reconciled you by Christ's physical body through death.'

There can be little doubt that God is the subject of reconciliation, the actor of it through the atonement, or that it is a two-sided affair.[37] If God is the one who restores man to his favour, it was because there was hostility and estrangement between himself and man. If on man's side there was unholy opposition against God, from God's side the situation was one of holy alienation from man. So God took steps to abolish the cause of antagonism between himself and man.[38]

Reconciliation is primarily the removal of the reasons for God's alienation from his creatures, before it is the removal of our opposition against God. In any normal kind of disagreement it is not the offended party who needs to say sorry to the offender. It is the opposite—the offended one needs to be reconciled to the offender.[39] When Scripture says we were 'enemies' to God, it expresses the estrangement from God to which we were subjected as sinners. God reconciles himself to us through Christ's atoning work, putting away the enmity, and we receive the reconciliation of which he is the author.

The two-fold barrier between God and man is removed in reconciliation. We can be reconciled to God, because in Christ God is reconciled to us. If in Scripture the accent falls on the sinner being reconciled, two facts are obvious. The sinner does not reconcile himself, he is passive in reconciliation and is saved from God's wrath by Christ: 'If, when we were God's enemies, we were reconciled to him through the death of his Son, how much more, having been reconciled, shall we be saved through his life' (Rom. 5: 9–11). Moreover, if man's reconciliation comes to the fore in Scripture, it is because man's need of a restored relationship is most strikingly apparent. His sin has marred communion between God and man. The accent falls on this perspective which is concordant with the gravity of man's sin and his striking need of salvation. God makes peace 'through the blood of Christ' and our reconciliation to God is included in God's reconciliation to us (Eph. 2: 13–18).[40]

RECONCILIATION IN CHRIST

Reconciliation is 'in' Christ and 'through' him (2 Cor. 5: 18–19, 21). The peace afforded is the consequence of the righteousness established in the atonement and accounted to believers by imputation. For this reason, it follows that there is a closeness between justification and reconciliation. In Romans 5: 9–10 there is a parallel between 'justified by Christ's blood' and 'reconciled to God through the death of his Son.' As peace with God, reconciliation is a consequence of justification: 'Therefore, since we have been justified through faith, we have peace with God though our Lord Jesus Christ, through whom we have gained access by faith into this grace in which we now stand' (Rom. 5: 1). This is positive objective peace, over against real enmity expressed by sin and rebellion:

> Justification is always forensic and does not refer to any subjective change in man's disposition. Since this is so, the expression 'reconciled to God' must be given a similar juridical force and can only mean that which came to pass in the objective sphere of divine action and judgment.[41]

The peace treaty between God and man is signed with the blood of the cross. Justification involves the abrogation of sin, because of the non-imputation of guilt. Reconciliation is renewed harmony with God through Christ, the reconciler in the work of redemption. Grace and peace with God are both received through faith in Christ.

If God is the author of reconciliation, Christ is the agent acting on God's behalf to negotiate the peace. God is the 'God of peace, who through the blood of the eternal covenant brought back from the dead our Lord Jesus, the great shepherd of the sheep' (Heb. 13: 20).[42] Peace with God is an objective state, and through Christ it has subjective consequences. When two countries make peace, communication is re-established, commerce resumes again, common projects are made, and cultural exchanges develop in an atmosphere of growing confidence. So also for the sinner, peace with God is not just a formal cessation of hostile attitudes. It is new life with God in the positive and subjective sense of talking with God, desiring to obey his will, to know more about his ways and works. Inner peace pervades the heart of the reconciled sinner in all his activities, with joy, hope, trust, and the power of the Holy Spirit (Rom. 15: 13).

The cosmic perspectives of reconciliation in texts like Colossians 1: 15–22, which branch out to embrace 'all things' in their scope, indicate that peace with God puts man in a position to serve the Lord of all his creation as a new covenant creature. New perspectives for service open up in God's reign of peace as the believer 'continues in faith, established and firm, not moved from the hope held out in the gospel' (v. 23). Reconciliation 'effects peace as the fruit of justification and thus prepares the way to receiving a share in the new creation, the new things, peace as the all-embracing conclusion of salvation.'[43]

Reconciliation has to be received. Sinners must enter into a state of peace with God, not to make it effective, but to benefit from its blessings. The pressing exhortation of the apostle as an ambassador of Christ—'We implore you on Christ's behalf: Be reconciled to God' (2 Cor. 5: 20)—is to enter a new relationship of favour with God because of the reconciliation established by the work of the cross. Repentance, new life in Christ, conversion and faith in him are not reasons why sinners get to be reconciled. They are consequences of the end of hostilities through the finished work of the cross. Just as justification finds its reflection in faith and is received through faith, so also reconciliation is connected with confidence in Christ as the one in whom the sinner can find peace. The work of Christ applies to sinners as they enter into a new covenantal relationship with God by becoming reconciled themselves. The grace of God who makes peace in Christ finds a home in the hearts of those who receive the gospel through faith and enter God's family. Reconciliation not only deals with hostility between God and man, it also takes away enmity between people, because the cross has removed the cause of human antagonism (Eph. 2: 16).

From its centre in God, reconciliation radiates out through Christ to embrace renewed individuals saved by grace, the new community of Christ's people, and cosmic peace in the new creation when 'God will be all in all'. (1 Cor. 15: 26, 28)

CONCLUSION

God's redemption, righteousness, and reconciliation are great answers for anyone trying to get by as a human being or looking for some happiness in life. The story the 'three Rs' tell us is this: Once upon a time there was a poor and miserable someone who was profoundly dissatisfied with life, felt oppressed by the world, and who lashed out continually at the hydra of injustice. That person was liberated from slavery by the payment of a ransom. Dressed in new clothes, placed in a new environment, offered friendship and given a future, life became as different as light is from dark. A promise was given that this situation would never change and that there would never ever be a return to slavery.

This is a picture of salvation in Christ. Redemption delivers from the slavery of the sin system. Righteousness is the believer's new attire. Peace with God and others, in a new community of faith, hope and love, gives a reason for living.

If the 'three Rs' present three different metaphors to describe the results of atonement, their message is totally consistent: as far as salvation is concerned, God did it—he did it in Christ and he did it for our benefit. The grace of God frees sinners for lives of faith and gratitude, quite the opposite to the slave mentality that protests 'I want it, I want it all and I want it now'. Shakespeare was right, 'Nothing will come of nothing: speak again.'[44]

ENDNOTES

[1] See also J. Stott, *The Cross of Christ*, ch. 7 on the aspects of salvation.

[2] J. I. Packer, 'What did the Cross Achieve', 20.

[3] J. Murray, *Redemption Accomplished and Applied*, 43.

[4] L. Morris, *The Apostolic Preaching of the Cross*, ch. 1.

[5] E. Brunner, *The Mediator*, 516.

[6] J. Murray, op. cit., 63.

[7] Cf. Psalm 26: 11; 31: 5; 49: 15; 69: 18; 71: 23; 72: 12–14, and many other references.

[8] Only in Isaiah 43: 1–3 where Egypt is called the given ransom are redemption and ransom connected.

[9] G. Vos, *Biblical Theology*, 114.

[10] Ibid., 109.

[11] H. Ridderbos, *Paul: An Outline of His Theology*, 194, who adds: 'The thought of the sacral propitiatory death and the idea of redemption borrowed from legal life would then be coupled very closely together.'

[12] These references use the word *exagorazo*, to indicate that redemption is from the 'forum (*agora*) of sin'. Cf. Ephesians 5: 16; Colossians 4: 5; Revelation 5: 9; 14: 3–4.

[13] Cf. 1 Peter 1: 2, 'sprinkling by his blood', a reference to the death of Christ as a sacrifice. Cf. L. Morris, *The Cross in the New Testament*, 321 f.

[14] H. Ridderbos, op. cit., 196.

[15] Cf. J. B. Green, M. D. Baker, *Recovering the Scandal of the Cross*, 38–46, 99–102.

[16] T. J. Crawford, *The Doctrine of Holy Scripture Respecting the Atonement* (Grand Rapids:Baker, 1954–1871), 194–6. Cf.2 Corinthians 5: 15; Ephesians 5: 25–7; Colossians 1: 21–2; Titus 2: 14; Hebrews 9: 14; 1 Peter 2: 24.

[17] As in N. T. Wright, *What Saint Paul Really Said. Was Paul the Real Founder of Christianity?* (Grand Rapids: Eerdmans, 1977) 119–24.

[18] 'Imputation' means 'accounted to, counted to or credited to'. Something belonging naturally to a person is imputed to that person, or something belonging to a person can be legally imputed to another person by transfer. An illustration is Philemon 1: 18 where Paul assumed the debt of the slave Onesimus on his own account.

[19] J. Murray, 'Justification' in *Collected Writings*, II, (Edinburgh: Banner of Truth, 1977) 213. Cf. J. Buchanan, *The Doctrine of Justification* (Edinburgh: Banner of Truth, 1984–1867), 318: 'It means a righteousness by which, and not merely a method in which, we are justified.'

[20] Concerning righteousness as belonging uniquely to God, see Isaiah 45: 24–5; 54: 14; 63: 1–3; 64: 13; 65: 24–5; Romans 8: 33.

[21] H. Ridderbos, op. cit., 167: 'God has shown the adjudicating power of his righteousness in Christ, by giving him for others as a means of propitiation in death.'

[22] J. Buchanan, op. cit., 318 f.

[23] Hebrews 4: 15; 7: 26; 1 Peter 2: 22; 1 John 3: 5.

[24] Reasons against 'sin-offering' are given by C. Hodge, *The Second Epistle to the Corinthians* (Edinburgh: Banner of Truth, London, 1959), 148 and P. E. Hughes, *The Second Epistle to the Corinthians* (Grand Rapids: Eerdmans, 1962), 214 f.

[25] P. E. Hughes, op. cit., 213. Hughes remarks that Christ was not made a sinner, and believers are not made 'righteous', but 'the righteousness of God'.

[26] H. Ridderbos, op. cit., 168.

[27] The word 'impute' (*logizomai*) is used in Romans 4 in verses 6, 8, 11, 22–4, cf. 2 Corinthians 5: 19. The NKJV translates 'imputed or accounted' and the NIV 'counted or credited'. See B. B. Warfield, 'Imputation' in *Works*, IX, 301–9.

[28] H. Ridderbos, op. cit., 176. 'The ground for this imputation cannot be the situation in that which man himself works or is, but just in that which not he, but God is able to effect and in which man can only receive a share through faith, that is by grace.'

[29] J. Murray, *Works*, II, 210

[30] J. Murray, *Redemption Accomplished and Applied*, 124. 'Justification is both a declarative and a constitutive act of God's free grace. It is constitutive in order that it may be truly declarative.'

[31] J. Owen, 'The Doctrine of Justification by Faith' in *Works*, V, (London, Banner of Truth, 1967–1850), 169. Chapters VII and VIII of Owen's work are one of the high points of Protestant theology on the subject of double imputation.

[32] J. Murray, *Redemption Accomplished and Applied*, 125. Murray also comments: 'Faith is not the response of the person to the justifying act, but is presupposed in the justifying act, and this faith is not the faith that we have been justified but is rather directed to the proper object in order that we may be justified.' *Works*, II, 215

[33] Taken from R. L. Dabney, *Systematic Theology* (Grand Rapids: Zondervan, 1972–1878), 639.

[34] Cf. M. Winter, *The Atonement*, ch. 5. Cf. J. Denney's remarks on 'free forgiveness' in *The Christian Doctrine of Reconciliation*, 12ff.

[35] Cf. The detailed examinations of the New Testament texts in L. Morris, *The Apostolic Preaching of the Cross*, 214–250 and H. Ridderbos, op. cit., 182–204.

[36] 'God was in Christ reconciling the world'—note the past tense to denote a completed work; the reference is not to the incarnation but to the cross.

[37] When the New Testament uses the verb 'reconciled' in the active tense, God is the subject and when it is used in the passive, man is the subject who has been reconciled. Cf. J. Denney, op. cit., 233 ff.

[38] E. Brunner, *The Mediator*, 516.

[39] Cf. Matthew 5: 23–4; Romans 11: 15; 1 Corinthians 7: 11.

[40] Cf. F. Turretin, *Institutes of Elenctic Theology*, II, 433–4; *The Atonement*, 49–53; J. Murray, *Redemption Accomplished and Applied*, 38–42; R. Gaffin, 'Atonement in the Pauline Corpus', in C. E. Hill, F. E. James, eds., *The Glory of the Atonement*, 156–60.

[41] J. Murray, op. cit., 39. Cf. H. Ridderbos, op. cit., 186 f.

[42] 'The God of peace'—see Romans 15: 33; 2 Corinthians 13: 11; Philemon 4: 9; 1 Thessalonians 5: 23; 2 Thessalonians 3: 16.

[43] H. Ridderbos, op. cit., 185.

[44] *King Lear*, I.1.

16

Satisfaction

Satisfaction describes, more comprehensively and precisely than the word atonement, all that is involved in the completed work of Christ as mediator between God and man.[1] Although it has often been criticised on the grounds that it is not a biblical term, satisfaction lies close to the meaning expressed by several words in Scripture.[2] It joins in one global description the religious cultic features of sacrifice (expiation, curse, propitiation, purification, blood) and the legal language of condemnation (guilt, penalty, judgment, remission). 'The satisfaction of justice lies near the heart of sacrificial atonement.'[3]

Anselm was the pioneer of the theology of satisfaction. Calvin and the Reformers used it in a different way: not in the sense of making redress to God's honour, but in the legal context of meeting the requirements of divine justice through punishment.[4] Later, satisfaction was described in the double sense of the active and passive obedience of Christ. His sinless life and undefiled death together make a perfect answer to the divine conditions for salvation and acceptance. 'Active and passive' are not altogether appropriate for, as we shall see, Jesus was never more active than in his 'passive' obedience in death.

THE COMPLETED WORK OF JESUS

We propose an approach to the question of satisfaction along different lines, although the background idea is that all the conditions necessary for salvation are fulfilled in Christ.

Death, after birth, is the most important moment in our lives, as not only is it irrevocable, but it completes life. People often die in a way that mirrors how they have lived. Lenin is said to have died fantasising about electricity, while Stalin imagined himself to be attacked by wolves. Death is a spiritual litmus indicating where our real values, hopes, and fears lie. Sometimes deathbed conversations express the feeling that looking back, life is complete, because what people set out to do has been accomplished.

For Jesus the time of death was also the most important moment in his life, as it brought his whole life's work to completion. He had achieved everything he set out to do as a divine-human person with a mission. No more profound way of expressing his fulfilment of purpose can be imagined than his prayer, 'The time has come...I have completed the work you gave me to do...' (John 17: 1, 4). This is the satisfaction that dwelt in the conscious mind of Jesus. No misplaced words or false teaching, no bad feelings, no unloving acts, no evil thoughts had sullied him. Moreover, he had done everything uprightly, in a way that corresponded to God's blueprint for what a human being should be. 'After the suffering of his soul, he will see the light of life and be satisfied' was eminently true for him. He also knew that he had fulfilled the prophecy that 'my righteous servant will justify many, and he will bear their iniquities' (Isa. 53: 11).

When the ultimate moment came, Jesus could look back on the whole of his experience, gather it up in a conscious act, and call out with a loud voice, 'Father, into your hands I commit my spirit.' When he had said this, he breathed his last breath (Luke 23: 46). This was satisfaction in death in a full and complete sense.[5] The remarkable fact is that no gospel writers actually say that Jesus died. 'Committing the spirit' to the Father and 'giving up the spirit' are not normal ways of describing death.[6] When Jesus died he did not do so in a spirit of defeat and anguish, but he was sure that death could not maintain its hold on him. He went before death not as its victim, but as its conqueror. A hymn used in the early church puts it in a striking way: 'It was not death that approached Christ, but Christ death; he died without death.'[7] Christ did not die because death had a right to him, but because it had rights to us, and for this reason the death of Christ is part of salvation. He died as its master not as its slave; his death was the first instalment of the triumph of grace.

Faced with death, in the seventh word on the cross, Jesus placed himself in the hands of the Father. Despite his suffering and humiliation Jesus' last act is a demonstration of satisfaction in three ways: it is accomplished with complete confidence of success in respect to the Father's approval of his work, it reveals legitimate self-satisfaction in what has been accomplished, and it shows that these two together are the foundation of eternal salvation for sinners.

SATISFACTION AND GOD THE FATHER

When Jesus reached adult life he replied to his parents' anxious questions: 'Don't you know that I must be in my Father's house?' (Luke 2: 49). Twenty years later, his work on earth having been completed, he committed himself again to the Father. In between times, he perfectly obeyed the Father's will, which meant he was subjected to the alien will of men. In his own words, 'The Son of Man is going to be betrayed into the hands of men. They will kill him, and on the third day he will be raised to life' (Matt. 17: 22–3, 26: 45). The cross was the culminating point of the actions of men against him. Placing himself in his Father's hands Jesus' suffering ceased to be that of active obedience. It became passive suffering in which he addresses the Father as the representative of men in the perfect offering of his completed work.[8]

The sixth word of Jesus on the cross—'It is finished' (John 19: 30)—indicates that his messianic activity among men is over. When Jesus gave his spirit into the Father's hands, he turned in a new direction, no longer that of identity with man's adamic nature, but that of his return to glory and the power that awaited him.[9] The second Adam acts in the Spirit, as he is on the point of becoming 'life-giving spirit' (1 Cor. 15: 45–9). Jesus gave up the spirit and henceforth will be the one who gives the Spirit once he has returned to the Father. The death of Jesus was a victorious act. He returned to renewed communion with the Father, having satisfied, for sinners, all the conditions necessary to inaugurate his ministry as glorified Lord. His communion with men would no longer be in the flesh, but through the gift of the Holy Spirit. The seventh word was the hinge between his Christological ministry and his mission in the Spirit—to impart salvation and life to his people.

Jesus was fully assured of becoming the 'Lord who is the Spirit' and surrendered the earthly spirit of humiliation with this end in view (2 Cor. 3: 17–18). He died a human death in the world of men, but by placing his spirit in the hands of the Father, he passed mentally into glory, where communion with the Father will be the eternal foundation of redemption and fellowship with his own. Before this time, 'the Spirit had not yet been given, since Jesus was not yet glorified' (John 7: 39).[10] Paradoxically, at the moment when everything seemed lost in human terms, Jesus rose above death as its master and defeated death in death itself. He had already tasted 'the second death', the pains of hell in judgment, and abandonment by the Father. But now that was past. Everything was accomplished and he thirsted for communion with the Father and his own in the kingdom. He would rejoin the Father in glory.[11] By giving his life over to the Father, Jesus affirmed his finished work to be entirely acceptable. He claimed his stake in the privileges that were his by right. He was fully entitled to the adoption to sonship with power (Rom. 1: 3–4; Heb. 1: 3–14).

There is a further aspect to the complete nature of the work of salvation achieved when Jesus placed himself in the divine hands. Jesus spoke seven times from the cross, not by accident, nor by a simple ploy, but by design. The seventh word is the one that brings finality to the others. More than that, just as God worked for six days and rested on the seventh, by giving his spirit over to the Father, Jesus entered into divine rest after his labour. Redemption goes a step further than creation and completes it. In Genesis 1, six times we read 'God said'. Jesus spoke one more time on the cross to introduce creation into a new creation. The creative word of God is the origin of creation, but Jesus' seventh word is the beginning of a new creation, and Jesus is the first to enter in. If God's creative word and Jesus' redemptive words bear the divine stamp by being powerful and effective, Jesus brought newness out of the old. The creation can never complete itself. It is only Christ who can complete creation and bring it to its goal in rest.

Christ did the opposite of Adam. By the first sinful act, humanity 'lost it' and was removed from the presence of God. But now the second Adam entered into the fray bringing his perfect humanity into the presence of God in eternity. Christ concluded the work of creation in Adam's place and for Adam's race: 'Anyone who enters God's rest also rests from his own work, just as God did from his.' In this way he brought the divine plan to fruition—God's work 'that has been finished since the creation of the world' (Heb. 4: 11, 3). 'Just as the seventh day was the day of rest and satisfaction, so the seventh utterance of the saviour brings him to the place of rest—the Father's hands.'[12] Christ rests his case, a perfect humanity, in the hands of God. This is the beginning of the new creation, humanity restored and renewed in Christ, a foretaste of a creation to be eventually liberated from sin and evil (Rom. 8: 21).

THE SON OF MAN'S SELF-SATISFACTION

At around 3 p.m. on an overcast Friday afternoon, Christ's earthly work was over. But none of those watching could have known it! Pain diminished his physical strength and there was apparently no difference between his fate and that of two terrorists. Would death not be Satan's last chance of victory? Not to Jesus' way of thinking! Just as his first word from the cross revealed the certainty that he could obtain forgiveness for his torturers (Luke 23: 34), in his last word Jesus cried out with supreme self-confidence—hardly the attitude of someone succumbing to the inevitable. He acted as the one in control. The biblical witness confirms that in his death, Jesus acted with the same serenity of spirit and cool self-assurance that had characterised his life. The Son of Man—

- poured out his life unto death (Isa. 53: 12);
- loved us and gave himself for us (Gal. 2: 20);
- loved us and gave himself up for us as a fragrant offering and sacrifice to God (Eph. 5: 2);
- loved the church and gave himself up for her (Eph. 5: 25);
- provided purification for sins and sat down on the right hand of the Majesty in heaven (Heb. 1: 3).

The power of divinity was at work in the humanity of the suffering servant. No human power, no sombre destiny robbed him of his life. He was the one who had the authority to lay it down and to take it up again, because his divine mission was to have power over all flesh, including his own (John 10: 18; 17: 2). Surely we must agree with the following appreciation:

How dishonourable, to imagine that the body of the Word made flesh was, in death, torn and reaved away from him! How melancholy, even to have indistinct views of the glorious truth that it was not so! Alike in death and after death, both the soul and the body of Emmanuel were in his own power. In the very grave, his dead body was in his own power, for it was in his own person—in union indissoluble with his Godhead...And here, in death, was a check to death, such as that last enemy had never hitherto received.[13]

This comes over with great clarity in Psalm 31, which is the source of the words Jesus uttered on the cross. The context is one of great confidence, despite the anguish due to the suffering at the hands of an enemy:

> Into your hands I commit my spirit;
>   redeem me, O Lord, the God of truth...
> I will be glad and rejoice in your love,
>   for you saw my affliction
>   and knew the anguish of my soul.
> You have not handed me over to the enemy
>   but have set my feet in a spacious place.
>
> Ps. 31.5–8

The one who described his suffering in these lines was not on the verge of dying, but was grappling with the problems of life and unscrupulous enemies. God is trusted as 'a rock, a strong fortress' who can provide permanent protection: 'I trust in the Lord.' The words of this Psalm are in complete harmony with Jesus' situation, despite the different setting. He suffered rejection at the hands of sinners who abused him (v. 10–14). He turned to the Lord and commited himself to his delivering power (v. 1–5, 14–16).

Jesus made some modifications to the words of Psalm 31: 5. He changed the future tense to the present, added the word 'Father' and eliminated the second part of the verse: 'redeem me, O Lord.' This could have been from lack of breath, but it is more likely to be because it was hardly appropriate in the light of the preceding words he had uttered. Not only had the moment of abandonment passed, but Christ also knew that everything had been accomplished and the right to enter God's presence was his. Jesus had no need of being redeemed from death. By placing his spirit in the Father's hands he denied any rights to his enemies, either death or Satan. In this way, Christ took the sting out of his own death. He was safe with the Father.[14]

The death of Christ took place as a continuity with all that he was and all that he had done during his life. Throughout his ministry he demonstrated the power of life over death by healing the sick, by raising Jairus' daughter, the widow of Nain's son, and Lazarus. Was he not capable now of rising above the mockery that he saved others, but could not save himself? (Luke 23: 36). On the cross the power of his words were an enigma to the spectators, but he accomplished his will in death. For his enemies, his last word was simply a proof that he was resigned to fate.

However, he is the resurrection and the life. In his ultimate trial when he placed himself in the Father's hands he fulfilled his own words to Martha: 'I am the resurrection and the life. He who believes in me will live, even though he dies; and whoever lives and believes in me will never die' (John 11: 25–6). Jesus had all the power of the great 'I AM', the God of the covenant. 'I am the resurrection'—the one who has power to give new life over death, 'I am the life'—the one who is the fount of life itself. So, contrary to appearances, Jesus' last word on the cross was one of supreme self-confidence. The Father would welcome him. He would defeat death. The resurrection was the consequence and the confirmation of Jesus' power over death.

Messianic consciousness is the key to the death of Christ. He died as the representative, the first to fray the passage through death for his people. The apostle Paul comments:

> But Christ indeed has been raised from the dead, the first fruits of those who have fallen asleep. For since death came through a man, the resurrection of the dead comes also through a man...But each in his own turn: Christ the first fruits; then, when he comes, those who belong to him. Then the end will come, when he hands over the kingdom to God the Father after he has destroyed all dominion, authority and power. For he must reign until he has put all his enemies under his feet. The last enemy to be destroyed is death.
>
> 1 Cor. 15: 20–8

Christ died and was the first to be raised to life. The captain of salvation leads his team into the arena of eternal life. Placing his spirit in the Father's hands was the first demonstration of the power of the kingdom, to be handed over to the Father after his return in glory and the resurrection to life of those he captains (Eph. 4: 8). His defeat of death is the promise of final victory because sin and death have already been overcome.

As the author and finisher of salvation (Heb. 2: 10), Christ places himself between death and his people. 'He died the just for the unjust in order to bring us to God' (1 Pet. 3: 18). His death was not for himself, but to cancel out the reason for our eternal condemnation. When he died he broke his body in an offering for sin, to fulfil the sign given to the disciples in the Last Supper, when he broke the bread: 'This is my body given for you' (Luke 22: 19). 'In this way, Christ broke his body before God in an instant of time...nothing human was alien to him...the moment of dying is a natural part of the sacrifice precisely because the sacrifice is voluntary. It is a presentation, an offering, in the basic sense of that word.'[15] But death will never hold him:

> You will not abandon me to the grave,
>   nor will you let your Holy One see decay.
> You have made known to me
>   the path of life;
> you will fill me with joy in your presence,
>   with eternal pleasures at your right hand.
>
> Ps. 16: 10; Acts 2: 27, 31

In his ultimate moment Jesus acted with the same lucidity that characterised all his doings on the cross. He forgave his persecutors, redeemed a wasted life, took care of his mother in making the beloved disciple responsible for her, and declared that his work is complete. Jesus remained conscious to the bitter end, refusing the pain-killing draught of wine and myrrh offered by the women of Jerusalem, but accepting the vinegar that rouses the spirits (Prov. 31: 6; Mark 15: 23). Jesus desired to undergo everything with a clear head. 'No one takes my life from me, I lay it down of my own accord' (John 10: 18a).

Why such determination? Would unconsciousness have compromised the outcome of Jesus' death? Was it not enough for him to die? The key lies in the divine will: 'This command I received from my Father' (John 10: 18c). Conscious obedience is of the essence throughout Jesus' life. His calling to represent others had to continue right to the gates of death. His struggle with death, the result of the sin he was bearing, had to be impressed on his holy humanity in a complete way. He had to experience the humiliation, physical suffering, isolation, fear, and uncertainty that characterise the death of human beings, because he was bearing sin in the place of others. Were it not so, Christ would not have experienced the lot of fallen humanity. But he accepted all this to fulfil his high-priestly ministry and become 'perfect through suffering...to make atonement for the sins of the people. Because he himself suffered when he was tempted, he is able to help those who are being tempted' (Heb. 2: 10, 17–18). Jesus drained the cup of death to the dregs.

When the end came, in the words of John's gospel, 'He bowed his head and gave up his spirit' (John 19: 30). Biblical commentators on this passage have shunned the idea that this was a sign of resignation. Some interpretations of this act have been highly imaginative, such as Augustine's suggestion that he bowed his head for us to embrace him, or Origen's idea that he placed his head on the Father's knee. Such flights of imagination are hardly necessary! Jesus died a normal human death. A life in which he found 'no place to lay his head' had been brought to a satisfying end (Matt. 8: 20; Luke 9: 58); Jesus rested in peace.[16] He entered a rest he had not found during his lifetime and the Father who received his spirit welcomed him in a way totally different from men.

It is fitting in this context to remember the words of Psalm 110, a messianic hymn of victory frequently referred to by the New Testament writers. The Eternal God requests that the Lord take his place at the right hand. The conqueror, also priest for ever in the order of Melchizedek, is to exercise judgment among the nations:

> The Lord is at your right hand:
>   he will crush kings
>   on the day of his wrath.
> He will judge the nations,
>   heaping up the dead
>   and crushing the rulers
>   of the whole earth.
> He will drink from the brook
>   beside the way;
>   therefore he will lift up his head.
>
> Ps. 110: 5–7[17]

Psalm 110 is about Christ exalted, the Messiah who is priest and king. 'Lifting up his head' is a sign of final triumph following combat and defeat of his enemies. Christ would be victorious and rule over all (Ps. 3: 3; 27: 6). Having crushed Satan and all powers, he bowed his head, secure in the assurance of his victory over death to lift it up anew in the resurrection.

The Son 'has been made perfect forever…holy, pure, blameless, set apart from sinners and exalted above the heavens', and like Melchizedek, the king of peace, established as a priest for ever (Heb. 7: 28, 26, 21). This final gesture which was totally natural was also a chosen sign of rest in triumph. Jesus placed himself finally in the Father's hands, awaiting the next step, which would be justification and glory in the Spirit: 'Christ died for sins once for all, the righteous for the unrighteous to bring us to God. He was put to death in the body but made alive by the Spirit…by the resurrection Jesus went into heaven and is at God's right hand' (1 Pet. 3: 18–22).[18]

Jesus did not slip away into death, but faced it with a clear head, as its Lord. He was in full possession of his senses to the end, obedient to the Father's will, in order 'to fulfil all righteousness' as he had set out to do at the start of his ministry (Matt. 3: 15). Nothing is accidental in the passion of the Saviour. Everything was accomplished according to the Father's good pleasure and would be the source of blessing.

ETERNAL SATISFACTION

The temporal death of Jesus has eternal consequences. At the moment of death all is lost for men. Jesus consciously lifted himself to the level of eternity in the expectation of divine exoneration. The last word on the cross, expressing victory and satisfaction, was also the first word of the new creation. Because Jesus placed himself in the Father's hand, all would be henceforth placed in his hands. In the abyss of suffering, Jesus laid hold of his right to eternal power and glory.

> If Christ died a mere passive victim, he did not die a victor: and no subsequent glory can in that case redeem what was defeat. But he died a triumphant agent. He prevailed against death to live and then to die, not merely voluntarily, but by a positive priestly action, giving himself to God. The cross itself is glorious; not from the subsequent resurrection and

enthronement, but glorious from itself. It is itself a chariot of triumph. There is more agency and power in Christ's cross, than in all his work as creator of the universe. There is as much spiritual glory in the cross of Calvary, as in the throne of the lamb in heaven. Christ crucified is—not after, but in being crucified—the power of God.[19]

The power and the glory were hidden from the world under contrary appearances, but in offering himself to the Father Jesus was already on the road to resurrection, ascension and glory. Jesus did not need to force entry into heaven. Because of the Father's welcome the door of the new creation swung wide open. 'I am returning to my Father and your Father, to my God and your God' (John 20: 17).[20]

In offering his body, bruised in sacrifice, and in committing himself to the Father, Jesus brought the old creation and its redemption into God's eternal presence. In his body there was the reconciliation of the old creation and the beginning of the new creation in resurrection and life. A humanity bearing the marks of sin is to become the new and glorified humanity. Nothing could hold Christ back; his departure from the world of suffering was victorious because of how he died. He did not enter the new world by and for himself, but with those he represented:

On the cross Christ hung as the representative of his people, and therefore we view his last act as a representative one. When the Lord Jesus commended his sprit into the hands of his Father, he also presented our spirits along with his to the Father's acceptance. Jesus Christ neither lived nor died for himself, but for believers; what he did in this last act referred to them as much as to himself. We must look then on Christ as gathering all the souls of the elect together, and making a solemn tender of them, with his own spirit, to God.[21]

Satisfaction made to God the Father, the self-satisfaction of the Son, and satisfaction for humanity are all contained in the ultimate word of suffering pronounced by Jesus. What this amounted to was the judgment of death, which is the natural end of sinful humanity. When Jesus presented himself to God he did so as the one who reconciled God and man. Believers, knowing that they are already accepted by the Father, with Christ and because of him, can use Jesus' words as a prayer, as some of the great saints have done: Polycarp, Bernard of Clairvaux, Jean Hus, Martin Luther, and many others. Christ's victory over death means that believers die 'in Christ' and nothing can separate them from the love of God (Rom. 8: 38–9).The new humanity of faith in Christ remains for ever united to him, in life and in death; nothing can intervene to destroy newness of life in him.[22] 'Thank God there is a refuge from the gales of life and the terrors of death—the Father's hand—the heart's true heaven!'[23]

CONCLUSION

The great defender of evangelical faith in the first half of the twentieth century, J. Gresham Machen, died in 1937 while on a lecture tour in midwinter in North Dakota. He sent a telegram to John Murray saying, 'I'm so thankful for active obedience of Christ. No hope without it.' Machen understood that we are as much saved by Christ's life as we are by his death. As his biographer stated: 'He gave expression to the conviction that he had assurance not only of remission of sin and its penalty, but also of being accepted as perfectly obedient and righteous, and so an heir of eternal life, because of the perfect obedience of Christ to the divine will.'[24]

Christ talked the talk and walked the walk in a way that was wholly satisfying to God. He did so on our behalf and did so to the end. The death of Christ was the final human demonstration of the active obedience of the Lord Jesus. Humanity was not made for death, but for life. In death Jesus lived and trampled it under his feet. Not only did he assume human frailty but 'he endured the cross, scorning its shame' on our behalf. In death he triumphed over it and placed himself as the conqueror in the Father's hands. He did so 'for the joy set before him...and sat down at the right hand of the throne of God' (Heb. 12: 2).

This was perfect satisfaction. It was a complete compensation offered to God for the remission of sin. In his death, Christ offered what God demanded from sinners for the satisfaction of his justice.[25] He offered up a perfect life, one that had reached the goal of the holiness, goodness, and truth required of man to inherit the covenant blessings. In this way, Christ had a unique claim to the reward of eternal life, not only for himself, but also for those who would believe in him.

In the conclusion to his comments on the Apostles' Creed, John Calvin beautifully sums up the dimensions of the satisfaction provided by Christ:

> We see that our whole salvation and all its parts are comprehended in Christ...If we seek strength, it lies in his dominion; if purity, in his conception; if gentleness, it appears in his birth. For by his birth he was made like us in all respects that he might learn to feel our pain. If we seek redemption, it is in his passion; if acquittal, in his condemnation; if remission of the curse, in his cross; if satisfaction, in his sacrifice; if purification, in his blood; if reconciliation, in his descent into hell; if mortification of the flesh, in his tomb; if newness of life, in his resurrection; if immortality, in the same; if inheritance of the heavenly kingdom, in his entrance into heaven; if protection, if security, if abundant supply of all blessings, in his kingdom; if untroubled expectation of judgment, in the power given him to judge. In short, since rich store of every kind of good abounds in him, let us drink our fill from this fountain, and from no other.[26]

ENDNOTES

1 B. B. Warfield, 'Atonement', *Works*, IX, 261.

2 It is used in the A.V. to translate *kāpar* in Numbers 35: 31–2: later translations, such as the NIV or the NKJV use 'ransom'. Cf. F. Turretin, *Institutes of Elenctic Theology*, II, 243 f, The Atonement of Christ, 56 f.

3 H. Blocher, 'The Atonement in John Calvin's Theology', in *The Glory of the Atonement*, C. E. Hill, F. A. James, eds, 283 ff.

4 R. A. Peterson, *Calvin and the Atonement*, 130–35.

5 Cf. Mark 15: 37, Matt. 27: 50, John 19: 30. Luke is the only gospel to record the seventh word of Jesus on the cross. Mark and Matthew refer to it when they say that Jesus cried with a loud voice before breathing his last. John describes Jesus' action, 'he bowed his head and gave up his spirit.'

6 'To give up the spirit in the sense of dying does not exist in the ancient world...John invented a new turn of phrase...and he must have done so with a specific intention.' I. de la Potterie, *La passion de Jésus selon l'Evangile de Jean*, (Paris: Cerf, 1986), 179. Nor are the expressions used in Matthew and Luke habitual ones.

7 Attributed to Sedulius, quoted by A. Edersheim, *The Life and Times of Jesus the Messiah*, II, (London: Longmans, Green, nd.), 609.

8 Cf. K. Schilder, *Christ Crucified* (Grand Rapids: Eerdmans, 1940), 485 ff.

9 Cf. Ecclesiastes. 12: 7, Zechariah. 12: 1, Numbers. 16: 22.

[10] John 14: 26; 16: 7, 13.

[11] John 19: 28–9. Physical thirst is a metaphor for spiritual fellowship in Scripture, in the Psalms (42; 63: 1–5; 143: 6–8) but also in John (4: 13–14; 6: 27–40, 53–58; 7: 37–9). Cf. Luke 22: 18.

[12] A.W. Pink, *The Seven Sayings of the Saviour on the Cross*, (Grand Rapids: Baker, 1958), 23.

[13] H. Martin, *The Atonement*, 43.

[14] K. Schilder, op. cit., 474 ff.

[15] Ibid, 496. See on this, 490–97.

[16] Because of the rest expressed by this gesture, the last word of Jesus on the cross has been called the 'word of contentment'. See A.W. Pink, op. cit., ch. 7.

[17] See also Psalm 2: 4–12. Cf. 1 Kings 1: 38 (2 Samuel 5: 8)—perhaps a reference to drinking from the Gihon spring in the enthronement of the king in Jerusalem.

[18] Cf. R. Stier, *The Words of the Lord Jesus*, VIII, (Edinburgh: T. & T. Clark, 1873), 33. The 'right hand' in the Psalms is a symbol of power.

[19] H. Martin, op. cit., 36–7.

[20] On the resurrection of the body, see S. Olyott, *Son of Mary, Son of God* (Darlington: Evangelical Press 1988), ch. 6.

[21] A. W. Pink, op. cit., 131.

[22] 2 Corinthians 5: 1, 6, 8; Philemon 1: 23; Hebrews 12: 23; 2 Timothy 1: 12; Acts 3: 21.

[23] A. W. Pink, op. cit., 134.

[24] N. B. Stonehouse, *J. Gresham Machen. A Biographical Memoir* (Grand Rapids: Eerdmans, 1954), 508.

[25] On satisfaction as equivalence see H. Blocher, art. cit., 297–9; F. Turretin, *Institutes of Elenctic Theology*, II, 446 ff and *The Atonement of Christ*, 86 ff.

[26] J. Calvin, *Institutes of the Christian Religion*, II.xvi,19.

17

Grace

The completed work of Christ on the cross tells us not just about man's need of salvation, nor about how it was accomplished, but most of all about the God who saves. God is a God of grace.

The more we understand how salvation was enacted, the more we can begin to fathom the wonder of God's wisdom and grace. The Lord of glory himself, the beloved Son, accepted the agony and woe of sinful humanity when 'he bore our sins in his own body on the tree' (1 Pet. 2: 24). He died the death of one bearing the curse of sin. There are no human parallels to the momentous event of the cross, no repetitions and no appendices to be added to this once for all salvation. 'It is God in our nature forsaken of God.'[1] Nothing is comparable to this.

The justice of God was fully satisfied in a mysterious way. One act was sufficient to save rebellious sinners from sin and efficient for the redemption of lost human beings. This was not enacted without personal involvement or with the mathematical precision of moves on a chess board. 'God was in Christ' suffusing the whole work with amazing grace and love, making the events of one day 'Good Friday' for ever.

The result of the cross is that God saves sinners. This can be fully appreciated if each of these three small words is given its full significance.[2] When God saves, his whole person, Father, Son, and Spirit is active in a display of his holiness, justice, power and love. When God saves, he does so in a way that is effective and adequate for all the needs of sinners. Salvation accomplished on the cross is once for all, it is unrepeatable and needs no supplements. Christ's death really saved; it was all that was required to accomplish salvation. God saved sinners—lost, dead in sin, under divine judgment, incapable of doing anything for themselves. Redemption is full, complete, and perfect. It is the triumph of all that God is in his holy justice, infinite mercy, and boundless love.

THE FACE OF GRACE

Grace in and of itself is not an attribute of God. It is the quality that expresses all the characteristics of God's person in his relation to his creatures and his creation at large. 'God's grace to men appears in spite of man's unrighteousness and by God's utterly sovereign decision...it is his "unmerited favour, given to those who deserve his wrath".'[3]

The divine name God used to make himself known to Moses reveals him as the God of grace (Exod. 33: 19; 34: 6). God shows mercy, goodness, and unmerited favour to his old covenant people by delivering them from slavery in Egypt (Exod. 15: 13; 20: 6; 34: 7) and declares, despite their unworthiness, 'I have loved you with everlasting love and drawn you with loving kindness' (Jer. 31: 3; 33: 11; Lam. 3: 22). The praise of Israel celebrates the grace of God in terms such as those of Psalm 25: 10: 'All the ways of the Lord are loving and faithful for those who keep the demands of his covenant.'

The New Testament revelation of God crystallises the grace of God in the person of the Lord Jesus Christ. God shows 'the incomparable riches of his grace, expressed in his kindness to us in Christ Jesus' (Eph. 2: 7). Jesus is grace incarnate in all his ways. Grace and truth are present in his person, in the fulfilment of Exodus 34: 6: 'in him we have received grace upon grace' (John 1: 16–17). As the face of grace, Jesus is the bodily tabernacle of the glory of God, 'the glory of the only begotten of the Father, full of grace and truth'. He is the divine Word of God in the flesh who remains mysteriously in the bosom of the Father, and makes him known on earth (John 1: 14, 18).

Because of this staggering personal disclosure of God as the God of grace, the expression 'the grace of our Lord Jesus Christ' is prominent in the experience of new covenant believers. It is the prelude and the conclusion of many of the epistles, as the beginning and the end of instruction about living in Christ. The grace of God in Christ cuts the Gordian knot that ties salvation to human achievements and self-righteousness. God shows himself to be favourable to sinners in a concrete demonstration of personal condescension and acceptance. 'The grace of God that brings salvation has appeared to all men' (Titus 2: 11). Grace is focussed in the sacrifice of Christ, by whom 'we have redemption through his blood, the forgiveness of sins, in accordance with the riches of God's grace that he lavished on us with all wisdom and understanding' (Eph. 1: 7). God has shown himself to be 'for us'. In Christ, the whole of God's redemptive purpose from election before the foundation of the world to future glorification finds its unity (Eph. 1: 6; Rom. 8: 29, 31). The sum of the blessings Paul presents in his overview of salvation from start to finish—foreknowledge, predestination, calling, justification, conformity to Christ's image, and glorification—is summed up by John's simple expression 'eternal life'. Although the beloved disciple does not often use the word 'grace' outside the first chapter of his Gospel it is present in his writings: 'My sheep know my voice; I know them, and they follow me. I give them eternal life and they shall never perish; no one can snatch them out of my hand. My Father who has given them to me, is greater than all' (John 10: 28–9).

'Divine grace precedes all. That is the whole point of grace.'[4] The fullness of grace is illustrated by the condition in which it finds man, an alienated enemy of God, a child of wrath, dead in sin, a stranger to the promise of salvation, without God and without hope in the world (Eph. 2: 3, 12; Col. 1: 21). Without God's grace sinners are nothing, they are but a breath away from eternal death. With God's grace, sinners become rich, inheritors of life. They come to know 'the grace of the Lord Jesus Christ, that though he was rich, yet for their sakes became poor, so that through his poverty they might become rich' (2 Cor. 8: 9).

Grace calls forth faith. Believers are not saved by faith, a common misconception, but by grace via faith. The apostle speaks precisely about the pairing of these two in his great statement on the subject in Ephesians 2: 8: 'It is by grace you have been saved though faith—and that not from yourselves, it is the gift of God—not by works, so that no one can boast.'

Grace calls forth faith because of the content of the gospel, Christ in our stead, because it touches our hearts, feelings, emotions, and wills with the wonder of divine love. Faith is not a work that contributes to salvation, it is the gift of God that recognises salvation in Christ. Faith is a part of grace not something added to it. Faith receives life from grace and its receptive character locks in to the promises of God. Without the promises of grace in the gospel, faith can neither stand nor bear fruit.

The grace of God in the salvation of sinners has three parameters. It is the good news of God's gracious design for salvation, of his accomplishment of redemption in Christ's death and resurrection, and of its implementation for individuals in need of newness of life. In saving sinners, what God purposed he accomplished; what he accomplished he applies according to his design. Grace has three concentric circles that develop with the historical progress of redemption.

CUSTOM-MADE GRACE

The grace of God is as broad as creation and since the fall of man has a general application.[5] God allows human life to continue despite sin and keeps evil in check by his judgments. Men also receive general blessings from God through the development of human culture.

In a saving sense, however, God's grace is specific. He does not simply provide an indefinite salvation through Christ's death on the cross and allow men to make of it what they will. That God saves sinners indicates a purpose that goes beyond the provision of something merely possible. The fundamental question is: what did God intend to do when Christ died on the cross? Did Christ die for all men in an indefinite way, or was his purpose to accomplish the salvation of specific sinners? This is often referred to as 'limited atonement', which is far from being an attractive term, so 'particular redemption' is preferable.

'Purposeful redemption' is perhaps an even better way of putting it. God's purpose or intention is the crux of the matter. The question involved in 'particular redemption' in plain language is: for whom did Christ die? 'On whose behalf did Christ offer himself a sacrifice? On whose behalf did he propitiate the wrath of God? Who did he reconcile to God

in the body of his flesh through death? Whom did he redeem
from the curse of the law, from the power of sin, from the
enthralling power and bondage of Satan?'⁶ To put it bluntly,
did God just leave the issue hanging and allow men to make
their own reply by accepting or rejecting the good news?

It has been remarked that this issue has become over-inflated
as a test of orthodoxy, whereas the New Testament writers do
not single it out as a doctrine of major importance or make it
the subject of explicit theological discussion.⁷ This might be
the case, yet the design of the atonement cannot be separated
from its accomplishment and its application without seriously
impairing our understanding of the wisdom of God.

An illustration might help. While teaching in Guadeloupe,
I stayed in a tacky tourist hotel, noisy and run-down, with
air-conditioning that sounded like an approaching tornado.
Imagine the feelings of the tourists who had signed up for a
dream holiday! They had planned one thing but got something
else, because they lacked information—the holiday brochures
did not allow them to foresee the outcomes of their choice.
When we make decisions, generally we like to know what is
involved. Deciding without knowledge of the implications
often turns out to be an unwise choice.

The cross of Christ is the central event of history. On its
outcome depend not only the effectiveness of God's own
work, but also the fate of lost sinners in need of salvation. It
also involved enormous cost—the self-giving of Christ, his
suffering and his death. What does it say about God's wisdom
to think that he would leave the end uncertain when the means
involved were so important? If humans know that outcomes
are vital in planning, why should it be less so with God?

The cross is linked specifically to the 'power and wisdom'
of God in redemption (1 Cor. 1: 20–30). Christ himself is
the treasure store of 'wisdom and knowledge' (Col. 2: 3).
The outcome of redemption as service through 'good works'
is fulfilled in those who are 'God's workmanship, created in
Christ Jesus' and were also 'prepared in advance for us to do'
(Eph. 2: 7). One thing we can be sure about is that God was not
unwise in his plans for the outcome of the cross. It is difficult
to avoid the fact that the grace of God is custom-made grace!

When people object to the purposeful grace of God, Christ
dying to actually save some people, it is because for them it

seems to smack of favouritism by making men unequal with regard to the possibility of salvation. This is a highly debatable issue, but despite the complexity of the question, two things can be said. It is almost impossible for human beings to determine the specific intentions even of other human beings. It is equally difficult to speculate about God's intentions, as no one has access to the hidden information in the divine mind, so there is little sense in quibbling over what God's hidden purposes might be. Whether one like it or not, we are obliged to follow Scripture.

Secondly, we know that God's intentions are inspired by grace, and God's grace is worked out through the historical demonstration of his love in the cross and by the preaching of the gospel. Together these are the means of differentiation that make a distinction between those who believe and those who do not. The way the grace of God is revealed places the people who hear the good news in a situation of responsibility. God's purposes are accomplished in the declaration of his intention to save those who believe. His sincerity to do so cannot be doubted.[8] That God has specific purposes does not preclude that his grace is declared to all in a public way. On the contrary, it requires it. 'A free offer of the gospel can rightly be made to every person ever born. It is completely true that 'whoever will' may come to Christ for salvation, and no one who comes to him will be turned away. This free offer of the gospel is extended in good faith to every person.'[9]

Sometimes jokes are made about people who love humanity in general, but don't love any one in particular. These two kinds of love are not exclusive, but they are different, as we certainly can't and don't love 'humanity' in the same kind of way as we love our nearest and dearest. Similarly, if God does show grace in a specific way according to his divine intentions, it does not mean he does not make his grace known to others. Nor would we consider it a form of favouritism for someone to love their partner or their best friend in a special sense. It is a personal choice and they can hardly be blamed for it. Nor is God open to the criticism of 'favouritism' if his grace is purposeful and particular. Saving grace is real grace in God's intention because it is effective:

The true evangelical evaluation of the claim that Christ died for every man, even those who perish (is that) far from magnifying the love and grace of God, this claim dishonours both it and him, for it reduces God's love to an impotent wish and turns the whole economy of 'saving' grace, so called, into a monumental divine failure. Also, so far from magnifying the merit and worth of Christ's death, it cheapens it, for it makes Christ die in vain.[10]

NOT 'DEFINITELY MAYBE' GRACE

It would be wrong to separate the divine intention in the atonement from what the cross actually accomplished. Scripture does not do so. The purposeful nature of grace is revealed in what was enacted at Calvary. The grace revealed at the cross did not have a general and indefinite reference to one and all.

Of course the argument is always advanced that some texts in Scripture say that Christ died with a universal reference, for 'all men', 'the whole world', or that God 'loved the world'.[11] Some other cases appear to speak of Christ dying for those who will not actually be saved.[12] We will not discuss these texts here, as the problems they raise have been adequately dealt with a multitude of times.[13] Suffice it to say that it has to be recognised that when 'universalising' expressions such as 'all men' and the 'world' are used in Scripture, the reference does not constitute a global generalisation including every individual. 'Christ is nowhere in Scripture said to have died for all, unless some limitation is added...these Scriptures do not teach that he suffered for all men of all nations, but that the object of his death is restricted according to the circumstances.'[14]

In fact, even in the passages thought to state that Christ died for all, it is clear that the 'all' refers to specific individuals. So for instance, in 2 Corinthians 5: 19, 'God was reconciling the world to himself in Christ, not counting men's sins against them', is immediately qualified by 'God made him sin for us, so that we might become the righteousness of God' (v. 21). In other words, God's reconciling act for the 'world' is one and the same in its extent with those for whom Christ died and who were made righteous in him. Likewise in Romans 8: 32 it is said that God gave up his Son 'for us all'. This is linked directly not only with justification, but also to the intercession of Christ at God's right hand. When Jesus died and rose again, it was in the interest of 'those whom God has chosen'. The application of the fruit of Christ's mediation is specific.[15]

More to the point, there are several texts that define the extent of the atonement in a precise way. If the death of Christ is public, like the serpent in the wilderness (John 3: 14–15), and is made known to all who hear the gospel, redemption is focussed in the following ways:

- the good shepherd lays down his life for the sheep (John 10: 11, 15);
- it is the will of God that Christ should lose none of those given him, but raise them at the last day (John 6: 38–9; 17: 9);
- the church was bought with the blood of God's own Son (Acts. 20: 28);
- Paul says Christ loved him and gave himself for him (Gal. 2: 20), which is broadened in scope to say he loved the church and gave himself for her to make her holy (Eph. 5: 25);
- Christ was made a curse for us (Gal. 3: 13);
- Christ gave himself for us to redeem us and purify a people for himself (Titus 2: 14);
- Christ obtained redemption for sin, for the people of the new covenant (Heb. 9: 12);
- Christ purchased men from every nation and made them a kingdom of priests (Rev. 5: 9–10).

These references are not produced like rabbits out of a hat in a way that betrays the meaning of Scripture as a whole. On the contrary, three fundamental features of the biblical doctrine of atonement developed in the preceding chapters provide the background to them and give them weight.

Firstly, it has been argued that the death of Christ was a vicarious penal substitution. Christ stood in the place of others, he died for their sin, and on their behalf. His penal substitution and punishment is the only way in which they can be reconciled to God. Substitution itself implies a specific relationship. It must be done for someone in particular. Indefinite substitution would not be substitution at all.[16] It is precisely this special relation brought into play by substitution that allows the apostle to make the daring statement about God's grace: 'The Son of God loved me, and gave himself for me' (Gal. 2: 20–1)—a cause of wonder indeed for one who never forgot that he had been the chief among sinners! (1 Tim. 1: 15). The vicarious death of Christ, expiation of sin, propitiation, reconciliation, righteousness, and redemption all have the same reference—to God's covenant people of the Old and New Testaments, and the individuals who by faith have the privilege of belonging.

Secondly, salvation was accomplished before we even had the opportunity to believe. Absolute priority, temporal and logical, belongs to God in redemption. Some passages in Scripture speak about a definite action on the part of the Father and the Son in favour of those who would believe, but who were not yet in the running to do so. 'While we were still sinners Christ died for us…when we were enemies we were reconciled to God through the death of his Son…' (Rom. 5: 8, 10). Far from depending on our reply, redemption was completed in Christ and reconciliation was already a reality in his death. So by the grace of God, atonement was accomplished in Christ for those who would (and will) believe, and its effectiveness does not stem from their response. The cross itself is the procuring cause of redemption. It ensures the salvation of all those who will believe in Christ.

Thirdly, there is the sequel to the death of Christ in the atonement, namely his resurrection. Those for whom Christ died also died in him and with him because he was their covenant representative, acting on their behalf: 'one died for all and therefore all died' (2 Cor. 5: 14).[17] But the same people were also raised to life by Christ and in him. Romans 6 tells us that 'if we died with Christ, we believe that we will also live with him. For we know that since Christ was raised from the dead, he cannot die again…If we have been united with him like this in his death, we will certainly also be united with him in his resurrection' (v. 8–9, 5). Those for whom Christ died also died in him, were raised with him, and will be raised with him. Newness of life in the present (v. 4) is a manifestation that one has been raised with Christ and is also a promise for the future resurrection.

The point is that the same body of people are 'in Christ' in his death and resurrection, and the same individuals walk in newness of life in the blessed hope. What this means is that Christ's death achieves exactly what it set out to do. While history runs on, the people for whom Christ died continue to come to him in faith, but at the end, none of those for whom he died will be lost and there will be none saved for whom he did not die. This makes the atonement efficient in the salvation of God's people. If there were people for whom atonement and redemption were made and who were finally lost, then the grace of God in salvation is in vain. It is hard to avoid the conclusion that 'if we universalize the extent of the atonement, we limit the efficacy.'[18]

God, in Christ, saves sinners. God's people, known to him and purchased by the blood of Christ, may be made up of asylum-seekers, but there are no illegal immigrants, nor will there be any extraditions from among the children of the kingdom.

THE GRACE OF SALVATION

If the design of the atonement and its accomplishment in the cross and resurrection of Christ have a specific destination, so also does their actual application in the case of those who believe and are saved.

To some people, this seems to restrict God's love to a small number and undermine the freedom of choice that all men must have. Divine sovereignty appears to block out human responsibility. They draw the conclusion that salvation is like a blank cheque handed out indiscriminately, on which those who want to be saved write their names. Their argument goes something like this: God sent Christ to make salvation possible for all, but the final decision belongs to the ones who open the door and believe in Christ. The sinner is able to make that decision for himself. By the death of Christ, man is placed in a redeemable position and is capable of taking the necessary steps to accept him. If everyone is not free to do this, how can they be held responsible or condemned because of their unbelief?

The meaning of election and what Christ actually accomplished in the atonement are changed by this line of argument: God's election concerns those whom he foresees accepting the gospel, and Christ died for no one in particular, but to give everyone the choice.

For this to be possible, the extent of sin has to be limited in some sort of way, so that sinners are capable of believing when they hear the gospel. The capacity of 'free will' contradicts what Scripture says about human beings being 'dead in sins' and incapable of self-help. In the New Testament there are many images to describe the salvation that comes to sinners in their lost condition. Three come to mind. In Christ and because of him, there is new birth, rising from the dead and a new creation.[19]

- 'The wind blows where it pleases...So it is with everyone born of the Spirit' (John 3: 8).
- 'God made us alive together with Christ even when we were dead in transgressions...and raised us up' (Eph. 2: 5–6).
- 'God who said 'let light shine out of darkness' made his light shine in our hearts...' (2 Cor. 4: 6).

Each of these instances underlines the priority of God's act when he confers new life on the spiritually helpless. No one thinks, after all, that we chose our own birth, that Lazarus was capable of hearing Christ and coming out of the tomb, or that the light of creation generated itself out of darkness. Any of these acts of salvation depend on the intervention of divine grace in giving sinners newness of life. Without a prior work of the Holy Spirit in regeneration, the believer cannot take his first spiritual breath or look to Christ to be saved. In salvation God chooses those who will be saved. The same are redeemed by the blood of Christ. God intervenes to give them new life.

Nonetheless, they are not saved unless they believe in Christ (John 1: 12; 3: 15–16, 36; 5: 24; 20: 31) and those who do not believe will die because of their own sins:

> The full story is this: God sent his Son with both hypothetical and categorical intentions. Categorically, Christ died only for the elect—what is called 'limited atonement'. Hypothetically, he died so that if anyone at all should believe, he would be saved. His death makes that hypothetical statement true. So Christ died to guarantee salvation to the elect and to provide the opportunity of salvation for all.[20]

Of course this statement is soon met with the objection that the opportunity of salvation does not exist at all because of divine election and because man is not capable of making the choice for himself. This, however, is not the case. As the gospel goes out, it places men in a situation where they are called to faith. God sincerely promises salvation to all who repent and believe. God, as we have said, is perfectly sincere in this promise. That people do not believe does not detract from the reality of grace; it indicates the hardness of unbelief and the seriousness of the refusal to believe.

The goodness of God in sending sun and rain on the just and the unjust alike does not mean that sunshine is a fake blessing (Matt. 5: 45). It underlines the ingratitude of those who do not thank God for his good gifts. In the same way, the free offer of the gospel is not an unreal blessing. Anyone believing in Jesus will most certainly be saved, and those who do not answer with repentance and faith are bringing judgment on themselves. They stand responsible. 'Whoever believes is not condemned, but whoever does not believe is condemned already, because he has not believed in the name of God's one and only Son' (John 3: 18).

What has been said up to this point about the grace of salvation is only half the story. By dying on the cross, Jesus not only fulfilled the conditions for giving new life to those who believe in him. His grace is much greater than that! Christ obtained the grace that works in the life of faith from start to finish. Through his atonement he obtained the grace and blessings that are applied throughout the whole process of the salvation of his people.

There is no grace known to believers that does not come directly from the Lord Jesus himself. Faith is the gift of God, because Christ believed and trusted in God. Justification is by grace because Jesus is the holy one who was justified in his resurrection. Holiness of life depends on his perfect holiness. Future glorification is the promise of God because Christ is already glorified. Jesus is the redeemer and redemption flows out from him. He is 'the author and the perfecter of our faith' (Heb. 12: 2). That faith allowed the Old Testament saints to live lives of faith (Heb. 11) and the same faith works perseverance in believers today.

This profound understanding of faith's dependence on the work of Christ allows the apostle Paul to speak about the gospel he received by revelation from Jesus Christ (Gal. 1: 11–12). He can say God 'set me apart from birth, called me by his grace and was pleased to reveal his Son in me' (Gal. 1: 15). He goes further and states that his justification is 'by faith in Jesus

Christ', that 'Christ lives in him' and that he lives 'by faith in
the Son of God' (2: 16, 20). Faith in Christ is the faith of Christ
and comes from him alone. 'We are saved entirely by divine
grace through a faith which is itself God's gift and flows to us
from Calvary.'[21]

The atonement secures all the gifts and graces of salvation;
believers receive them by faith in Christ. They fan out into
the whole of life until those for whom Christ died reach the
destination of the glorious liberty of the children of God in
the eternal kingdom.

CONCLUSION

In a world plagued by uncertainty of all kinds one thing is sure,
other than that we will all die, that is the security of those who
rest in Christ for salvation.

A sense of security is necessary for growth in any personal
relationship. This is nowhere more so than in the relationship
between believers and God through salvation in Christ. It
stimulates personal growth in grace. To know that Christ
died for us in 'purposeful redemption' makes our lot sure
and certain. Down the line of faith, confidence blossoms, as
do love, joy, and peace of mind. Faced with trials and even
death, we can have the unshakeable assurance that our fate is
wrapped up with that of Christ and nothing can sever us from
his love (Rom. 8: 38). Like the Christians at Philippi, we can
be confident at least of this, 'that he who began a good work in
us will carry it on to completion until the day of Christ Jesus'
(Phil. 1: 6).

On the other hand, uncertainty and lack of confidence are
corrosive to any relationship. Anyone who has been betrayed,
particularly by someone they trusted, knows just how
destructive it is. 'Purposeful redemption' indicates that God
never goes back on the promises given to us in Christ. Christ's
life and death won God's complete approval and we can rest
our eternal destiny in that. We are accepted 'in the beloved'.

If, in and of ourselves, we are 'hateful to God, his fatherly
love must flow to us in Christ'.[22] We can be certain of this
because Christ has been given to us as the guarantee that in
him we are really God's own children. Faith holds on to that
pledge for dear life.

Jesus was forsaken of God for our sakes. Consequently, God's promise is: 'I will never leave nor forsake you' (Heb. 13: 5).

ENDNOTES

1. J. Murray, *Redemption Accomplished and Applied*, 77.
2. J. I. Packer, '"Saved by his Precious Blood": an Introduction to John Owen's "The Death of Death in the Death of Christ"', *Among God's Giants*, 169.
3. J. Frame, *The Doctrine of God*, 426. Cf. P. E. Hughes, *But for the Grace of God* (London: Hodder and Stoughton, 1964), ch. 1.
4. P. E. Hughes, op. cit., 10.
5. Often called 'common grace'. See J. Murray, *Collected Writings*, II, ch. 10.
6. J. Murray, op. cit., 62.
7. W. Grudem in his *Systematic Theology* (Grand Rapids: Zondervan, 1994), 603. Grudem singles out Louis Berkhof for criticism, although nearly every Reformed discussion from F. Turretin onwards makes this a key issue. He says that it is a 'mistake to focus on the purpose of the Father and the Son, rather than what actually happened in the atonement.'
8. Cf. R. L. Dabney, 'God's Indiscriminate Proposals of Mercy, as related to his Power, Wisdom and Sincerity' in *Discussions Evangelical and Theological*, I, (London: Banner of Truth, 1967).
9. W. Grudem, op. cit., 597.
10. J. I. Packer, op. cit., 177. Packer is describing John Owen's criticism of the idea that Christ died for every man.
11. The main references are to John 1: 29; 3: 16; 6: 51; 2 Corinthians 5: 19; 1 John 2: 2; 1 Timothy 2: 6; 4: 10; Hebrews 2:9.
12. Such as 2 Peter 3: 9; Romans 14: 15; 1 Corinthians 8: 11; Hebrews 10: 29.
13. The reader can refer to Wayne Grudem's discussion in his *Systematic Theology*, 598–600.
14. F. Turretin, *The Atonement of Christ*, 161ff. and his *Institutes of Elenctic Theology*, II, 471 ff.
15. On this passage see J. Murray, op. cit., 65 ff.
16. J. I. Packer, 'What did the Cross Achieve?' 36 ff.
17. Cf. Romans 6: 3–11; Ephesians 2: 4–7; Colossians 3: 3.
18. J. Murray, op. cit., 64.
19. Cf. P. Helm, *The Beginnings* (Edinburgh: Banner of Truth, 1986), 15.
20. J. Frame, op. cit., 419–20.
21. J. I. Packer, *Among God's Giants*, 179.
22. Calvin's comment on Matthew 3: 17, quoted by R. A. Peterson, *Calvin and the Atonement*, 17.

18

No More Cross Words

The idea that the atonement accomplished by Jesus Christ on the cross was a vicarious and penal sacrifice for sin has often been criticised for being a cold, rationalistic, legal transaction that does not involve us. When it is not rejected outright and replaced by other constructions more acceptable to the 'modern mind', the temptation is to water it down by emphasizing the need to 'accept' Christ. People are invited to look at themselves and see how happy they could be if they would only open the door to Jesus. The focus of the message invariably shifts to other apparently more appealing aspects of Christ's work: Christ defeats sin, evil, and violence and we are invited to share his victory…by following his example of loving self-sacrifice we can become better human beings…

It is easy to forget that the victory of Christ over evil is a reality because Christ took on himself the condemnation of our sin and abolished it by his death. The example of Jesus' life is certainly peerless. His patience, humility, obedience, altruistic love, righteousness, and forbearance in the face of injustice are truly wonderful. But Scripture never suggests his example could be a way of obtaining salvation. It is a model for life 'in Christ'.[1]

The penal substitutionary doctrine of the atonement presented in this book gets down to brass tacks because it accounts for how God dealt with sin and saved lost humanity. It does so by centring on the unique position Jesus accepted as the mediator between God and man. Other versions of the atonement ultimately fall short of the biblical picture of the role assumed by Christ and what he accomplished on the cross. In his death and resurrection Christ opened the way into the presence of God through his work of mediation and intercession. He made peace with God on our behalf and obtained forgiveness for sin. In his person and work, justice and love are joined together, and convey a genuine knowledge of God in salvation. Christ is the redeemer who really did redeem.

The cross was a sacrifice for sin. It turned away God's legitimate anger at man's rebellion. It abolished sin and established righteousness. It satisfied God's conditions for redemption. It made peace between God and sinners. It laid the foundation for a new creation. Whenever the glory of the cross is fully appreciated it inspires faith, hope, and love.

In all he did Jesus acted as the mediator and the head of the covenant. He represented his people throughout: in his life of perfect righteousness, in his death when he suffered for sin and when he rose again as the first victor over the power of death. By faith believers are united to him communally and individually in all that he underwent on their behalf. In him they died to sin, in him they rose again, and in him they have new life. Everyone who receives Christ as mediator and trusts him for salvation can say: 'I have been crucified with Christ and I no longer live, but Christ lives in me. The life I live in the body, I live by faith in the Son of God, who loved me and gave himself for me.' (Gal. 2: 20).

The apostle's words are not an inflated expression of self-satisfaction, nor are they an invitation to 'look within'. On the contrary, they point to the marvel of divine grace that is objectively real, independent of our feelings, because it was accomplished by one act, at a moment in time, once and for all: 'He loved even me and gave himself for me'! These words are an invitation to look 'to him', to the cross where he died, and to glory where he lives and reigns.

In our day and age, Christianity has become fuzzy about its central beliefs. The lines that separate the Christian faith from well-meaning sentimentality, new age mysticism, or even other religions are increasingly vague. Methods are what matter, better communication, more attractive packaging to sell this fine product, or so we are told. It is not, however, the medium that provides the answer to the problem of unbelief, but the message. If the whole counsel of God in the atonement is lost, so is Christianity. Because 'not only is the doctrine of the sacrificial death of Christ embodied in Christianity as an essential element of the system, but in a very real sense it constitutes Christianity. It is this which differentiates Christianity from other religions.'[2]

It is vitally important today that the gospel be, and become once again, the gospel of the cross in the fullest sense of the word. The good news is not a message of love that allows us be ourselves for ourselves. It saves us from ourselves for God the creator and meets our deep needs as people naturally alienated from him. The truth is not 'in us', nor is it 'out there' somewhere. The gospel of the cross allows us to find out who we really are—God's creatures saved by grace, redeemed by Christ's death, made new in him, at peace with him, and dependent daily on his love and care.

Christian witness and discipleship lose their cutting edge when they lack the tonic accent indicated by the apostle: 'What I received I passed on to you as of first importance: that Christ died for our sins according to the Scriptures, that he was raised on the third day according to the Scriptures and that he appeared alive...' The consequences of losing this focus are disastrous. 'By this gospel you are saved, if you hold firmly to the word I preached to you. Otherwise, you have believed in vain' (1 Cor. 15: 2–5).

In 1 Corinthians 15, Paul simply echoed what Jesus understood about his own calling. At one of the turning points in his earthly ministry, Jesus was led to underline the same lesson that Paul later did, in dramatic circumstances. He laid down some hard conditions for being a disciple, 'If anyone would come after me he must deny himself and take up his cross and follow me. Whoever wants to save his life will lose it, but whoever loses his life for me will find it' (Matt. 16: 24–5). Simon Peter, it will be remembered, had just acknowledged Jesus to be the Messiah: 'You are the Christ, the son of the living God', and was blessed in his confession, because it was not 'revealed by man, but by my Father in heaven' (Matt. 16: 16, 18). This confession was 'the rock' suitable for building the community of Christ's people. There was not a shadow of doubt in Peter's mind that Jesus was the Christ, the promised One.

Yet, a couple of minutes later, when Jesus began to explain to his followers that he must go to Jerusalem, suffer many things at the hands of the Jewish authorities, that 'he must be killed and on the third day be raised to life' it was too much for Peter to stomach. No suffering and dying Messiahs here, please—'Never Lord! This shall never happen to you!' (Matt. 16: 22). Peter the confessor had become Peter the Satan, the liar, the divider, the murderer of truth. His words were a temptation thrown in Jesus' path as much as the temptation in the wilderness at the start of his ministry had been. Peter the rock had tragically become a 'stumbling block', a rock of offence for Jesus by advocating that the Master should take the fast track to glory without suffering and death. Unbeknown to him, Peter had set a trap for Jesus by denying the need of the cross and atonement.[3]

Jesus' unique and startling use of 'Satan' to rebuke his disciple serves to illustrate that 'there is no doctrine of Scripture so deeply important as the doctrine of Christ's atoning death.'[4] To deny the need of the death of Christ for salvation from sin is tantamount to a satanic perversion of the truth. The 'things of men' that seemed so plausible to Peter not only replaced the 'things of God', but were wholly contrary to divine revelation. It is a sobering thought that each time human considerations cause us, for reasons of respectability, honour, comfort, or self-defence, to downplay the atoning sacrifice of Christ, we stray from the things of God.

It is difficult not to conclude that the 'cross-bearing' and the self-denial required of Jesus' followers include the confession of Christ's atoning death, which is contrary to the wisdom of the princes of the world who crucified the Lord of glory (1 Cor. 2: 8). Taking up one's cross is not suffering in the sense of the expression 'everyone has their own cross to bear'. It is confessing Christ, the crucified Messiah, to be the Lord, following him out of recognition of what his death involves. 'Dying to self' involves dying to the worldly wisdom that scoffs at the dying Lord or makes light of his sacrificial death. 'Taking up the cross and following Christ' means perishing the idea that a truly benevolent God would have found an easier, softer way than the cross to solve man's sin problem. 'Losing one's life' for the sake of Christ is accepting that this scandal, the shameful and painful death of the cross, was necessary and that this is the wisdom of God for our salvation.

With ideas like these about the necessity of the atonement for salvation one certainly will not win friends and influence people, gain much academic credibility, or entertain the cathodic masses hooked on amusement. On the other hand, one will 'find life', and that is the essential thing. 'Gaining the whole world but forfeiting one's soul' (v. 26) does not hold much attraction when the ultimate stakes have been understood.

Any other 'gospel' is no gospel at all (Gal. 1: 7). Here lies the perennial danger. Modern evangelicalism seems sometimes to be sailing close to the wind and running the risk of losing its grip on the biblical gospel. Are not the following words, penned nearly half a century ago, doubly true today?—

> Without realising it, we have during the past century bartered the biblical gospel for a substitute product which, though it looks similar enough in points of detail, is as a whole a decidedly different thing. Hence our troubles; for the substitute product does not answer the ends for which the authentic gospel has in past days proved itself so mightily. The new gospel conspicuously fails to produce deep reverence, deep repentance, deep humility, a spirit of worship, a concern for the church...[5]

Jesus is the one mediator between God and men, God made man, the Son of God. He is the only one who could stand and who stands between God and us, but also between ourselves and death. He lives to do so because he died in our place. Thus the finality of the transaction that transpired at Golgotha becomes clear, even though our questions about how and why it should be so remain shrouded by the opaque mystery that characterises the being and the ways of God.

Bertrand Russell is supposed to have once said something along the lines that Christianity is based on the belief that fairy stories are agreeable. The crucifixion demonstrates the exact opposite. The nature of God whose works and ways are revealed at the cross is totally contrary to what we would imagine to be possible or acceptable for the salvation of sinners. That a God who met his own holy and just requirements when his own Son humbled himself, became a man, and accepted suffering and death to save those who were his natural enemies is beyond the wildest stretches of our imagination. God is gracious: he calls the wicked to abandon their ways and turn to the God who freely pardons: 'For my thoughts are not your thoughts, neither are your ways my ways, declares the Lord' (Isa. 55. 6–8). Happily, the ways of God are contrary to ours and overturn human rules and expectations. This is the trigger of the invitation to 'seek the Lord while he may be found and call on him while he is near.'

This is also the reason why the cross exercises such a peculiar attraction. Among the momentous events of history that come and go, buried in the sands of the past, it holds the fascination of eternal newness. When the dramatic events woven into the tapestry of time are consigned to the pages of the history books, or long forgotten, the message of the cross resurfaces ever anew with the same promise of salvation: 'Behold, the Lamb of God, who takes away the sin of the world!' (John 1: 29).

The cross words make for atonement, and because of God's love in Christ, there will be no more cross words.

Nothing else can satisfy our hearts' deep desires like the love of the cross.

Nothing could heal our sin like the forgiveness of the cross.

Nothing delivers us from certain death like the cross.

Nothing will make us hope for eternal life like the cross.

ENDNOTES

1. R. A. Peterson, *Calvin and the Atonement*, ch. 9.
2. B. B. Warfield, 'Christ our Sacrifice', Works, II, 435.
3. L. Morris, *The Gospel According to Matthew* (Grand Rapids: Eerdmans, 1992), 430.
4. J. C. Ryle, *Expository Thoughts on the Gospels: Matthew*, quoted by L. Morris.
5. J. I. Packer, '"Saved by his Precious Blood": an Introduction to John Owen's "The Death of Death in the Death of Christ"', *Among God's Giants*, 164.

Select Bibliography

H. Blocher, 'The Sacrifice of Jesus Christ. The Current Theological Situation' *European Journal of Theology*, 8:1 (1999)

H. Boersma, *Violence, Hospitality and the Cross. Reappropriating the Atonement Tradition* (Grand Rapids: Baker, 2004)

E. Brunner, *The Mediator* (London: Lutterworth, 1934)

R. L. Dabney, *Christ our Penal Substitute* (Harrisonburg, VA: Sprinkle, 1985)

———. 'God's Indiscriminate Proposals of Mercy, as related to his Power, Wisdom and Sincerity' in *Discussions Evangelical and Theological*, I, (London: Banner of Truth, 1967)

J. Denney, *The Christian Doctrine of Reconciliation* (Carlisle: Paternoster, 1998)

———. *The Death of Christ* (Carlisle: Paternoster, 1997)

J. B. Green, M.D. Baker, *Recovering the Scandal of the Cross. Atonement in New Testament and Contemporary Contexts* (Downers Grove: IVP, 2000)

C. E. Hill, F. A. James, eds., *The Glory of the Atonement. Essays in Honor of Roger Nicole* (Downers Grove: IVP, 2004)

R. Letham, *The Work of Christ* (Leicester: IVP, 1993)

P. Lewis, *The Glory of Christ* (Carlisle: Paternoster, 1992)

H. Martin, A. A. Hodge, *The Atonement* (Cherry Hill, NJ, Mack, nd)

L. Morris, *The Apostolic Preaching of the Cross* (Grand Rapids: Eerdmans, 1965)

———. *The Cross in the New Testament* (Grand Rapids: Eerdmans, 1965)

J. Murray, *Redemption Accomplished and Applied* (Edinburgh: Banner of Truth Trust, 1961)

J. I. Packer, 'What did the Cross Achieve? The Logic of Penal Substitution' *Tyndale Bulletin* 25 (1974)

———. '"Saved by his Precious Blood": an Introduction to John Owen's "The Death of Death in the Death of Christ."' in *Among God's Giants. Aspects of Puritan Christianity* (Eastbourne: Kingsway, 1991)

D. Petersen, ed., *Where Wrath and Mercy Meet* (Carlisle: Paternoster, 2001)

R. A. Peterson, *Calvin and the Atonement* (Fearn: Christian Focus, 1999)

A. W. Pink, *The Seven Sayings of the Saviour on the Cross* (Grand Rapids: Baker, 1968)

G. Smeaton, *The Apostles' Doctrine of the Atonement* (Edinburgh: Banner of Truth, 1991)

J. G. Stackhouse, ed., *What Does it Mean to be Saved? Broadening Evangelical Horizons of Salvation* (Grand Rapids: Baker, 2002)

J. Stott, *The Cross of Christ* (Leicester: IVP, 1987)

F. Turretin, *The Atonement of Christ* (Grand Rapids: Baker, 1978)

———. *Institutes of Elenctic Theology,* II, (Phillipsburg: Presbyterian and Reformed, 1994)

B. B. Warfield, 'Christ our Sacrifice', *Works*, II, (Grand Rapids: Baker, 1981)

———. 'Atonement', 'Modern Theories of the Atonement', *Works*, IX, (Grand Rapids: Baker, 1981)

P. Wells, *Entre ciel et terre. Les sept dernières paroles du Christ* (St. Légier: Ed. Contrastes, 1990)

Index of Principal Subjects

Adam, 33, 221.

Atonement, 7, 28, 32, 37, 68, 76, 79, 103, 127, 133, 139, 184, 219.
  Limited, 236.
  Necessity, 68.

Atonement Today, 141.

Blood, 88, 121, 128, 132.

Common grace, 47, 58, 65, 153, 160, 236.

Condemnation (penalty), 73, 144.

Covenant, 28, 33, 44, 51, 57, 62, 78, 98, 163, 168, 178, 200, 248.

Death, 111, 220.

Debt, 23, 71, 140.

Exchange, 21, 23, 28, 78, 110.

Example (Christ as), 19, 55, 69, 86, 107, 124, 133, 247.

Expiation, 183, 193.

Faith, 14, 38, 211, 235, 244.

God, 41, *passim*.
  Anger, 73, 149, 188, 248.
  Attributes, 48, 76, 82.
  Compassion, 58.
  Equity, 61.
  Forgiveness, 26, 78, 140, 191, 201.
  Goodness, 57, 72, 80, 244.
  Grace, 57, 84, 233, 248.
  Holiness, 50, 63, 122, 206.
  Justice, 60, 64, 208.
  Love, 56, 59, 85, 194.
  Patience, 61, 115, 247.
  Plan (purpose), 51, 102, 168, 223, 237.
  Righteousness, 60, 70, 104, 186, 206.

Guilt, 22, 28, 73, 201, 205.

Hell, 111, 161.

Incarnation, 34, 44, 94, 168.

Intercession, 184.

Imputation, 206, 209.

Justification, 209, 214, 217.

Law, 30, 73, 79, 114 137, 187, 203.

Lordship, 44.

Mediator, 76, 167, 174, 251.

Models, 17, 37, 91, 138.

Obedience, 101, 113, 208, 219, 230.

Penal Substitution, 17, 28, 36, 110, 127, 137.
  Criticisms of, 20, 141.

Propitiation, 183.

Reconciliation, 139, 175, 212.

Redemption, 171, 200, 233, 248.

Relationships, 27, 63, 78.

Remission (sin), 77, 184, 230.

Representation, 33, 88, 229, 241, 248.

Revelation, 42, 82, 95, 122.

Religions, 85, 93, 248.

Sacrifice, 22, 51, 84, 121, 137, 188.

Salvation, 199, 242.

Satan, 34, 109, 250.

Satisfaction, 23, 184, 219.

Scandal, 15.

Shame, 78.

Sin, 22, 29, 67, 190, 205, 208.

Three Offices, 34, 98, 174.

Victim, 22, 71, 81.

Victory, 18, 37, 108, 170, 181, 226.

Violence, 22, 81, 110.
  Non-violence, 86, 122.

World-view, 16, 133.

Christian Focus Publications
publishes books for all ages

Our mission statement –

STAYING FAITHFUL

In dependence upon God we seek to help make His infallible Word, the Bible, relevant. Our aim is to ensure that the Lord Jesus Christ is presented as the only hope to obtain forgiveness of sin, live a useful life and look forward to heaven with Him.

REACHING OUT

Christ's last command requires us to reach out to our world with His gospel. We seek to help fulfill that by publishing books that point people towards Jesus and help them develop a Christ-like maturity. We aim to equip all levels of readers for life, work, ministry and mission.

Books in our adult range are published in three imprints.

Christian Focus contains popular works including biographies, commentaries, basic doctrine and Christian living. Our children's books are also published in this imprint.

Mentor focuses on books written at a level suitable for Bible College and seminary students, pastors, and other serious readers. The imprint includes commentaries, doctrinal studies, examination of current issues and church history.

Christian Heritage contains classic writings from the past.

Christian Focus Publications, Ltd
Geanies House, Fearn,Ross-shire,
IV20 1TW, Scotland, United Kingdom
info@christianfocus.com

For details of our titles visit us on our website
www.christianfocus.com